W9-AWG-159

The Cognitive Behavioral Workbook for Depression *sets a new high sta___ for psychological self-help books. Within these pages, Knaus blends rational emotive behavioral therapy, cognitive therapy, and cognitive behavioral therapy with his insights and innovative techniques to create a powerful step-by-step program for defeating depressive thinking and preventing relapses.*

—Richard Sprinthall, Ph.D., professor of psychology and director of graduate studies in educational psychology at American International College in Springfield, MA

Here is a great source for anyone interested in learning the causes, consequences, and cures of depression. The book is a great resource for practitioners seeking effective and efficient ways to assist clients in working their way out of depressive states. It's an easy read, both informative and well-organized.

—Joseph R. Ferrari, Ph.D., professor of psychology at DePaul University and editor of the *Journal of Prevention and Intervention in the Community*

Using the REBT format, Knaus' Cognitive Behavioral Workbook for Depression *is much more than a workbook. It is accessible and practical and simply the best self-help guide to the nature and non-pharmacologic treatment of depression available to sufferers—and their families. It is also a wonderful supplement to professional help.*

—Joseph Gerstein, MD, FACP, assistant clinical professor of medicine at Harvard Medical School (ret.) and diplomate of the American Academy of Pain Management

How to conquer depression with self-education is Knaus' gift to readers in his new book, The Cognitive Behavior Workbook for Depression. *Drawing on the wisdom of depression experts as well as his own innovative PURRRRS & Depression Inventory, Knaus shows how to reduce the depth and shorten the duration of most depression. He teaches the reader how to quickly identify and overcome the main components of his or her individual depression. Self-disclosure and case examples offer a realistic perspective and encouragement to anyone struggling with depression's demons. Knaus offers us here a most hopeful book on depression!*

—Deborah Steinberg, MSW, private practitioner and coauthor of *How to Stick to a Diet*

The Cognitive Behavioral Workbook for Depression *is the best bet and the best book I've seen for tackling one's depression. It admirably blends a wealth of research and well-chosen examples into step-by-step procedures for understanding and undermining one's misery. It is fun to read, easy to follow, and full of optimism.*

—Emmett Velten, Ph.D., clinical psychologist, board of trustees member of the Albert Ellis Institute of New York, and founding member of the self-help recovery system that became SMART Recovery®

I am very impressed with Knaus' focus on breaking out of the procrastination and debilitating inertia that usually accompanies depression. His expertise on procrastination sets his book apart as a resource that can really make a difference to those seeking to reduce their depressive thoughts and feelings. If you're struggling with depression and this book is in your hands, I encourage you to follow Knaus' advice and "do it now!" The tools and strategies in this book will certainly help you better understand yourself and move out of the misery of depression.

—Timothy A. Pychyl, Ph.D., associate professor of psychology at Carleton University in Ottawa, Canada, and director of the Procrastination Research Group

The Cognitive Behavioral Workbook *for* Depression

A STEP-BY-STEP PROGRAM

WILLIAM J. KNAUS, ED.D.

New Harbinger Publications, Inc.

Publisher's Note

This publication is designed to provide accurate and authoritative information in regard to the subject matter covered. It is sold with the understanding that the publisher is not engaged in rendering psychological, financial, legal, or other professional services. If expert assistance or counseling is needed, the services of a competent professional should be sought.

Distributed in Canada by Raincoast Books

Copyright © 2006 by William J. Knaus, Ed.D.
New Harbinger Publications, Inc.
5674 Shattuck Avenue
Oakland, CA 94609

Cover design by Amy Shoup; Acquired by Jess O'Brien;
Text design by Tracy Marie Carlson; Edited by Brady Kahn

All Rights Reserved
Printed in the United States of America

Library of Congress Cataloging-in-Publication Data

Knaus, William J.
   Cognitive behavioral workbook for depression : a step-by-step program / William J. Knaus.
      p. cm.
   Includes bibliographical references.
   ISBN-13: 978-1-57224-473-3
   ISBN-10: 1-57224-473-9
   1. Depression, Mental. 2. Cognitive therapy. I. Title.
RC537.K57 2006
616.85'27—dc22
                                    2006024515

New Harbinger Publications' website address: www.newharbinger.com

09   08   07
10   9   8   7   6   5   4

Starting in the mid nineteen-fifties, psychologist Dr. Albert Ellis pioneered a revolution in the field of psychotherapy when he boldly asserted that people feel the way that they think. By this he meant that evocative events, such as a job loss or depressive change in biochemistry, are the tip of the iceberg. Because most of these events filter through our belief systems, the way we define, interpret, and judge activating situations stimulates what we feel and guides what we do. Our beliefs, attitudes, and related cognitive processes are the deep base of an iceberg that is more massive than what is seen at its tip.

Some environmental, psychological, social, and biochemical events activate self-harming thought associations and beliefs. Ellis saw that by recognizing, examining, and purging harmful, irrational beliefs and other forms of unrealistic thinking, surplus suffering and misery could go the way of the dinosaur. Over the past fifty years, a continuing line of research has demonstrated the validity of this position.

Albert Ellis brilliantly helped change the psychotherapeutic landscape by tirelessly working for over fifty years, fifteen to eighteen hours a day, directly helping thousands through his counseling and millions more through his books and the network of counselors and psychotherapists that he helped train. The rational emotive behavior therapy (REBT) system he pioneered inspired the evolution of numerous complementary systems, such as psychiatrist Aaron Beck's evidence-based cognitive therapy and the generic and popular cognitive behavioral therapy approach. REBT is the bedrock system for these and many other associated systems.

In honor of his magnificent achievements and his enormous, tireless contributions to the emotional health and welfare of others, I dedicate this book to my longtime friend and colleague, Albert Ellis.

Contents

Foreword - vii

Acknowledgments - xi

Introduction - 1

CHAPTER 1   The Echoes of Depression - - - - - - - - - - - - - - 15

CHAPTER 2   Preparing for Positive Changes - - - - - - - - - - - 33

CHAPTER 3   A Master Plan to Defeat Depression - - - - - - - - - 53

CHAPTER 4   Recognizing Depressive Thinking - - - - - - - - - - 69

CHAPTER 5   Using Reason Against Depressive Thinking - - - - - 87

CHAPTER 6   Shedding a Cloak of Mental Misery - - - - - - - - 103

CHAPTER 7   Defeating Depressive Beliefs- - - - - - - - - - - - - - 119

CHAPTER 8   Ending Worthlessness Thinking - - - - - - - - - - - - 141

CHAPTER 9   Defeating Helplessness Thinking- - - - - - - - - - - - 153

CHAPTER 10   Hopelessness and Optimism - - - - - - - - - - - - - 165

CHAPTER 11   Restraining Blame - - - - - - - - - - - - - - - - - - 177

CHAPTER 12   Avoiding the Perils of Perfectionism - - - - - - - - - 189

CHAPTER 13   Low Frustration Tolerance and Depression - - - - - - 203

CHAPTER 14   Coping with Depressive Sensations- - - - - - - - - - 221

CHAPTER 15   Dealing with Emotional Stresses - - - - - - - - - - - 233

CHAPTER 16   Special Cognitive and Behavioral Techniques - - - - - 261

CHAPTER 17   A Multimodal Way to Defeat Depression- - - - - - - - 281

CHAPTER 18   Five Changes to Defeat Depression - - - - - - - - - - 291

References - 309

Foreword

Dr. Bill Knaus's *The Cognitive Behavioral Workbook for Depression* is not exactly a wonderful book, because, as Alfred Korzybski showed in *Science and Sanity*, to say it is wonderful is to overgeneralize, and to imply that it is 100 percent filled with wonderful things. Inevitably, this book has omissions as do all books on depression, including outstanding ones like those of Aaron Beck, David Burns, and my own *Guide to Rational Living*. Be that as it may, *The Cognitive Behavioral Workbook for Depression* is wonderfully thorough, and if consistently followed, is exceptionally helpful.

Bill Knaus, whom I helped train in rational emotive behavior therapy (REBT) in the late 1960s, used REBT particularly well in dealing with human problems, and then became an authority on overcoming procrastination. Our 1977 book by that title is still a best seller, as are other of Bill's books.

Not content with helping his readers with their fears of failure and low frustration tolerances, Bill decided to tackle the extremely prevalent and serious problem of depression. He has done so with a vengeance. He has thoroughly investigated and therapeutically dealt with its many related issues of hopelessness, blame, perfectionism, and emotional stresses. He shows readers how to deal with the most important aspects of depression, and he has covered it beautifully.

In his eighteen excellent chapters, Bill Knaus has researched and cited scores of studies on depression and shown how these findings can be used by readers who are in various depressed states. In many of his chapters, he emphasizes the use of the well-known ABCs of REBT. He shows how to look for and apply the ABCDE technique to depressive thoughts, feelings, and actions. A stands for the activating event, such as an imperfect performance. *B* stands for your rational beliefs ("I acted stupidly, and I'd prefer to do better next time") and your irrational beliefs ("I should have done better, and I am a stupid person"). C stands for your emotional and behavioral consequences. This includes healthy feelings such as regret and the emotional results of unhealthy thinking such as self-downing. D stands for disputing your irrational beliefs by questioning them and through taking problem-solving actions ("Where is it written that I absolutely must behave flawlessly?"). *E* stands for an effective new philosophy (you may be dissatisfied with certain performances, and accept yourself despite them).

Bill Knaus also shows you how to change your basic self-defeating depressive philosophies to help achieve the REBT choice of unconditional self-acceptance, unconditional acceptance of others, and unconditional life acceptance. Then, you will rarely depress yourself about anything!

Simple, isn't it? Yes, but as Bill Knaus shows, it takes much work and practice—thinking, feeling, and behavioral homework. Apply his many methods and strategies to your depressiveness. Don't wait. Get going.

—Albert Ellis

Acknowledgments

I especially want to acknowledge my friend, Atlanta artist and psychotherapist Edward Garcia, for his review of this book and numerous insightful contributions, and my wife, Nancy Knaus, who graciously reviewed all chapters and offered many helpful comments for people with depression. I would like to acknowledge my friends Diana Cleary and Dale Jarvis, who worked with me to create original jointly written poetry for this book. I also would like to acknowledge the following people, who contributed tips and ideas and who reviewed chapters to help assure that the material would be meaningful to people struggling with depression: Dr. Robert Arthur, Stafford Springs, CT; Dr. Barry Morris, Vancouver; Dr. Bernie and Diana Pardell, Englewood, NJ; Dr. Bill Golden, New York City; Dr. Leon Pomeroy, Richmond, VA; Dr. Daniel David, Cluj-Napoca, Romania; Dr. Dom DiMattia, Goshen, CT; Dr. Emmett Velten, Phoenix, AZ; Dr. Matthew Israel, Canton, MA; Dr. Diana Richman, New York City; Dr. Robert Heller, Boca Raton, FL; Dr. Robert Morris, Clearwater, FL; Dr. Arnold Lazarus, Princeton, NJ; Dr. Russell Grieger, Charlottesville, VA; Dr. Michael Edelstein, San Francisco; Dr. George Morelli, San Diego, CA; James Byrnes, MA, Hebden Bridge and Halifax, England; Will Ross, Mesa, AZ; Dr. Windy Dryden, London; Dr. Richard Wessler, New York City; Deborah Steinberg, MSW, Boca Raton, FL; Dr. Tony Kidman, Sydney Australia; Dr. John Minor, Manhattan Beach, CA; Dr. Nando Pelusi, New York, NY; Dr. Albert Ellis, New York, NY.

Introduction

Talk show host Dick Cavett suffered a severe depression. Later, when reflecting on his depressive state, he said that if a magic pill had been an arm's length away, he would have felt too tired to reach for it. He said this to emphasize the potency of depression and its debilitating effects. On the other hand, he also said that he could muster his resources to read about depression.

Would most people with depression stretch for a way to break a cycle of depression? I suspect yes! By picking up this book, you have reached out to do something to relieve yourself of depression.

You can use this book as a springboard for positive change. You can use it as a cookbook and follow the recipes, or you can adapt from it what you believe will work for you. Throughout, you will find many ways to build on your positive capabilities and to decrease your depressive thoughts and depression-inspired actions.

Now, at the start of this process of overcoming depression, you may face your first dilemma. If you bought this self-help book on dealing with depression while also thinking you are helpless to change, this is a paradox. By taking the step to purchase the book, you have accessed an important resource. By acting upon what you read, you can help defuse depressive thinking and break the inertia of depression.

A KNOWLEDGE EXPLOSION IN DEPRESSION

There is an overwhelming amount of information on defeating depression, including many different ideas on how this might be done. Over the past decade, we have witnessed a knowledge explosion about the causes of depression and how to treat it.

Information about depression is ballooning. As of March 9, 2006, the key word "depression" appeared in more than 160 million citations on the Internet Google search engine. On this same date, the word "depression" appeared in 109,815 articles, books, chapters, and dissertations listed in the American Psychological Association (APA) database and in 185,596 PubMed articles. These days, popular magazines, newspapers, and books also cover the topic of depression and how to defeat it. This knowledge explosion offers sound reason for hope. With greater public awareness about the personal and economic costs of depression, people who feel depressed are increasingly showing a greater willingness to come forward to learn how to get relief.

> As much as it can be daunting, the rapid growth of knowledge about depression is encouraging.

Depression is a complex area, but it is one that is becoming increasingly manageable. New information is coming into play every day, helping to streamline what we know and can do about depression.

There is considerable controversy regarding how best to address depression, and this has as much to do with differences in how individuals respond to various approaches as to the differences between therapists working with clients who feel depressed. Yet despite all this variability, the vast majority of people can and do learn how to significantly reduce their level of depression or gain full relief from the distresses visited upon them by this dark demon. People who gain relief from depression include those who think they can never overcome their personal problems and that their depression will stubbornly linger forever.

Defeating depression rarely follows a straight line. Many events can occur in the gap between where you start and where you want to be. A prime impediment to overcoming depression, for example, is depression itself. When laboring under a down mood, sluggish feelings, and depressive thinking, you may experience difficulties in concentrating on what you think is desirable to do. Fortunately, you don't have to be 100 percent knowledgeable to defeat depression, nor do you have to be 100 percent effective. Defeating depression is a process of progressive mastery, and doing 10 percent better can feel like paradise.

FOUR PRIME ASSUMPTIONS FOR POSITIVE CHANGE

This book describes cognitive and behavioral ways of knowing and doing to overcome depression, to help boost your chances for defeating depression. It begins with four prime assumptions.

1. Some people develop depression without concurrent depressive thinking. However, this is an atypical response, especially for people who suffer from depression for months and years, or for whom depression keeps coming back. Although depression can exist independent of negative thought, when coupled with depressive thoughts such as hopelessness, helplessness, and uselessness, depressive misery can intensify. Deactivating depressive thinking can lead to a significant reduction, if not elimination, of depression.

2. How you think about your world and yourself influences your perceptions and perspective on reality. If the words and ideas that you use to describe your experiences are reasoned and can be confirmed, you are likely to experience a realistic sense of control over yourself, which increases your chances for effectively managing the events around you. In contrast,

when major aspects of your experiences are triggered by depression-related misconceptions and misunderstandings, you can feel both an added degree of misery and disadvantage.

3. You can teach yourself to recognize depressive distortions and extinguish them. For example, if you believe *nothing will ever change and you'll be depressed forever*, you can learn to label the idea as depressive and then apply techniques you'll learn from this book to deactivate this form of depressive thinking that goes along with depressive moods and depression-related activities.

4. Antidepressive problem-solving behavioral actions are a time-proven remedy for overcoming depression. Engaging in actions such as exercise, using techniques to disrupt the inertia of depression, and reasonably structuring your activities of daily living can help reduce the misery of depression and depressive thoughts, and increase your sense of well-being and control over your life.

Hope is an illusion, unless made realistic by what you do. This book's four assumptions provide a hopeful, tested direction for making positive changes to get out of the abyss of depression. These same assumptions are platforms for going forward and enjoying your life.

PROMOTING AWARENESS AND ACTION

Effective therapists of different persuasions promote realistic *awarenesses*, and they serve as catalysts for constructive *action*. Working collaboratively with their clients, they talk out problems and engage people in problem-solving activities. This book can serve a similar purpose. Here you are your own coach, but learning the skills to be an effective self-development coach carries a lifetime of benefits.

The awareness and action approach describes how to do the following:

■   Reduce unnecessary negative thinking that links to distressful emotions, unpleasant physical sensations, and self-defeating actions.

■   Increase purposeful and functional thinking that links to positive actions.

■   Promote positive self-development activities, such as building personal resources, promoting positive relationships, and pursuing passions and interests.

Throughout this book, you'll read about awareness and action steps that you can take to gain relief from your depressive thinking, feelings, and behaviors. By learning to act against the mental negativity of depression and by engaging in antidepressant actions, you can bring yourself a sense of valued relief. But negating the negative is only part of the story. Building positives provides an important self-development direction for defeating depression and for keeping it from coming back.

As you engage in self-development activities to overcome depression, you can build psychological skills that you will be able to transfer to other venues of life. For example, in chapter 5, you'll learn how to apply critical thinking skills to depression. These skills apply to judging different life situations.

By learning and applying self-development skills to depression, you can simultaneously—and with no significant extra effort—learn to defeat depression while developing yourself. This self-development direction serves to prevent future depression, helps to advance your major goals, and allows you to gain greater satisfaction in living. So view the techniques within as having a purpose beyond defeating depression, and you are likely to find ways to put them to use to advance the quality of your future life.

A REVOLUTION FOR POSITIVE CHANGE

In the past few thousand years, we have learned a lot about depression, its causes, and corrective actions. In the past fifty years, a cognitive revolution in psychotherapy has come to pass, gained speed, and now offers many tested and innovative cognitive and behavioral ways to address depression.

This revolution in cognitive and behavioral methods to alleviate the excessive stresses of depression, anxiety, and related forms of human suffering started around 1956 with New York psychologist Albert Ellis's invention of rational emotive behavior therapy (REBT). Through his writings and presentations, Ellis described how people needlessly distress themselves and what they can do to make positive changes (Ellis 2003b). Ellis's system provided the bedrock from which the cognitive and behavioral system used in this book grew, as well as other popular methods such as cognitive therapy. Research on Ellis's cognitive and behavioral methods affirm REBT as an effective therapeutic method.

> Changing depressive thoughts is within your control. By defeating them, you can reduce or eliminate the physical and emotional strains associated with them.

In the early 1960s, University of Pennsylvania psychiatrist Aaron Beck developed cognitive therapy (Beck 1963). Research on Beck's cognitive and behavioral methods affirm cognitive therapy (CT) as an effective method for dealing with depression and other negative psychological conditions. Whereas Ellis placed more of his emphasis upon presenting scientific thinking and a philosophy for reducing needless disturbances, such as depressive thinking, Beck placed more emphasis on experimentally testing his cognitively based system.

This book gives many practical examples for defeating depression from the pioneering work of many who have contributed to our understanding of depression. You will also find many techniques that are unique to this workbook, such as a self-scoring depression inventory that helps you identify key aspects of your depression. The book describes a stepping-stone approach to defeat depressive thinking, the PURRRRS method, and many other innovative methods. You will also find tips from depression experts who submitted ideas specifically for this book. But described throughout, you will also find many tried and true methods for defeating depression.

In defeating depression, there is not one method, plan, or program that fits all. However, depressive thinking is such a typical part of the human experience of depression that it presents a big target in a campaign to overcome depression and to prevent it from coming back. That cognitive aspect of depression is therefore emphasized, along with behavioral ways of knowing and doing that are designed to defeat depression.

DEFEATING DEPRESSIVE THINKING

What is this thing called *depressive thinking?* Depressive thoughts are pessimistic, demoralizing, motivation-sapping thoughts that typically precede or accompany depression. For example, thoughts such as "I'm helpless. My life is hopeless. I'll never get better" can help promote as well as dramatically worsen a depressed mood. Discharging this thinking lessens depression.

This workbook gives guidelines for recognizing depressive thinking and depression-related behaviors. It describes many ways to improve your mood. But there is an important intermediary step. When you accept that depressive thinking exists within your mind, and that this self-talk does not represent an unchangeable reality, you may find that getting rid of these thoughts runs a smoother course.

Although there is great variability in the content of depressive thought, it can be boiled down into categories such as helplessness, hopelessness, worthlessness, blame, low frustration tolerance, perfectionism, anxiety, and anger. Knowing how to identify and root out such depressive thoughts is a tested way to gain relief from depression and to prevent it from coming back.

USING PROCRASTINATION TECHNOLOGY TO DEFEAT DEPRESSION

Activity trumps depression. Increasing your activity level is associated with decreases in depression (Turner, Ward, and Turner 1979). Cognitive therapists David Burns and Susan Nolen-Hoeksema (1991) found that depressed people who follow through on behavioral assignments improve three times as much as those who don't act to finish the assignments. These assignments include self-help readings, such as this book.

When you feel depressed, you are likely to experience apathy for taking action. Difficulties in concentration, fatigue, and procrastination commonly fuel this retreat. You are more likely to procrastinate when depressed.

Fortunately, counteracting procrastination when you are depressed can lessen depression. In turn, lessening depression can reduce procrastination associated with depression.

Some forms of procrastination may link to some forms of depression, and this combination mutually links to neurotransmitter events (Braverman 2004). Neurotransmitters are chemical bridges that exist in the gap between brain synaptic nerve endings. Serotonin, acetylcholine, GABA, and dopamine are four primary neurotransmitter systems responsible for transmitting information across synaptic junctures. According to this theory, procrastination, depression, and fatigue relate to dopamine deficiencies. Dopamine is a neurotransmitter that is associated with high achievement and energized actions. It tends to be concentrated in the prefrontal lobe section of the brain, which is associated with the higher mental processes, such as reason.

Braverman's theoretical connection between brain chemistry, fatigue, procrastination, and depression is interesting. This hypothesized connection will eventually undergo scientific scrutiny. In the meanwhile, here is a hypothesis that you can test for yourself. Let's assume a linkage between the neurotransmitter dopamine, depression, procrastination, and fatigue. Let's further assume that by engaging in counter-procrastination activities, with reasonable consistency, your efforts will correlate with increased dopamine efficiency, decreased depression, increased energy, and decreases in procrastination. Let's assume that even forced follow-through actions are likely to be accompanied by a subjective experience of greater enjoyment of life. Now, what do you do?

The innovative application of procrastination technology to depression holds considerable promise. Throughout this book, you'll find counter-procrastination strategies to use to help defeat depression.

What is *procrastination technology*? Procrastination technology involves applying practical knowledge and techniques to mobilize your personal resources to follow through on what is important to do. This process involves the use of tested techniques to not only get a jump on deadline activities (paying bills) but to follow through on self-development activities such as engaging in problem-solving actions for defeating depressive thinking.

The application of procrastination technology is an innovative strategy for overcoming depression. You will find many procrastination technology innovations from this author that weave through the book. They include the five-minute plan and cross-out sheet methods for getting into action and following through on what is important to do to deal effectively with both procrastination and depression.

IS SELF-HELP HELPFUL?

An effective therapist helps promote a realistic *awareness* by identifying and clarifying problem areas and serving as a catalyst for constructive *actions*. This involves a collaborative effort between a person who wants to bring about specific change(s) and an empathic, knowledgeable professional. That collaborative effort is what is known as a *therapeutic alliance*. When talking out problems with a trained counselor, it is important that

1. You believe that your counselor is empathic to your cause.

2. You and your counselor are working toward agreed goals.

3. You have a sense of rapport with your counselor.

Bibliotherapy, or what is known as healing through reading, compares favorably to individual psychotherapy (Gregory et al. 2004). If a therapeutic alliance, empathy, rapport, and agreed-upon goals are important aspects to a therapeutic process, a book can't supply this same form of therapeutic interaction. However, the interactive therapeutic process and a self-help reading program share a common ingredient. Both processes involve self-education. The main difference is in the way the information is given.

Professionally written self-help programs can be effective for addressing a broad range of distressful states such as anxiety (Marrs 1995) and problem drinking (Apodaca and Miller 2003). But is reading about the application of psychological principles to depression effective for addressing depression?

Self-help bibliotherapy approaches are effective for defeating mild and moderate forms of depression (Wampold et al. 2002). In some cases, a cognitive behavioral self-help approach can be helpful in dealing with the more severe forms of depression (Cuijpers 1998). It now appears that a self-help bibliotherapy approach may profitably apply to a subgroup of people with depression who have an interest in using evidence-based cognitive and behavioral self-help methods for self-improvement.

Why might professionally written bibliotherapy manuals prove effective when you deal with depression? A well-designed self-help book can deliver information that is specific to depression. The book can flesh out key issues in depression within a shorter time span than the therapeutic setting can provide. Educational self-help books on depression describe exercises you can use to promote positive changes. You can return, as many times as you choose, to review a section of the book that you once found helpful. You can take your time to study an idea or exercise in greater depth.

Professionally written self-help books on depression typically contain evidence-based information on depression. They describe structured steps for addressing and overcoming depression. Books do lack the flexibility of a skilled counselor who can ask questions to gain clarity and to help move the process forward. Although self-help bibliotherapy and individual counseling represent different ways to get to the same result, they can be used in combination with each other, along with exercise, an antidepressant medication program, or other scientifically valid interventions for depression.

Bibliotherapy is helpful for some people, but not for all. Some of my depressed and nondepressed clients will read materials I offer and actively underline statements and exercises and then use the ideas. Some report going back over highlighted sections when their depression (distress) deepens, in order to regain a sense of perspective. Some have no interest in reading and will politely take resource materials that I offer and place them in a corner where they lie fallow. I have also found that some clients use the materials on their own and do quite well following written prescriptions. Since you have acquired this book and are in the process of reading it, you are probably a member of the group who is willing to test the waters to see if the approaches described within can be made useful.

GAINING GROUND WITH BIBLIOTHERAPY

People who believe that they can apply practical, hands-on methods are likely to profit using a cognitive behavioral self-help manual (Mahalik and Kivlighan 1988). Bibliotherapy can be especially useful for people who think that they can address depression if they have the tools (Burns and Nolen-Hoeksema 1991). However, in applying self-help methods, persistence is important. Robert Gould and George Clum (1993), who looked at the effectiveness of self-help approaches for anxiety and depression, found that persistence was a significant factor leading to successful outcomes.

Here is how to take advantage of the self-help methods described in this workbook:

- Learn as much as you can about recognizing depressive thinking in its many guises.

- Emphasize and complete the exercises in this book that you think are most relevant for overcoming your depression. If it is hopelessness thinking, concentrate on that. If it is a combined set of conditions (which is likely for most), identify the most oppressive, break it down into digestible bites, and deal with it. Then, move on to the next. If it is structuring your time so that you increase your activity level, take those steps.

- Force yourself to follow through on meaningful exercises that you feel tempted to put off because you tell yourself that you are too depressed to try. These may be the exercises most worth pursuing. (If you tend to put off timely and relevant exercises, you will find many ways throughout this workbook to get past this form of procrastination thinking.) Much as exercising with weights can produce a productive strain, well-targeted self-help activities can temporarily provoke added discomfort. But discomfort is nothing to either fear or to avoid. How many things have you accomplished in your life that did not involve some discomfort and frustration?

- Pace yourself based upon the time and resources you have available to learn and apply the various techniques. Recognize that it takes time to build skills that are useful for defeating depression. In the Aesop's fable about the tortoise and the hare, the idea of "slow but steady wins the race" aptly applies to defeating depressive thinking and gaining relief from the unpleasant sensations and mood that accompany this distressful state.

■   Practice and repractice tested ways to question the validity of depressive thinking. Build upon this knowledge. This process can lead to defeating depression and preventing it from coming back.

If you believe that you can take steps to defeat depression, read on. Even if you don't think you can help yourself, read on. If you are in this latter group, you'll discover ways to address the sort of depressive thinking that stirs a pot of unrealistic depressive pessimism.

LEVELS OF CHANGE

It is probable that depression will eventually lift, even if you take no formal action to end this form of misery. However, since depression tends to be complex and often includes coexisting conditions such as perfectionism, anger, and anxiety, waiting depression out may be like sitting in a winter swamp while awaiting the warmth of summer. This passive approach has some value, providing you don't withdraw into yourself and preoccupy yourself with personal problems and depressive thoughts. But it also relies on chance.

Through purposeful, directed, focused actions you can boost your chances to defeat depression. You can dramatically shorten the duration of a depression and prevent depression from coming back. You can rid yourself of the unpleasant and often painful aspects of depression, such as the mental miseries of self-doubt and downing, inertia, apathy, fatigue, and absence of enthusiasm for life.

PRACTICAL, EMPIRICAL, AND CORE CHANGES

You can target your efforts to overcome depression at practical, empirical, and core problem-solving levels. Practical problem-solving solutions are specific things that you can do, such as logging your thoughts when you feel tense. This helps make depressive thinking visible and vulnerable. Practical methods include educational information about depression, along with common sense tips your grandmother might give you, such as getting out into the sun to break the gloom of a midwinter funk. Through the development of practical knowledge, and by engaging in practical actions, you can interrupt the flow of negative beliefs, alter depression-laden behaviors, and engage in higher level positive awarenesses and actions.

Empirical problem-solving solutions involve working as a scientist, where you use observations and knowledge to connect the dots between depressing situations, thoughts, emotions, and consequences. The process involves the application of reason and scientific ways of knowing to cope with depression. Through this process, you train yourself to see depressive premonitions as testable hypotheses, as opposed to absolute truths. For example, if you think that your future is always going to be bleak, define this as a hypothesis. Then look for exceptions to contest this view.

At the level of core problem-solving solutions, you dig deeper. You examine your personal views of your self, your level of tolerance for frustration, your perspective, the themes that characterize your life, and your beliefs, values, and personal philosophies. Core problem-solving includes examining your beliefs, revising those that are irrational, and reinforcing those that are fact-based and constructive.

In this workbook, you will find many ways to address depression at the practical, empirical, and core problem-solving levels. Techniques from these three levels can fill a toolbox for positive change.

A TOOLBOX FOR CHANGE

The alphabet has twenty-six letters. You can use them to develop millions of words. You can blend the words into infinite phrases, sentences, and paragraphs. In a similar sense, you can take basic self-help strategies and build these ideas into your life. You can start this process at any time. It doesn't matter if you are nine or ninety. Within this book, you'll find many tools to defeat depression that you can also apply to advance your best self-interests.

Defeating depression is a trek. Your toolbox of coping methods can help speed the journey. This toolbox includes the following:

1. Lists of ideas to curb depression.

2. Practice exercises to counter and debunk depressive thinking and strengthen coping skills.

3. Sidebars and text boxes that highlight key ideas.

4. Reinforcement of key ideas in different contexts. If you miss a point in, say, chapter 2, you'll likely find a different application of that basic idea in a different area of depression.

5. Optional ways to counteract depressive thinking.

6. Guiding principles.

7. Metaphors, similes, analogies, fables, and parables to make important ideas memorable.

8. Stories of people who faced depression and prevailed, and how they did it.

9. Encouragement.

10. New technologies and innovations for defeating depression.

Some ideas and techniques will be relevant for one person that are not so important to another. For example, perfectionism is a state of mind that commonly coexists with depression and increases the risk for depression (Hewitt et al. 1998). People plagued by this form of stressful thinking can find help in chapter 12. If you find that perfectionist thinking is an extraordinary burden, you'll likely spend a lot of time with that chapter. But if you are relatively free from perfectionism, chapter 12 is likely to be what is called a quick read.

There is no universally applicable system for ending depression. Some depressed people do well with recognizing and challenging depressive thoughts. Exercise is a proven remedy for defeating depression, and some people improve dramatically after following a daily exercise routine. Developing and following a highly structured routine can make a positive difference for others. Antidepressant medication works for some. A combination of approaches is more likely to provide the foundation for building positive change for others. There is no universally perfect single solution or combination of solutions for depression. But whatever approach you decide, give the approach a fair test. This test can involve a period of weeks and months.

With multiple techniques directed toward addressing depressive conditions, it may not be possible to know which is having the most favorable impact. Perhaps, like a good spaghetti sauce, many ingredients can lead to a positive result.

IS THIS APPROACH FOR YOU?

This workbook is for those who feel mildly to moderately depressed, as well as for others with more severe depressions who can stretch and chip away at their depressive thoughts and stretch to establish routines that compete with depressive moods, sensations, and behaviors.

How do you know if you are in the subgroup of people who can potentially benefit from self-help measures to defeat depressive thinking? Here is a basic question: If you had the tools, do you think you could take small steps to defeat depression? If your answer is yes, then cognitive and behavioral approaches merit consideration.

The majority of people in a major depression can help themselves address their depression through cognitive and behavioral methods. However, for someone in an extremely immobilized depressive state, medical interventions are often necessary. Someone who seriously contemplates suicide, and has the plan and the means, should immediately seek professional help. If depression is threatening important relationships and career, working with a counselor is normally a conservative step. There is a very high probability that you can find ways to overcome depression. As far as seeking outside help goes, with all the publicity and public education about depression, no one need feel stigmatized by seeking help for depression—or by buying a book on how to deal with depression and then using it.

A TIME FOR SELF-HELP ACTIONS

What is a reasonable amount of time to engage in self-help work to defeat depression? The matter of how far to take self-help is an individual decision, but it is useful to establish time boundaries for determining how long to try on your own to defeat depression.

There is no simple answer to the question of how long to use a bibliotherapy self-help approach. Boundary setting is often subjective. People are different. Tolerances for depressive symptoms differ. Degrees of depression differ. Causes differ. Depression follows different courses. A lot also depends on how stoic you are about your depression. The progress you make can be a determining factor.

Past experiences with depression can be used to predict the probable course of depression, as well as what has worked and what has not. If you've fought your way out of a prior depression, you have evidence that you can break a depressive cycle. If you are new to the challenge of defeating depression, applying tested techniques can tell you what you can do on your own.

If, after a reasonable time of testing self-help methods, you find yourself treading water, consider working with a counselor. Depending on your situation, a reasonable time may be anywhere from two weeks to three months.

The more you do on your own, the more credit you can give yourself for your progress. Still, this need not be the trek of a lone traveler. Positive support from friends, family members, exercise groups, groups for people with depression, and so on is associated with progress in getting up from depression. However, some people are naturally inclined to work on their own. They prefer their own company. There is nothing wrong with learning and applying techniques to defeat depression on your own.

BRIDGING THE GAP OF DEPRESSION

Between a desire to stop depression and the end of depression, you are likely to find a gap that takes time to bridge. The reward from crossing this gap comes in the form of relief from depressive thoughts and sensations. However, as the saying goes, "Rome wasn't built in a day." It takes time and practice to build antidepressant skills and strengths.

Although you can learn about how to defeat depressive thinking within hours or days, applying the principles to uproot depressive thinking can take weeks or sometimes even months. That is because it is one thing to know what to do and another to put to use what you know. You can, for example, read about how to drive an automobile. You read about starting the car. You read about steering the car. This information helps. But by simply reading about it, do you really know how to coordinate your thoughts and movements so that you drive safely and effectively? Or does learning how to drive require getting behind the wheel? In a similar sense, you can learn to become an expert in defeating depressive thinking and keeping out of future depressions. But the gap between knowing and doing closes with practice.

> Each person who suffers from depression has an individual story to tell. What might trigger depression in one may leave another untarnished.

Although you may want to immediately defeat depressive thoughts, the structural parts of your brain that are involved with depression will probably change at a slower pace. However, as you work at defeating depressive thinking, your brain is creating structures that code the counter-depression skills that you develop.

It is normal for people with depression to have coexisting thoughts that can have a destabilizing effect on their psychic life. Such thoughts usually take additional time to change. Common coexisting thought patterns include perfectionist thoughts, anxious thoughts, and low frustration tolerance self-talk, where the smallest hassle becomes intolerable. Recognizing and defusing these emotionally laden patterns of thought reduces a major source of distress. This book describes common unpleasant conditions that coexist with depression and what to do about them.

A STRUCTURE FOR POSITIVE CHANGE

If you begin this book not knowing what to do to defeat depression, you are like many others. The presence of depression, as part of the human condition, has baffled people for thousands of years. But there are many tried and true ways, as well as new innovations, for defeating this ancient nemesis. Recent innovations for unlinking depressive thinking from a depressed mood, for example, open enormous opportunities for gaining relief.

However burdensome the mood, thoughts, and sensations of depression may be, they are addressable. What can you do to curb them? Between the covers of this workbook, you'll find a comprehensive course consisting of dozens of prescriptions to do better, get better, and stay better.

I designed this book to show how to identify and counteract depressive thinking and other conditions of depression. As you look through the table of contents and index of this book, you'll find scores of action prescriptions for gaining relief from depression.

As you move through the chapters, you will find something familiar and something new. This building block approach provides a way for you to organize your thinking about depression, expand upon what you learn, and progressively master depression.

If you find yourself having difficulty concentrating on understanding an idea, this is normal. You can mark the pages(s) and come back to it later. Meanwhile, important ideas and exercises will appear in different forms throughout the book. If you miss something useful in one chapter, you are likely to find a variation later. This design helps reinforce key methods for defeating depression.

You'll naturally move at your own pace. But it is important to work at a pace that can eventually lead to a progressive mastery over depression. Try to stretch a little.

Few put as much concentrated time into their development as they would a one-semester college course. By putting as much time into mastering this "course" on depression as you would into English 101, you set the stage to significantly profit from what you learn.

> Neutralizing depressive thinking provides an added bonus. You sharpen your reasoning skills. You can transfer these skills to other areas of your life and benefit.

BUILDING A WALL AGAINST DEPRESSION

This book describes not only what you can do to address depression but also how to go about this business in a step-by-step manner. The interventions for addressing depression are drawn from evidence-based systems; they are clinically tested and theoretically sound. These steps are important building blocks.

The process of ending depressive thinking is like building a wall. Putting the pieces together, step by step, builds the wall.

This introduction describes what to expect from this book and the part you play in dealing with your own depression. The first three chapters give foundation ideas for dealing with depressive thinking. Chapter 1 is a warm-up chapter. You'll find a history of depression and general information on depression. Chapter 2 provides a self-administered depression test you can use as a self-inventory to help detect prime factors that are common to your experience of depression. This chapter includes a twelve-step method to defeat depression and other techniques to get started. In chapter 3, you'll find a master plan for defeating depression.

The second layer in your wall against depression includes multiple techniques for defeating depressive thinking. In chapter 4, you'll learn basic ideas for recognizing depressive thinking. Chapter 5 describes how to use fundamental reasoning techniques to counteract depressive thinking. Chapter 6 describes cognitive distortions in depression and techniques to counteract them. In chapter 7, you'll learn how to use a time-tested ABCDE approach for defeating depressive thinking. This approach includes a powerful stepping-stone method.

Through reading chapters 8 through 11, you raise your wall to a higher level. These chapters expand on the core depressive thinking themes of worthlessness, helplessness, hopelessness, and self-blame. By expanding upon these issues and dealing with them in depth, you take proactive steps to gain control of your time and life.

Chapters 12 through 15 show how to manage core problems that commonly coexist with depression. Ignoring these conditions when they exist increases the chances that depression will come back. These common conditions include perfectionism, low frustration tolerance, sensation sensitivity, and troublesome emotions such as anxiety and anger. When you get to this point in your wall, you'll learn many techniques for dealing with depression that apply to states that ordinarily mingle with depression. By overcoming these states, you innoculate yourself against a future depression.

Chapters 16 through 18 top off your wall. Chapter 16 describes special cognitive and behavioral methods for defeating depression. Chapter 17 describes a multimodal approach for organizing your efforts to defeat depression. Chapter 18 describes a unique five-phase process for positive change. Through following this five-phases-of-change system, you'll learn a unique way to exit from your depressive labyrinth. For a further look at the science behind this book, you can refer to the appendix at http://www.newharbinger.com/client/client_pages/bookexcerptARCHIVE.cfm. There, you can find more information on depression research and explore how cognitive behavioral professionals address depression. You'll also read about the science behind a broad range of antidepressant methods, such as natural emotive behavioral therapy, Omega-3 fatty acid, magnetic and electrical therapies, exercise, and antidepressant medication.

There can be situations related to depression that go beyond the information in a self-help book. If you think of yourself as defeated by depression or think you are getting worse, consider talking with a professional. If you are at risk of losing your job or a vital relationship due to depression, again, consider talking with a professional. Depressive thinking contains many twists of logic and misrepresentations of reality. Getting some external feedback and clarity can help. A trusted friend or service provider might suggest a referral. In combating depression, it is wise to keep your options open.

The philosopher Aristotle said about 2,500 years ago that life and events have a beginning, middle, and an end. So does depression. You can bring it to its end. Taking the tiniest step signals that you have started the process of making positive personal changes. Knowing what to do about defeating your depression is a start. Using what you know can hasten its demise.

Overcoming depression very likely won't happen overnight. But you can start the progression of change overnight. I won't wish you luck. This leaves too much to chance. By engaging in directed awareness and action work, ridding yourself of depression gets done. In this process of progressive mastery, pace yourself, but stretch a little and you will gain a lot.

CHAPTER I

The Echoes of Depression

When mired in depression, happiness eludes you. Pleasure is nowhere to be found. Your ambitions clot. Your strength leaves you. You worry. You lack confidence. You think you are unlovable. Your thoughts fill with cries of helplessness and hopelessness. You feel trapped. Your attention is adrift. You try to disappear. Your relationships sour. You feel stuck, numbed, dull, lifeless. Paradoxically, you may feel irritable and angry. Encapsulated within a persistently negative mood, gloom seems impenetrable. Interests are dampened. This process practically always includes patterns of negative, depressive thoughts including helplessness, hopelessness, and worthlessness. What is behind depression?

Here is depression's point of view: "I am depression. Cold like an arctic mist, I dampen your spirit and your soul. I fill your thoughts with gloom. When I am with you, you are but a withered leaf beneath wet snow with nowhere to go. Still, I can do much more. I can fill your mind with graveyard thoughts and make you teary. I can cause you to complain and bicker. I can make you feel uncertain. I can drain all pleasure from your life. I can drive laughter into the shadows. I can dig you into a hole so deep that you can't see the top. I can then overwhelm you with thoughts of helplessness and hopelessness, so you won't try to get out. For I am the mood of depression. I alone can control what you feel and do."

This description of depression may sound a bit dramatic. Nevertheless, you'll find a tone of desperation in depression that you can't ignore. Like a destructive tenant, depression rarely leaves without strong urging.

Depression is a normal phase of living for millions. Sadness, feeling down, bereavement, and feeling depressed are all part of the human condition. Practically everybody will, over their lifetime, experience some degree of depression, some much more so than others.

> "Depression" comes from the Latin *depressio,* meaning to press down and make lower.

Depression comes with a melancholic mood that is ordinarily weighted with negative thinking. It ordinarily follows an extraordinary stress, but for some, depression (and avoiding depression) is a way of life. Yet depression is not in charge of your life. Although depression can feel numbing, this mood is vulnerable. As you detect and debunk droning depressive thoughts and engage in antidepressive behaviors, depression tends to lift.

There is sound reason to be optimistic that you can get relief from depression. The National Institute of Mental Health estimates that 80 percent of depressed people respond to evidence-based interventions, such as cognitive behavioral therapies, antidepressant medications, exercise, and allied techniques (National Institute of Mental Health 1999). Depression is addressable!

If the odds are 80 percent for getting relief from the depression you are currently in, would you bet on yourself to defeat depression? If you count yourself among the 80 percent, you are probably seeking tools to gain relief. This book provides such tools to accomplish this result.

If you think that you are one of the 20 percent that will tread water with depression, or you fear you can never control conditions you associate with your depression, then you've identified a strain of depressive thinking called *hopelessness thinking*. Unlike the composition of a granite rock, however, this thinking is changeable. The trick is to know how to recognize and expose the fallacies in thinking that typically accompanies depression and relieve yourself of the weight of this added tension. This book describes how.

DEPRESSION THROUGH THE AGES

Help is on the way. Before looking at how you can free yourself from depression, you might find it comforting to know that you are not alone.

Depression has existed for thousands of years, perhaps from the time our ancestors first stood on two legs and peered over the grasses on the plains of Africa. Since then, hundreds of millions of people have fought depression and won.

Depression has a history that is at least as old as civilization. We can find descriptions of depression in the hieroglyphics, paintings, and statues of ancient Egypt (Okasha and Okasha 2000). When the pyramids were still new, the Egyptians depicted this dispiriting mood in many of the ways that we see depression today. The Egyptian remedies included sleep, excursions, and dance. These ancients understood that sleep disturbances add to the burden of depression and activity counteracts the inertia of depression.

Depression appears in *The Odyssey*. The ancient blind poet Homer described a depression in Odysseus's son Telemachus. We also read about depression in the Bible. The Old Testament described Job and Saul in melancholic pain.

As long as depression has existed, people have tried to understand and "cure" this ailment. Hippocrates, the ancient Greek founder of medicine, was the first to recognize the relationship between the environment, bodily state, and emotions. He correctly saw the brain as the seat of thoughts and emotions. His first stage of treatment for depression involved diet and exercise. Thereafter, the second century Greek physician Galen and eleventh century Arabian physician Avicenna also prescribed diet and exercise. Today, exercise and diet continue to be a prescription for helping people overcome depression.

The seventeenth-century British scholar Robert Burton (2001), who wrote *The Anatomy of Melancholy*, described depression as a broken-winged goose that droops and pines away. In this fifteen-hundred-page tome, Burton noted that depression can exist without obvious cause or go beyond the reason of the cause. He insightfully saw that depression had a variety of symptoms, including false beliefs, an expansive imagination, despondent mood, sleeplessness, and other signs that we see today. He thought, as did Hippocrates, that depression included both physical and psychological aspects. He recommended various therapies, many of which are standard practices today.

During the Dark Ages, the Roman Catholic Church preached that depression was the work of Satan. Following this big setback in progress, the eighteenth century French physician Philippe Pinel disputed the Church's demoniacal possession dictum. He saw depression as the result of social and psychological stresses, heredity, and physiological factors.

According to California psychologist and priest George Morelli (pers. comm.), the Church in the East took a totally different approach from the Western Church. The Eastern Desert Fathers saw depression as a passion called despondency that was triggered by thoughts (*logismi*) which lead individuals to *amartia*, which means "to miss the mark." This miss-the-mark view is consistent with what contemporary mental health clinicians would term "inappropriate and self-defeating thinking and behaving." They addressed despondency through *diakresis*, or right thinking.

> Your mind can ignite depression, as well as serve as a mirror to a depressed mood. But depression is not all in your mind. There are real biological symptoms. Social factors are often involved. Environmental stresses can contribute. Psychological factors can dominate.

Psychiatrist Adolph Meyer (1948) introduced the idea that depression was a reaction to life events, and not a medical illness. His psychobiological studies showed that thoughts and feelings affect a person's physiological state.

In *On Murder, Mourning and Melancholia*, the founder of psychoanalysis, Sigmund Freud (2005), wrote that melancholia has various definitions and meanings, and various somatic and psychological causes. Freud viewed depression as complex and believed that it resulted from early childhood trauma.

A contemporary view of depression is that it is a psycho-social-biological condition that involves dispositional factors, stress triggers, and depressive thoughts. Harsh and dangerous environments can increase the risk for depression.

Compared to earlier solutions for defeating depression, a current emphasis on changing depressive thoughts has scientific backing. Whatever the causes of depression, and differences between people in their expression of depression, by curbing depressive thoughts, you decrease other parts of depression, such as fatigue and troubled sleep.

DEPRESSION: AN EQUAL OPPORTUNITY CONDITION

Depression is an equal opportunity condition that can occur independently of life status, religious beliefs, power, or wealth. In a depressed state, people of different races, income levels, intelligence, and cultures describe very similar thinking, biological, and emotive conditions. However, the poor and disadvantaged are more susceptible to depression.

Depression can affect anyone. Abraham Lincoln suffered from depression. So did Winston Churchill. Other well-known people who suffered from depression include the founder of American psychology, William James; the poets Edgar Allan Poe, Walt Whitman, and Emily Dickinson; comedian Rodney Dangerfield; talk show host Dick Cavett; 60 Minutes commentator Mike Wallace; and television entrepreneur Ted Turner. Their depressions were not hopeless conditions. Each person found a way to contribute despite a sometimes paralyzing depressed mood.

Famous People with Depression

Dick Cavett
Winston Churchill
Rodney Dangerfield
Emily Dickinson
William James
Abraham Lincoln
Edgar Allan Poe
Ted Turner
Mike Wallace
Walt Whitman

Nineteenth century American poet Emily Dickinson's depression motivated her to examine depressive suffering. Her poem "After Great Pain" conveys an understanding of her own depression.

Depression is a form of suffering. The fifteenth Dalai Lama (2002) noted that a disciplined mind is the path away from suffering. To create a state of peace of mind involves looking within for "inner strength because no one else can provide this for us—no deities, no gurus, and no friends. That is why the Buddha says you must be your own master" (p. 169).

In the Buddhist world of the Dalai Lama, time is transitory. There is time for detachment from negativity. From a Western viewpoint, actions to decrease depressive thinking provide opportunities to emerge from pain with a directional force. Each view can complement the other.

Depressive thoughts that accompany depression can dominate attention, thus disrupting concentration. Recognizing, labeling, and contesting them are ways to defeat them. Although there is great variability in the content of depressive thought, it typically boils down to categories, such as helplessness, hopelessness, worthlessness, blame, low frustration tolerance, perfectionism, anxiety, and anger.

Knowing the depressive thinking categories and how to contest their content is a tested path to set the stage for an uncoupling of depressive thoughts from the physical side of depression. But there is an intermediary step. This step involves accepting that depressive thinking comes closer to reflecting a mood of depression than your ultimate sense of reality. It involves accepting the reality that depressive thoughts that accompany depression are more a reflection of your mood. This intermediary step sets the stage for uncoupling depressive thinking from depression, and this uncoupling is associated with reductions in depression (Beevers and Miller 2005).

YOU ARE NOT ALONE

When you feel depressed, it may seem like no one cares or that nothing matters. But you are not alone. The World Health Organization (WHO) estimates that 340 million people currently suffer from depression. By the year 2020, WHO predicts depression will rank second among the most serious health conditions behind ischemic heart disease (Murray and Lopez 1996). It is already the number one disability for women. Depression is no trivial matter!

During the course of a year, 9.5 percent of the people in the United States will have a significant depression or mood-related disability (Robins and Regier 1997). As some gain relief from depression, others cross the portal into depression.

The statistics represent a rotating-door phenomenon. Worldwide, they also represent hundreds of millions of people. Although some think the incidence of depression may be overstated (Waraich et al. 2004), others think that because of poor recall, reports of depression may be skewed and underestimated (Patten 2003). Despite variances among the estimates and predictions about depression, there is persuasive evidence that depression is a major disability and that the incidence of depression is rising.

As of March 8, 2006, the U.S. population was 298 million. According to depression statistics, approximately 28 million people in the United States will suffer from a significant depression during any one-year time span. Millions of others will exhibit what are called "subclinical" symptoms of depression. They feel depressed, but not to the extent that they feel so miserable as to feel incapacitated. Because there are so many different kinds of depression, variations in the incidence of depression, and variances in depression statistics, the best we can do is to estimate the prevalence of depression. Whatever way you want to cut up the depressive pie, depression is common, and currently it seems on the increase.

The date of your birth partially determines your risk for depression. For example, the incidence of depression has dramatically risen in the past one hundred years. People born after 1936 have an earlier age of onset and higher rates of major depression than those born before that date (Weissman et al. 1984).

The prevalence of depression has accelerated in the past fifty years (Kessler et al. 1994). How is this to be explained? There are many interacting physical and social conditions including earlier onset pubescence, rapid technical and social changes, social-moral changes, and mass migration from small communities of families and neighbors to larger urban centers and communities that have fewer traditional social supports. Change—even the positive kind—promotes stress.

Depression statistics are more than dry words on paper. They show that you are not alone in your battle with depression. Although it is not your fault that you are depressed, no more than it is the fault of others who are depressed, it is your responsibility to deal with this demon.

In your struggle to end depression, you join hands with hundreds of millions who face a similar challenge. But dealing with depression is also an individual pursuit. No one can do this for you. This is something that you can do for yourself by taking advantage of what we know about depression and how to evict this dark tenant. It is your challenge. But you do have lots of support, even from people you may never know. There is no shame in asking for help.

CAUSES OF DEPRESSION

The ancient Greek physician Hippocrates thought that depression was the result of personal vulnerability combined with stressful circumstance. You're born with a vulnerability for depression. Stressful circumstances evoke it.

The modern version of Hippocrates' theory is called the *diathesis-stress theory*. According to this model for depression, you have to have both a vulnerability for depression (diathesis) and a triggering situation (Sullivan, Nealee, and Kendler 2000). The diathesis can be a neurochemical event, negative early experience, illness, or something else. Psychologist Leon Pomeroy (2005) uses a computer analogy to describe this diathesis-stress process as an interaction between the *hardware* of the brain and the *software* of the mind. He suggests a strong interplay between brain and thought (mind) dysfunctions.

Hippocrates' observation has stood the test of time. A predisposition for depression coupled with a significant life stress can trigger depression.

Depression That Starts from Events

There is scarcely a person alive who has not experienced a sinking feeling following a tragic event. We all suffer setbacks and losses and face unpleasant situations. These are part of the normal fluctuations of life. Such events can affect perspective and biochemistry.

When a depression-triggering event is known, such depressions are called *situational*, *reactive*, or *exogenous depressions*. Such triggering events include major life stresses such as job loss, divorce, the death of a mate, traumatic shock, feeling stuck in a situation without an exit, living for years in a moribund marriage, or a cumulation of continuing hassles.

Events alone do not necessarily cause depression. You can slump into a depression following a pattern of viewing life through dark glasses. A preexisting condition such as loneliness, anxiety, or perfectionism can evolve into depression. Such coexisting conditions can complicate depression.

Depression That Comes from Within

You may awaken one morning in a super mood. Nothing has changed except for the mood. Throughout different periods of life, we will have pleasant surprises, make unexpected progress, and have joyful experiences and feel uplifted. But as the old saying goes, life is not all peaches and cream. You can awaken one morning in a dreadful mood, and nothing has changed in your life, except for the mood.

It is not always loneliness, loss, misfortune, or preexisting negative patterns of thinking that spiral into a depression. Some folks have an idyllic existence. For no visible reason, they get depressed, and life no longer seems worth living. Depression can come out of the blue, even when life seems good. This type of physical depression is sometimes called an *endogenous depression*.

Sylvia Plath (1972), author of *The Bell Jar*, tells us she had it made. She had an adoring handsome boyfriend and a career she loved. Then like a bell jar descending over her head, she felt enclosed by depression. For Plath, a depressive state came upon her when her life was going well.

The Bell Jar describes Plath's feelings of hopelessness, suffering, and sense of worthlessness. This was not Plath's first experience with depression, nor would it be her last. She suffered from a bipolar depression. Her depression came and went from her early adolescence forward. In her time, however, too little was known about dealing with this form of depression and the depressive thinking that accompanied it.

The causes of endogenous depressions seem more to do with changes in biochemical brain processes than with life conditions. However, once in motion, these primarily physical depressions can adversely affect the quality of your thoughts, relationships, career, and normal life experiences.

When depression arrives, and you have no noteworthy negative events in your life, the physical symptoms of depression can seem bewildering. You have aches and pains, and you have trouble sleeping. Your concentration seems shot. You dwell on the negative and find ways to discount positive events (mental filtering). You worry that your fatigue is a symptom of some dread disease. So you go to your physician, who runs tests. There is nothing to be seen or found. You keep going back, looking for a cure for the intense malaise that hazes your life. But part of the solution lies in recognizing that you're suffering from depression so that you can take advantage of what we know to subdue this condition.

The various causes of depression can frustrate theorists when different forms of depression don't snugly fit a single model. But that is as it is. People are different. Circumstances are different. Histories are different. Perceptions and perspectives are different. Vulnerabilities are different. There are different kinds of depression. Despite this diversity, there are common threads that weave through depression.

Without a depressed mood, you would not be depressed. Depression and depressive thinking typically walk hand in hand.

Without depressive thinking, a depressed mood is much more tolerable and more readily changeable. By expelling depressive thinking from your thoughts, you can change your mood!

WHEN IS DEPRESSION SERIOUS?

When does depression rise to the point where it is serious? Perhaps this happens when you think that it has. But there are standard criteria to consider.

A dysphoric mood which lasts for several days or weeks is not necessarily a cause for concern. This can be part of the normal ups and downs of life. So, not all that we call depression is depression.

Some think that they feel depressed when they feel the blues, get bummed out, feel sad, have a down day, get into a "mood," or experience a disappointment. You fight with your mate and you say you feel depressed, but how does this differ from hurt or anger? You get a flat tire on the highway and your jack is missing. You say you feel depressed. But how does this differ from frustration? You don't get selected for a promotion. You think this is depression. But how does this differ from disappointment? Your best friend moves out of the country. But how is this more than sad? These ups and downs of life can get confused with depression.

Depression is far more numbing, painful, and enduring than the blues, blahs, and down moods that practically everyone experiences. In the pits of depressive despair, most report that this condition grinds on from day to day and is difficult to bear.

Depression is beyond the limits of the normal sense of disappointment, loss, bereavement, sadness, bad days, holiday blues, or down moods. It is more than temporarily feeling down in the dumps. For example, disappointment can pass within hours. Bereavement diminishes over time. On the other hand, depression of the mind, body, and spirit can feel like the life is sucked out of you. It's a mean beast that hangs on for weeks, months, and sometimes for years. This enveloping condition of emptiness is not the kind of situation where you just pull yourself up by your bootstraps and get on with your life. Depression is debilitating in significant and often dramatic ways. The sense of painful inertia and immobilization that weaves through depression just doesn't disappear when you—or others—tell you to "get over it." Like a broken leg that takes time to heal, depression takes time to defeat.

The cognitive and behavioral skills you develop through this book can decrease the number of times you feel depressed; they can decrease the depth of your depression; and they can decrease the duration of your depression.

WHEN IS DEPRESSION A SYMPTOM OF SOMETHING ELSE?

Depression can reflect deficiencies in certain classes of neurotransmitters, physical disease, and illness. No amount of self-help reading or psychotherapy will cure disease conditions, such as a thyroid condition, that change the body chemistry to promote the sensations of depression.

Between 20 percent and 25 percent of those with major medical conditions will experience a significant depression sometime during their disease (American Psychiatric Association 2000). Chronic conditions that can evoke this type of reactive depression include AIDS, arthritis, cancer, coronary heart disease, stroke, diabetes, pain, thyroid conditions, liver disease, allergies, hormonal imbalances, fibromyalgia, Crohn's disease, Parkinson's disease, and rheumatoid arthritis. The view you take of such conditions can influence your mood.

When in doubt as to the causes of your depression, get a medical checkup. However, regardless of whether depression arises from trauma, comes from out of the blue, or is a symptom of an underlying disease, depressive thinking and depression-related behaviors remain high target areas for cognitive and behavioral interventions. By dropping excessively negative thoughts, you've freed yourself of a major double trouble that is commonly associated with depression.

THE MANY FACES OF DEPRESSION

There are many reasons for depression, and there can be different forms and expressions of depression. For some people, depression runs in the family, and they are prone to feel unhappy. Others slump into depression because they think badly about themselves, have a persistently pessimistic outlook, feel bound by worries and troubles, or stress themselves because of the gap between their expectations and reality. Depression can erupt following a traumatic event, an ongoing stressful situation, or a perceived loss. It can come out of the blue.

The voice of depression can be obvious, such as when you tell yourself that life will only get worse. However, it is not unusual for people to project a sense of surface cordiality to disguise their pain.

Some feel depressed but don't publicly show it. In Ruggero Leoncavallo's opera I Pagliacci, we are introduced to a smiling face of sadness. Though sorrowful, the smiling Pagliacci clown hid his tears. In "Tears of a Clown," Smokey Robinson echoed this same sentiment of crying when no one was around to hear. Can you be sad and depressed and still smile? Yes! But however the smile may look to an observer, it may not feel real to you.

Disguising depression is understandable. It is functional when it serves the purpose of maintaining positive relationships. It is nonadaptive when pretense detracts from problem solving.

Depression is rarely a simple matter that links to a single cause. When linked to a poor self-concept and the tendency to catastrophize about disappointment, unfairness, and inconvenience, depression can be recurrent. Although catastrophizing is not a universal sign of depression, people increase their risk of depression when they magnify and dramatize their difficulties beyond a normal response so that they rise to reach cataclysmic proportions.

You may think that when you are depressed, the type of depression you experience is immaterial. That's partially correct. All forms of depression involve a profoundly sad or down mood and a high probability of distorted depressive thinking. This workbook provides an approach that applies to different types of depression where depressive thoughts and behaviors are present. But if you know the general type of depression you face, you can then access the literature on that particular type of depression.

What follows is a discussion of seven common varieties of depression: major depression, adjustment disorder with depression, dysthymic depression, postpartum depression, seasonal affective disorder (SAD), atypical depression, and bipolar depression. Each form has its own literature. Depending on the type of depression, you may approach it with different combinations of therapies, and sometimes in different ways. For example, you can address the form of depression known as seasonal affective disorder by intensifying your exposure to light.

Each form of depression carries a risk of depressive thinking. Each is addressable by techniques that unlink depressive thoughts from depression and unhealthy activities from depression, such as withdrawal. This uncoupling process can both promote relief and reduce the risk of a relapse.

Major Depression

Although depression always involves a profoundly sad and down mood, there are other unpleasant physical symptoms and negative psychological processes that normally accompany a major depression. A major depression (*unipolar depression*) is defined by the conditions that accompany it, such as a lengthy, depressed mood that includes several or more of the following:

- depressive thinking

- reductions in frustration tolerance

- sleep disturbances

- appetite disturbances

- difficulties attending and concentrating

- a diminished sense of personal worth, self-doubts, and indecisiveness

- a loss of ambition and enthusiasm

- a loss of pleasure

- a loss of sexual desire

- sluggish movements

- fatigue

- suicidal thoughts

Major depressions can follow a normal bereavement, a catastrophic loss of property, or any condition you perceive as traumatic. It can grow from a pattern of general anxiety or negative self-talk. Whatever the causes, this common form of depression carries a 10 percent lifetime prevalence rate for men and 20 percent for women. Major depressions are costly in human suffering, loss of productivity, and in medical expenses. Powerful psychological as well as medical interventions may help alleviate this suffering.

Adjustment Disorders with Depression

Adjustment disorders with depression follow a significant and unwanted change, such as divorce, job loss, sudden financial loss, or a betrayal of confidence. What makes this adjustment disorder different from a major depression? The difference is measured in perception and vulnerability, along with lesser intensity and shorter duration.

In this time-limited state, your mood is down. You feel preoccupied with and strained by negative thoughts about the troubling situation. However, you continue to have ample resources available that you can expend in making an adjustment to the situation. There are periods when you feel fine. Nevertheless, this lingering misery is deepened by recurrent distracting thoughts and stressful sensations and emotions.

Accepting that this form of depression is a normal phase of adjustment can be a step toward gaining perspective. In the backwash of strongly unwanted events, however, such healthy mental disengagement takes time to work through and adjust to. Antidepressant medications are typically counterindicated.

Dysthymic Depression

A dysthymic depression is a persistently mild depression where you experience many aspects of a major depression but in milder degree. Dysthymic depressions tend to linger, sometimes for two years or more. In that sense, they also differ from adjustment disorders with depression. Along with a down mood, restlessness, and a sense of going through the motions of living, anxiety often accompanies this state of mind and body. Procrastination is common.

This depression may not be linked to any noteworthy event. You may experience yourself as vulnerable because you don't feel right. In a dysthymic state of mind, you may experience a recurrent fear, and because of the energy drawn to mobilize against the fear, you can experience periods of intensified depression. Lots of times you may feel like you are slogging through the day with minimal energy and enthusiasm, with a cloud over your head. Nearing the end of the day, you may look forward to falling to sleep.

Life brings little pleasure. You may feel cranky, irritable, and testy. You may take for granted that life will continue this way. Dousing your troubles with alcohol can seem like an appealing solution. But that is not the way to break free. Alcohol and drug abuse will only aggravate an already festering condition.

People in a dysthymic cycle can spend 70 percent of their lives feeling down (Klein et al. 2000). Dysthymic depressions often predate major depressions. The combination of dysthymic and major depression is called a double depression. By recognizing and addressing this depression early, you can reduce the risk of a double depression. Here, an ounce of prevention can truly be worth a pound of cure.

Postpartum Depression

Women have an increased risk of depression for physical reasons associated with childbirth. For that reason, their highest risk of depression is between pubescence and menopause. One such depression is postpartum depression.

Approximately one in thirteen women experiences depression shortly after the birth of a child. Sometimes called "baby blues," this euphemism can detract from the significant importance of a condition that affects both mother and child, and, perhaps, future generations.

Postpartum depression has features in common with other forms of depression:

- depressed mood

- eating difficulties (overweight, excessive loss of weight)

- difficulties sleeping

- loss of interest, including sexual interest

- headaches, backaches, and other unpleasant aches and pains

- difficulties attending, focusing, and remembering things to do

- overanxiety about the baby or fear of hurting the baby or yourself

- depressive thoughts, such as helplessness, hopelessness, worthlessness, shame, guilt, anger, and blame

After living with postpartum depression, uncoupling depressive thinking from the unpleasant physical sensations of the depression can feel like living in Shangri-la. You might still have a depressed mood and unpleasant sensations, but a marked reduction in depressive thinking can have a positive effect on your general level of stress and ability to tolerate frustration.

Seasonal Affective Disorder

When winter looms in northern climates, we experience shorter days, cold, snow, slush, and cloudiness. For many, this is a dreary time of the year. Life can seem oppressive compared with the balmy days of summer.

With the changes in temperature, a shorter day, and a sense of being cooped up, some feel a negative mood change. The technical term for this form of depression is seasonal affective disorder (SAD). This malaise starts around November and lasts until about April. You rarely hear of SAD cases in Southern California. SAD is primarily concentrated in northern latitudes where about 10 percent of people experience a major SAD depression.

Compared with balmier times of the year, in a SAD state of mind and body, you might plant yourself with glazed eyes fixed on the TV. You might get testy with mates and friends. You might worry excessively about the future. You could feel immobilized.

With longer days, SAD wains. If you suffer from SAD, chapter 16 describes multiple ways to get a lift from SAD during the winter months.

Atypical Depression

An atypical depression is a common form of depression. It is called "atypical" because of the differences between it and a major depression. This form of depression involves sleeping excessively and weight gain. However, unlike people with major depressions, where even a surprise visit from a good friend has no mood-changing effect, any positive changes in your life can temporarily lead to a lifting of the depression.

The atypical depression is distinctive in other ways. Brain research suggests that there is a stronger right hemisphere involvement than with major depressions (Bruder et al. 2002). As with major and other forms of depression, you can profitably address atypical depressions with cognitive and behavioral forms of intervention.

Bipolar Depression

The ancient Roman physician Arateus was the first to see that the radical mood swings between depression and elation were part of the same condition which is now called a bipolar disorder. He also saw this condition as an extension of normal human moods and that it existed on a continuum.

In milder forms of manic euphoria, you may have thoughts racing through your head, talk faster than usual, have a greater interest in sex than usual, and spend much more money than usual. These elevated times are relatively brief compared to depressive cycles. In these phases you might experience a persistent agitation.

People with bipolar depressions often spend up to 33 percent of their adult lives in depression. They may languish in depression for months or even years without seeking help (Kupfer et al. 2002). Antidepressants can make a bipolar depression worse.

Over the millennium this condition has been associated with noteworthy accomplishments. On the list of those with bipolar disorders we find composer Ludwig van Beethoven, actors Jim Carrey and Robin Williams, the humorist Mark Twain, and Clifford Beers, the founder of the mental health movement in the United States.

Today, you might start out with education about a bipolar condition, accepting it as a lifetime condition that needs to be managed. There are many stories of people who've accepted that they had a bipolar depression, much as others accept a diabetic condition. They do what is necessary to contain and rise above it.

A bipolar disability requires a lifetime of maintenance efforts that include expunging depressive thoughts and guarding against manic episodes through medication. Managing a bipolar condition takes a special effort, much like sustaining weight loss takes effort. There are rewards in the form of gaining a sense of control and leading a more normalized life.

DISTRESSES AND DEPRESSION

Your experience with depression is more than a label and set of symptoms that fit a particular category. People experiencing depression have different stories to tell. These differences lie in the context in which depression arises, the content of thought associated with depression, and the concepts that underlie the content.

Independent of the type of depression and circumstances related to it, patterns of distorted thinking commonly coexist with a depressed mood. These coexisting depressive thoughts are, perhaps, the most personal as well as controllable aspects of depression. The effort taken to recognize and address them is strongly associated with putting an end to a depressive experience. For example, following a loss, you might believe that you can no longer go on. This form of hopelessness thinking may reflect a depressed mood, but it also can deepen the mood. Depressive thinking can be profitably changed without diminishing the meaning of a loss.

> If you can stoically accept depression without lament, this freedom from negative thinking about the unpleasantness of depression can hasten its demise.

Some depressions keep coming back coupled with complications such as hopelessness thinking, perfectionism, negative childhood experiences, anger, worry, panic, social difficulties, anxiety, rumination preoccupations, shame, guilt, neuroticism, and a low tolerance for frustration. Depressions that keep coming back ordinarily require a stepped-up effort to cope with depression-related thoughts and to develop skills to cope with conditions that parallel and complicate depression, such as perfectionism (Riso and Newman 2003).

This workbook targets prime issues linked to depressions that keep coming back. This workbook was designed to help make your first depression your last depression. Throughout, you'll find ways to reduce the intensity and duration of a current depression. The same tools apply to preventing a future depression.

HENRY'S EXPERIENCE WITH DEPRESSION

In chapter 4, we'll take a close look at depressive thinking and how this process complicates depression. In the chapters that follow chapter 4, you'll learn multiple ways to defuse this form of thinking. For now, let's say that depressive thinking is a pessimistic and somewhat catastrophic form of thought that accompanies depression and darkens present and future perspectives. Addressing this thinking often involves intermediary steps, including recognizing that the thinking is unhealthy and accepting that depressive thinking may reflect the reality of the depressive experience more than the reality of your situation. It sometimes involves *runaway ideation*, which is a series of stampeding, interconnected thoughts in which each thought associated to the next leads to a more catastrophic projection.

Let's take what might first appear like an extreme example of how stampeding depressive thinking can turn your inner world into a nightmare experience. Although extreme, the following form of depressive thinking occurs with notable frequency.

Henry had been in a depressed state for several weeks. His mood was down. His sleep was disrupted. He courageously moved through the day with a surface cordiality and an undercurrent of distressful thoughts.

Henry expected his tax refund to come within six weeks of filing his taxes. When he didn't receive the tax refund within the time he expected it, he imagined that an agent found fault with his return. He started to worry about an IRS audit. This worry escalated to anxiety when he inadvertently engaged in catastrophic thinking that the IRS would prosecute him and that he would lose his house and end up in federal prison. He imagined the horror of his family. He worried about how he would explain this to his wife and daughters. He imagined that while in prison, no one would take care of his pet poodle and that his mate would

> You have a depression that merits attention if you have a depressed mood and any two or more of these conditions:
>
> 1. You've had two weeks of a significant depressed mood.
>
> 2. You've lost interest and pleasure in life.
>
> 3. You have no desire for sex.
>
> 4. Your depression symptoms seem out of line with your life situation.
>
> 5. Depression significantly interferes with your day-to-day functioning.
>
> 6. You have persistent sleep and appetite problems.
>
> 7. Your psychological symptoms include a sense of hopelessness, helplessness, and worthlessness.
>
> 8. You've thought about suicide.

divorce him. He imagined that upon exiting prison he would be able to get only marginal jobs. He saw himself living out the remainder of his life in poverty and disgrace.

Within his deeply darkened mood, Henry experienced wave after wave of hopeless thoughts. At one point, he believed that death would be preferable to the disgrace he envisioned. He considered that cancer or a coronary would be a blessing compared to his troubles. He thought about crashing his car head-on into a tree.

Then, launching from this gloom, Henry's thoughts shifted to thinking about his contractor's sloppy work in fixing a drainage problem. He thought about the foot-deep pool of water that collected around his foundation after major rainstorms. He recalled the contractor's excuses and the fact that the problem was still not fixed. His level of anger rose as he thought about initiating a lawsuit. This anger cloaked his fears and depression to give him a temporary sense of power which was followed by a dread of a different sort, as he began to worry that his wife was having an affair, which then led to arguments with her over trivial matters.

Henry's exit from this distressful thinking followed three prime recognitions:

1. He recognized this process was an expression of depression which also sparked depression.

2. He recognized that he could change his anxious, depressive anger spiral.

3. He recognized that he could question the credibility of these catastrophic and depression-related patterns of thought.

Following these three recognitions, Henry progressively mastered the techniques described in this book. He learned to recognize and to think critically about his depressive thinking and to override it with reason. As he progressively mastered these techniques, his depression decreased. When I last heard from him, Henry reported a fifth-year anniversary of being largely free from his terrible trident of catastrophic, depressive, and angry thoughts.

Although Henry's catastrophic thoughts, depressive thoughts, and angry thoughts are uniquely his, the majority of people with depression will experience different levels and combinations of stressful thinking that contribute to, or reflect the experience of, depression. However, depressive thinking can be effectively addressed. Instructions for doing so are a primary subject of this book.

SEPARATING DEPRESSION FROM SADNESS

Live in fear of loss, and you fear to live. An uncontrollable feeling of loss, a welling of tears, a memory of what once was and that will never again be—this is sadness or a natural response to a loss of something or someone you value. Sadness is a bittersweet memory. It is a universal human response to loss.

Sadness is more than a thought about a loss. It is a profound awareness that comes deeply from within. It is a solemn emotion. It can be brief. It can linger.

Loss is inevitable. Sadness is inevitable. It is because we form attachments with people, with animals, and with ideals and places, that sadness becomes part of our lives. The size of the loss doesn't matter. A child who experiences the death of a cherished pet hamster weeps at a loss that some might think is trivial. But this is not trivial. The loss is as real as any other.

Losses come in different ways at different times. The loss of a tradition can be a shock to your psychological system. Children leaving home to live on their own are missed.

> Live in fear of loss, and you fear to live.

The death of a friend leaves a feeling of emptiness, perhaps for years thereafter. All sad. All inevitable.

When my childhood friend Al's daughter Erin died, I saw my six-foot-five 350-pound friend collapse in despair. He asked, "How will I ever get through this?" There was no answer. There was only time. All I could do was to be there. I wrote a poem in her memory. At that moment, I wished I could have done more.

Within the year of his daughter's death, Al died from cancer. I felt a great loss. Sadness still awakens within me when I think of memorable times from our boyhood until his death. When I visit his grave, I bury an old coin in the ground. Silly? Perhaps. Al loved to collect old coins.

When my dog Apollo died, I uncontrollably wept. I felt his absence and felt a profound sense of loneliness. You see, for fifteen years, Apollo was my companion, as I was his. Now when I look around to see him, he is no longer there. I hear a noise. I look up, expecting to see him. I see movement in a bush outside. But he is not there. Loss and loneliness are part of sadness. Still, the feeling of loss brings to me a sense of meaning. My new dog, Cider, helped mute the loss. Life goes on.

If there was no meaning to our relationships, there would be no sad feelings. There are sad times because there were once happy times, cherished times, and valued attachments.

Sadness reminds us that we are human. It is part of our biology and our heritage. If you accept that reality, you may find that you don't go through phases of denial, anger, and resignation following a major loss. Acceptance of sadness is enough. Meanwhile, write poetry. Organize a march to raise money for a cause. Paint. Walk. Solve a problem. As sadness ebbs, life continues.

There is a tranquility in sadness. The experience says that you cared.

If you could experience sadness safely, you might seek the experience. That is why sad movies are so popular. People read sad novels to get in touch with that feeling. So it isn't the feeling of sadness that people dread. It is the personal significance of the loss that sadness represents.

Factors That Correlate with Depression

- Depression tends to run in families.

- Alcohol and drug abuse are associated with depression.

- Preoccupations with unrealistic expectations, worry, anxiety, feelings of failure, and anger increase the risk for depression.

- Dispositions toward perfectionism, lack of assertiveness, and withdrawal are associated with depression.

- Major life changes connect with depression, whether they are the death of a mate or multiple, welcomed events such as marriage, the birth of a child, or moving into a new home. Such events can be stressful and connect with depression.

- For women, chemical or hormonal imbalance following childbirth or during menopause is associated with elevated risks for depression.

- For both sexes, chemical imbalances, such as a decreased efficiency in the neurochemical serotonin, are associated with depression.

- Traumatic experiences associated with an elevated risk for depression include a near-death experience and physical, sexual, or psychological abuse.

- Life circumstances that correlate with an elevated risk for depression include poverty, dangerous environments, and chronic illness.

Sadness and Tragic Loss

Loss. Sadness. Time to grieve. Time to heal. Time. Time. Time. It can go so slowly. There is acceptance. There is allowance. There is working through the process of loss. But in situations where the loss came from a tragedy that is followed by depression, it can take considerable time and work to come to grips with the experience.

Bob's fiancée, Jane, died hours before their wedding. It was a tragic automobile accident. Bob was shocked, numbed, and grief stricken.

Three years after this tragic event, Bob continued to feel a great guilt. He told himself, "If only I phoned Jane before she left, she would have gone through the intersection at another time." He told himself, "I can't live without her." He believed, "I will never find anyone like Jane."

> Ridding yourself of the burdens of depressive thinking does not obliterate the normal sadness and grief that come from repeated frustrations, major disappointments, or tragic losses.

As long as depression cloaked Bob's reality, he no longer did what he enjoyed. Once an avid tennis player, Bob's racquet gathered dust. There were no more dinners with his friends. After Jane's death, he withdrew from his family. Previously a successful accountant, Bob quit his job. Thereafter, he mostly did odd jobs, such as buffing automobiles at an auto detailing shop.

Bob felt overwhelmed by the details of daily living. His mood was despondent. He awakened in the middle of the night with a frightening image of the accident that took Jane's life. But the tragedy of this loss was compounded through his sense of defeatism, pessimism, and self-downing.

As he learned to defuse the negativity in his thoughts and accept his lack of control over Jane's tragic death, Bob's inner turmoil softened to sadness. Months later he resumed his accounting career. At the time of this writing, he is happily married with three children. His current family is a source of great joy. Jane lives on as a cherished memory.

Sadness is very different from depression. Sadness has meaning. Significant depressions are disabilities. Sadness is a reflection of what once was. Depression demonizes the mind with negative thoughts, such as helplessness and hopelessness. Sadness is a feeling reflected in the meaning of the loss. Depression is a drawing inward that can erupt in uncontrollable anger. In sadness, there is depth in experience. But both depression and sadness can coexist. Sadness, you accept. You deal with depression.

DECISION MAKING AND DEPRESSION

To break free from depression, some people will impulsively quit their jobs, move to a new location, or go on a spending spree. At the extreme, some will buy items they don't need or won't use. In this spree, you might buy a new wardrobe or a different automobile so that you can stimulate yourself and feel alive again. Some will divorce their mate. Such major impulse-driven changes can be distracting and often costly. For example, moving from a coastal city to a Southwest farmhouse brings no guarantee that you'll leave depression behind.

Normally, the worst time to make any major decision is when you are in a major depression. Judging the world from this pit of despair, you are unlikely to see the horizon.

Depression can have serious lifestyle consequences when dysphoric judgment dominates your actions. This is normally not the time to change mates, quit your job, or sell your house. This is not the time to seek refuge in a cabin deep in the woods. It also is not the time to give up on yourself. Instead, when depression clouds you in darkness, this is the time to look for a flashlight.

Most depression authorities suggest postponing major life changes during periods when you feel significantly depressed. Your judgment is likely to be fogged. However, there are practically always exceptions to this guideline. If you live in a high crime area and were recently assaulted, moving to a safer area (if possible) can, in the long run, help eliminate a prime cause for a stress-linked depression.

POSTSCRIPT

A depressed condition of the mind, body, and spirit has been a pox on hundreds of millions since the recording of history and before. As with millions before you, you may think you have no way out. Still, depression, the tenant that vaults through the halls of history, is vulnerable. Awesome as depression appears, you can learn to lift this haze from yourself. You can teach yourself to take charge of your life. You can leave depression fading in the rearview mirror. This is a process of progressive mastery. There can be no guarantees that focused and productive actions to defeat depression will lead to relief from depression. But there is a good probability.

CHAPTER 2

Preparing for Positive Changes

When depressed, you are likely to have trouble seeing your way out of it. You can feel so miserable about your present life and pessimistic about your future prospects that you may think that any light at the end of the tunnel is from a freight train heading your way. But the light to an open path ahead is there, awaiting discovery.

The universal ingredient of depression is a down mood that persists beyond what seems reasonable for the circumstances. In that sense, depression is like carrying a heavy rock in a knapsack. But this knapsack on your back can carry other unwanted rocks. Depressive thinking, anxiety, perfectionism, anger, and guilt are the rocks that commonly fill the knapsack. When these conditions coexist with a depressed mood, you can feel bent over by their weight.

Let's start by looking at some of these common conditions that go along with depression. The following depression inventory is a tool for finding out which of these conditions are part of your experience. Knowing what you face will put you in a better position to deal specifically with those aspects of depression that affect you the most.

The inventory can help isolate changeable features of depression. In this chapter, you'll also find a tested 12-step method to defeat depression that is followed by a set of techniques that can serve as a tailwind that blows in the direction of relief from depression. As you look over your inventory results and explore some of the steps you can take to break the grip of depression, know that you don't have to try to do everything at once. Instead you can look upon this chapter as providing a cornucopia of awareness and action ideas and exercises. Although it is unreasonable to expect yourself to do everything outlined in the book, zero in on what you believe you can do that will help, and start from there.

TAKING A DEPRESSION INVENTORY

I designed the Depression Inventory to help you to identify key components of your depression. Although this is not a standardized measure for depression, it identifies areas of subjective experience related to the features of depression addressed in this book.

People with depression universally experience a down mood, but depression carries many related components. Ninety percent of those with a major depression have sleep problems. Sixty percent of the time, people with depression have a history of anxiety. Fifty percent experience a coexisting anger. Some experience practically all the common conditions associated with depression, but in different degrees.

When you know what issues to target, you are better positioned to execute solutions. Identifying, clarifying, and pinning down the depression process is an important first step in combating depression.

Components included in the inventory are covered thoroughly in the book. Knowing what areas to target and steps to take to break a depressive cycle can give you an edge.

The page numbers following each inventory item point to a page or sections in the book that address issues referenced by the items. But these references are not exhaustive. You will find suggestions for mobilizing your resources in numerous sentences and paragraphs that are too extensive to list.

YOUR DEPRESSION INVENTORY

Instructions: Rate how true the following statements are for you, using a five-point scale where 1 means you strongly disagree, 2 means you somewhat disagree, 3 means you neither agree nor disagree, 4 means you agree, and 5 means you strongly agree. As a time frame, describe how you felt in the past two weeks.

1. *I feel anxious (nervous, tense). See pages 233-237.*   1 2 3 4 5

2. *I have sleep problems (waking early, interrupted sleep, sleeping more than usual).*   1 2 3 4 5
    See pages 273-276.

3. *I feel helpless to shake my depressed mood. See pages 136; 153-164.*   1 2 3 4 5

4. *I lost interest in life. See pages 221-259; 284-285.*   1 2 3 4 5

5. *My eating patterns have changed for the worse (loss of appetite, weight gain).*   1 2 3 4 5
    See pages 221-259.

6. *I can't stop blaming myself for my troubles. See pages 137; 177-188.*   1 2 3 4 5

7. *I feel distressed about making mistakes. See pages 189-202.*   1 2 3 4 5

8. *My body feels sluggish. See pages 221-259; 284-285.*   1 2 3 4 5

9. *I think about killing myself. See pages 10, 27, 37.*   1 2 3 4 5

10. *When I feel stressed, I use drugs (nicotine, cocaine, pot, alcohol, or some*   1 2 3 4 5
    other drug) to calm down. See pages 207-210.

11. *I get down on myself when I don't meet my expected expectations.*   1 2 3 4 5
    See pages 189-202.

12. *I've lost my energy. See pages 221-259; 284-285.*   1 2 3 4 5

13. *I've lost my ambition. See pages 221-259; 284-285.*   1 2 3 4 5

14. *I have no hope for the future. See pages 165-176.*   1 2 3 4 5

15. *I have difficulty attending and concentrating. See pages 221-259; 284-285.*   1 2 3 4 5

16. *I can't do anything right. See pages 189-202.*   1 2 3 4 5

17. *I put things off that I need to do. See pages 5-6; 49-50; 62-65; 182.*   1 2 3 4 5

18. *Inconveniences frustrate me. See pages 203-220.*   1 2 3 4 5

19. *I want to fall asleep and never wake up. See pages 10, 27, 37.*   1 2 3 4 5

20. *I feel sad and down most of the time. See pages 22-28.*   1 2 3 4 5

21. *I feel rushes of anger. See pages 246-248.*   1 2 3 4 5

22. *I have trouble making decisions. See pages 30-31.*   1 2 3 4 5

23. *I feel guilt over the things I have done.* See pages 249-250.   1   2   3   4   5

24. *I think badly of myself.* See pages 133-135; 141-152.   1   2   3   4   5

25. *I'm unable to experience pleasure.* See pages 221-259.   1   2   3   4   5

26. *I feel ill (chest pains, dizziness, stomachache, lower back pain, or other ailment).*   1   2   3   4   5
     See pages 221-259.

27. *I can't stand the way I feel.* See pages 203-221.   1   2   3   4   5

28. *I have panic attacks.* See pages 238-242.   1   2   3   4   5

29. *I get easily frustrated.* See pages 203-221.   1   2   3   4   5

30. *I feel ashamed of myself.* See pages 251-254; 284.   1   2   3   4   5

31. *I feel edgy (irritable, fidgety, agitated, can't sit still).* See pages 203-220; 221-259.   1   2   3   4   5

32. *I feel like a failure.* See pages 141-152; 189-202.   1   2   3   4   5

How to Interpret the Depression Inventory

The depression inventory demonstrates that depression has known characteristics. It serves as a tool to pin down significant issues that relate to your depression. After completing the inventory, you may better target depression zones that apply to you. You can use this information to identify helpful resources within this workbook.

When you rank an item 3 or above on the depression inventory, it is probably worth reviewing. The items you rank 4 and 5 can be core factors in your depression that merit special attention. Learning to deal effectively with core factors can light a path up from depression.

When you feel depressed, your response to the items are likely to be weighted on the negative side of the scale. You may rank the majority of the items in a negative direction. If you rank most items 4 and 5, here is something to consider: depressive themes tend to repeat themselves. Rather than have, say, 32 separate high-ranking conditions to deal with, you may have multiple examples of a few key ingredients. Use the following key to map your own themes and to help focus what areas you want to address.

Item 20 is the prime condition associated with depression. It refers to a depressed mood. A rank of 3 or higher on this item suggests that depression is a painful condition for you.

Items 3, 6, 7, 14, 16, 18, 24, 27, and 32 represent depressive thoughts. If you scored 3 or higher on any of these items, you've identified an area that can be gainfully addressed through the cognitive behavioral procedures described in this book.

Possible physical ingredients of depression appear in items 2, 4, 5, 8, 12, 13, 15, 25, 26, and 31. They can be addressed through exercise, diet, and antidepressant medication. Learning to tolerate these physical conditions, which is discussed in chapter 14, can bring relief.

Some inventory questions relate to common coexisting conditions. Anxiety, anger, guilt, and perfectionism, for instance, commonly coexist with depression. Items 1, 11, 17, 21, 22, 23, 28, 29, and 30 refer to cognitively toned conditions that commonly coexist with depression. You can address the negative thinking behind these unpleasant states using the same techniques you learn for dealing with depressive thinking.

Item 10 refers to substance abuse. If you use addictive substances to medicate yourself against depression, this typically backfires. It is especially difficult to address depression while trying to escape from depression through, say, using alcohol. Often depression deepens as people get addicted to these "cures." These problem habits of consumption typically include addictive thinking, such as "I need a drink to relax." You can address this addictive thinking using the same techniques that you would for dealing with depressive thinking.

Items 9 and 19 represent suicidal thoughts. When people feel depressed, such thoughts are common.

At one time or another, most people who experience a significant depression will wish they were dead. Although the topic of suicide prevention goes beyond the scope of this self-help book, there are many things to do. For example, relabeling suicidal thoughts *depressive thinking* can give you a different perspective on the meaning of the thoughts. Nevertheless, if you gave a 4 or 5 rating to either or both of items 9 and 19, and you have a plan to end your life, strongly consider talking with a licensed psychologist, psychiatrist, or social worker. Suicide is a leading preventable cause of death.

You can use the inventory as a progress measure. Copy it. Retake it every two weeks to track your progress. Once past your depressed mood, retaking the inventory every several months can serve as an early alert system. If you notice increases on the scale of depression, you can mobilize efforts to prevent depression from coming back.

TWELVE STEPS TO POSITIVE CHANGE

When you are depressed, it can be hard to think of positive steps to take. You may feel that you lack enough energy to think of what to do differently. If you choose not to use antidepressants, however, you can still take certain steps to improve your mood. This section discusses the best steps that I know of—I used them on myself when I was depressed and they worked. I would recommend them to family and friends.

Even psychologists are not exempt from depression. Twenty-nine years ago, I went through a moderately severe major depression. I definitely experienced a seriously depressed mood. My physical symptoms included early morning awakening (arising early and not being able to fall back to sleep), irritability, appetite problems, fatigue, and difficulties concentrating. I often felt like I was wading through knee-deep tar with a lodestone on my back.

My depression evolved slowly. It was connected to major changes in my life and long work days. First, there were signs of an approaching storm. Then I felt swamped.

I knew that it was important to deal with depression, and that it was important to take steps—even small steps—to counteract this process. Three thoughts helped:

1. Depression is time-limited.

2. Activity is a remedy for depression.

3. Depressive thinking is a state of mind, not a concrete reality.

I was not under any illusion that I could quickly fix myself, but I also knew that this was a condition that I could not afford to let fester. I recognized the signs of depression, so I knew what I was up against. I also had success helping others deal with their depressions. That knowledge and experience gave me a unique advantage. If I thought that the techniques I used were helpful with my clients, they were good enough to use on myself.

Fortunately I knew the cognitive signatures of depressive thoughts. The cognitive signatures of depression are thought patterns that commonly link with depression. They include helplessness and hopelessness thinking. Knowing that certain thoughts are normally present with depression made it simpler to accept their existence and to contest them. I repeatedly acted to defeat this depressive thinking when I caught the ideas weaving through my mind.

I admit that I was not always on top of this process. Nevertheless, by making a special effort to overcome depressive thoughts, I did myself considerable good and, I'm convinced, shortened the duration of my depression. Throughout this workbook, I'll share my thoughts with you on ways to go about this task.

The twelve steps I followed will normally apply, in one degree or other, to the different forms of depression. They're outlined below. These methods will be fleshed out in greater detail as you progress through the book.

Twelve Techniques for Alleviating Depression

1. Eat healthy.
2. Stick to priorities.
3. Look for the novel.
4. Persist.
5. Resolve conflicts.
6. Exercise.
7. Maintain relations.
8. Learn relaxation methods.
9. Dispute negative thinking.
10. Use downtime constructively.
11. Plan special activities.
12. Get fresh air and sun.

1. I made sure that I immediately avoided mental traps associated with depressive thinking. I monitored my self-talk and identified and contested depressive thinking.

2. I joined a health club and forced myself to exercise at least five times a week. This helped me break the depressive cycle, overcome fatigue, and improve my concentration.

3. Despite a poor appetite, I forced myself to eat a balanced diet.

4. I turned my early morning awakening to advantage. During the period between 4:00 A.M., when I awoke, and 9:00 A.M., when I started seeing clients, I used the time to write a book titled *Do It Now: How to Break the Procrastination Habit* (1998). I found this writing tedious. Often I felt bogged down. But I forced myself to attend, concentrate, and persist.

5. I acted to maintain good relationships with people and to seek opportunities to be with people. During those times, I refused to complain about how I felt. Instead, I encouraged people to speak more about themselves. Since most people like to hear themselves talk, this worked well.

6. I pushed myself to resolve conflicts and to overcome difficulties as they arose, and before they might fester.

7. I did not concern myself over interrupted sleep. Rather, I used a Jacobson's muscular relaxation technique when I couldn't fall back to sleep. I found that this had restorative value. (See chapter 14 for a description of this procedure.)

8. I stuck to my main priorities and drastically cut back on low priorities. Simultaneously, I backed off and tried not to overtax myself at low energy periods.

9. I made sure I got out in the sun and walked for about a half hour a day. I did this around noon.

10. Each day I tried to find something I hadn't seen before. This helped shift my focus from my depressed mood onto events that were novel. Seeking novelty served as a temporary distraction from depression.

11. Every day I planned one change in my routine. The change required an action initiative. I thought about this initiative the day before I executed it. I walked myself through the mental paces. Then, when the anointed hour arrived, I walked myself through the actual paces. These new activities were normally of low impact, such as eating breakfast at a new restaurant or walking around a block the opposite way.

12. I maintained a high level of trust and confidence in my plan and I persisted with it.

With regard to activity as a remedy for depression, practically anything will do, from cleaning bathroom tiles with a toothbrush to weeding the garden. You might find that a half hour a day or more of these activities can help you shift your focus away from depressive thoughts. Your body might feel less tense. Although this is a palliative technique, when practiced repeatedly, this approach can have a positive, cumulative effect.

Although I did not follow the twelve steps like clockwork, I managed to follow through in a reasonable way. The depression lasted about four months. But I had pretty much waded out of the worst part of the muck within two months. Since that time, I've been fairly consistent in maintaining the twelve-point routine, and I've rarely had a significant period when I felt in a depressed mood.

These activities are healthy to follow. You may also be taking or considering taking antidepressant medication. I decided against medication because I was concerned about possible side effects and I was unimpressed with the results I had seen in others. For some, however, the antidepressant option is a reasonable choice—different people have different responses to medication. When medication has positive effects, it can help make it easier to do some of the things outlined in this book.

Social supports can prove valuable as well. An understanding buddy or group can do these things:

■   Encourage you to engage in positive activities.

■   Give you a gentle push and accompany you, say, to a health club for exercise.

■   Help monitor your progress.

■   Help support a contract you make with yourself as to what you will do to address your depression.

Some people tend to be private and prefer to do things on their own, and this includes dealing with depression. For others, it is important to work with others to avert loneliness and for support. A friendly counselor, buddy, friend, spouse, brother, or sister can sometimes help. A guide, coach, or mentor obviously can't change depressive thinking and actions for you, but he or she can encourage you to engage in helpful activities. In approaching people for help, recognize that it is okay to admit to feeling depressed to people you have good reason to trust and who you believe could be helpful.

If you had a broken leg, you wouldn't hide it. Depression is like a broken spirit. Accepting the reality that depression is present, sharing that knowledge with others, opens other options for defeating depression, such as writing a contract with a buddy where there is a commitment to do reasonable activities.

Suppose you don't want to involve people you know in your antidepressant program, but you believe you can do better with some form of social support. What then? You may find a support group for people with depression in your community.

CATCHING THE TAILWIND TO BEAT DEPRESSION

In this section, you'll find some ideas to help get this process started. These techniques are brief methods that are like a helpful breeze that can blow the sails of your ship toward a safe harbor that is free of depression. They include both practical and imaginative "breezes."

The following techniques include the use of a benefits analysis to set the compass toward the harbor, the use of metaphor and poetry to help you find your way through the storm of depression, a way to end a double-trouble problem that often coexists and deepens the distress of depression, and a daily gratitude technique and other techniques that can further billow your sails.

Take a Long- and Short-Term Benefits Analysis

The following exercise can help put into perspective the advantages and disadvantages of antidepressant actions. In this analysis, you will consider the probable short- and long-term benefits of directly addressing depressive thinking. For example, the short-term benefits of acting against depressive thinking can include showing yourself that you are not helpless. This can feel relieving. Short-term benefits for waiting out the depression can include avoiding the initial strains that come with breaking a pattern of depressive thinking, emotions, and actions. But this passive approach can extend depression into long-term pain. Long-term benefits of taking action can include eliminating depression, crediting yourself for the results, and reducing the risk of a relapse.

LONG- AND SHORT-TERM BENEFITS ANALYSIS

Use the following chart to examine how you might benefit from addressing your depression now.

Action	Pushing Yourself to Break a Depression Pattern	Allowing a Depressive Process to Continue Unopposed
Short-Term Benefit		
Long-Term Benefit		

As you look over the results of your analysis, does it make more sense to let depression wind down on its own or to actively address depressive thinking now?

Find a Meaningful Pursuit

Life is so much more than trying to negate negatives. It is never too early in a process of curbing depression to think about engaging in a positive or passionate pursuit. Do you have to have had a passion or pursuit before you got depressed? No! You can choose a pursuit and make it happen.

The more time you spend in meaningful pursuits, the less time you spend with depressive thoughts. So plant a garden. Tend the garden. Watch the plants grow. Feed squirrels. Take that old multicolored rag that you've used to wipe paint from brushes. Stretch it, frame it, and call it something like "random art." Carve sculptures out of soap. Watch butterflies in flight. Photograph birds in a tree.

Positive activities distract from depressive thoughts. They can bring a change in your mood. What about simple, positive activities that you once enjoyed that are still within your power to do? For example, how *would* you spend your time if you were not depressed? What activities previously gave you pleasure? List these activities. Here are some examples: Soak in a warm bath. Listen to a favorite song. Crochet a tablecloth. Write a friend. Meet a friend for an athletic activity. Make a bird feeder. Play a video, computer, or board game. Watch a favorite comedy.

POSITIVE ACTIVITY LIST

Use this activity list to note former pleasures. Then reenact the pleasure—even if you don't feel like it.

1. _____

2. _____

3. _____

4. _____

5. _____

Plan to do at least one formerly pleasurable activity each day—whether you feel like it or not!

Another form of pursuit is to exercise your senses. When you feel drawn into a world of depression, your senses may feel dulled, but they are still available. Use your sensory powers to focus on external experiences. For example, I'll often have my depressed clients walk around their neighborhoods and pay attention with all their senses. I ask them to see something they had not seen before. I ask them to use their sense of smell to scan for different scents. They can listen for familiar sounds like the songs of birds, but also listen for something new. A sense of touch comes into play when they touch tree trunks or feel a breeze. I suggest they bring with them something they can taste, such as coffee or a favorite treat. This sensory experience demonstrates how to use sensory power to redirect your attention away from depression.

Atlanta psychotherapist Ed Garcia (pers. comm.) has a sensory exercise he reports that many of his depressed clients came to enjoy. The exercise involves charting the use of each of your five senses five times each day. For the sense of smell, you could smell the aroma of coffee, smell a favorite perfume, smell a rose, smell a blade of grass, smell the interior of a new automobile, or smell a collection of herbs. You can follow the same routine daily, or substitute in other sensory experiences.

FIVE-BY-FIVE SENSORY EXERCISE

Use the following chart to list your senses and how you intentionally use them during the day:

Sense	Experience 1	Experience 2	Experience 3	Experience 4	Experience 5
Touch					
Taste					
Smell					
Sight					
Sound					

Following the five-by-five sensory exercise daily can help interrupt your flow of depressive thoughts and increase the amount of time you stand aside from a cycle of depression.

Establish a Beacon

Beacons are powerful ideas that can override the onslaught of depressive thinking. Winston Churchill, the prime minister of Great Britain during World War II, suffered a horrific depression. He described his version of depression as a "black dog." He drank excessively to silence the dog. Some days he could not get himself out of bed. As to his role during the war, he wrote in his autobiography that the war kept him going. He thought it was his destiny to keep England mobilized to bring victory. Because of this mission, Churchill mobilized himself to rise above his depression. A key idea was his beacon. He saw his war responsibility as one of destiny.

President Abraham Lincoln suffered from ongoing bouts of depression. He held himself together because he saw the Civil War as a just war. Lincoln also recognized that his personal happiness was his personal responsibility. He once said, "A man is about as happy as he makes up his mind to be." Lincoln found his beacons.

Churchill and Lincoln send an important message to us. They show that you can use your mind to override an oppressive depression. Their efforts were even more impressive considering that cognitive types of therapy had not been invented. There was no antidepressant medication on the market. Philosophy, will, vision, and self-determination were the tools each used to cope with depression. Their beacons gave them reasons for going on.

> Beacon thought contributed by Edward Garcia:
>
> "My feelings have governed my thinking, and I shall now make my thinking govern my feelings" (pers. comm.).

Few snap their fingers and get a beacon. These are usually inventions of the mind, or they come from other sources. Beacon thoughts can come at any time, even when you least expect them.

Can you intentionally find an organizing principle that becomes a beacon for a constructive direction? Play with ideas. Find core themes from the lives of others. Recall what you wanted to accomplish when you were a child.

YOUR INSPIRATION BEACONS

Write down your beacon thoughts in the space below:

_____

_____

_____

Beacon thoughts can come to mind at any time. You may even awaken in the early hours with a thought that points to a cause or to a direction. Perhaps a beacon thought is *experience life*. Then the question becomes, what is it that you want to experience? When you get a new idea, write it down. Such powerful ideas will help you fight depression.

Use Metaphors, Similes, Allegories, and Poetry

One of the most consistent findings in brain research on depression is that depression is associated with relatively less activity in the left than the right frontal lobe (Heller and Nitschke 1997). The right hemisphere is associated with negativity and creativity. Perhaps that is where negative metaphors gain hold. By intentionally working to develop positive metaphors, you can compete with the negative variety associated with depression. Positive metaphors can serve as a means of guiding your positive actions to defeat depression.

Using Metaphors

Metaphor is a figurative comparison, such as "life is a cornucopia." Churchill, for example, metaphorically described depression as his black dog. These metaphors can evoke powerful images.

Churchill's "black dog" of depression grabs the imagination. "A prison beneath jimsonweed" calls forth another depressing image. "Trapped in a tomb" conjures a third. Such lyrical, visual, and sometimes poetic images are examples of the creative imagination stimulated by depression. We can describe depression as a crystal ball of gloom. But depressive images are not oracles. Mental images are different from the actual future.

Metaphors can describe depression. They also can point to exits from depression: Blind bats of depression fly in the blackness of night. Throw stones of reason and disable the fliers. (Note: Think of bats swarming with different depressive ideas inscribed on each. Inscribe stones with counter-depression facts, questions, or challenges.)

Use the box below to describe your sense of depression using metaphor. It can be something as brief as "my enemy." Then describe an action metaphor to counteract it. "Laser-guided missiles of reason quell the enemy." Whenever you think a depressed metaphor, contrast it with an action metaphor. This comparison can give you a sense that you can metaphorically shift your perspectives from gloom to control. By sticking with the antidepressant metaphor, you may find that you can use it to trump the despair of depression.

FIND A METAPHOR

Use the space below to create a positive action metaphor that contrasts with a depression metaphor.

Depression Metaphor: _____

_____

Action Metaphor: _____

_____

Using Similes

A simile draws a comparison between two things. "Dark as depression" is such a comparison. Depressive similes strike an emotional chord that you can reverse. If depression is like a chilling cold, then imagine a beam of light bathing your body in warmth. If life is like entrapment in a tomb, then imagine walking a path into the light with others who have defeated depression. This change in perspective can balance the language of depression with the language of optimism.

FIND A SIMILE

Use the space below to create a positive simile.

_____

_____

_____

Using Allegories

Allegories convey ideas of deeper meanings. In these narratives, characters represent abstract ideas used to convey a message. Here is an example of a depression allegory:

A denizen of depression awoke one morning in a temple of rationality. Still shrouded by a melancholic veil, the denizen moved like a snail with rubbery movements. As depression pounded on, the person recognized that the deadening sensations were as they were and thought, "If a dog experienced depression, would it distress itself by dwelling upon its condition? The dog would live from moment to moment. Although bound by depression, the dog would be free from the tyrannies of pessimistic expectations. And when the veil lifted, the dog would live from moment to moment but with quickened stride."

CREATE AN ALLEGORY

Make up an allegory that is meaningful to you that symbolizes the meaning of a realistic tolerance for depression. Through developing tolerance for depression, you can decrease the intensity of the experience.

_____

_____

_____

Using Poetry

Poems can provide a useful way to portray a personal meaning of depression. Normally, the poem describes this misery lyrically. But why not create both a depressing poem and a contrasting action poem that shows a pathway from depression?

By writing a poem that describes a path away from depression, you might titillate that part of your mind that links to more positive emotions. The following two collaboratively written poems illustrate this contrast.

A Shadow World

Into a mirror I see
A world of shadows surrounding me
As life faintly echoes through the hollow
The shadows cloak the path I follow.
Like a dog that hunts in darkness
With no scent, or sight
It experiences a dulling fright
As it climbs a lightless height.
Reflecting,
Detecting,
Suspecting,
Why has this struggle chosen me?

—Bill Knaus, Dale Jarvis, Diana Cleary

A World of Disengagement

On the trail of life one day
I met depression on the way
Although the burden sank me low
I decided to let depression go.
Now that the challenge is set
It's up to me to see it met
Perhaps the dog will get the scent
Through action, I'll see depression relent.
Farewell to my familiar guard
Who'd kept me sheltered within my nest.
I'll consider you a friend who protected me when
My heart wasn't ready to solo this quest.

—Bill Knaus, Diana Cleary

WRITE POETRY

Use the space below to write your own contrasting poems.

Avoid Double Troubles

Are you tired of feeling depressed? Do you agitate yourself about feeling depressed? Do you ever tell yourself something like "I'm sick of being sick?" If so, this is a form of double-trouble thinking where you layer a problem on top of a problem. The secondary problem can dramatically worsen your depression.

Sometimes called a double whammy, double-trouble thinking includes such ideas as "I must not feel this way," "it's awful that I feel depressed," and "I can't stand feeling depressed." Double troubles can also involve panic over panicking, worry over worry, or anxiety over anxiety. This reaction to tension can feel more stressful than the original strain.

The author of *Three Minute Therapy*, San Francisco psychotherapist Michael Edelstein, describes how getting upset about being upset is elusive, pervasive, and often not observed (Edelstein, Steele, and Ramsey 1997). Because the secondary condition is not attached to an observable external event, the psychoanalyst Sigmund Freud described it as free floating. Edelstein sees this condition as tied to irrational thinking about depression. Thus, it is not free floating.

To help separate one trouble from the other, Edelstein (pers. comm.) suggests these two questions:

1. "Am I depressed over feeling depressed?"

2. "Do I feel depressed about something(s) that happened that affected me directly?"

Here the idea is to figure out if you are facing one or two levels of distress.

Edelstein also suggests looking at whether you think you are depressed about nothing in particular, but practically everything in general. This condition of mind can be a prelude to being upset about feeling upset.

Questions for Ending Double Troubles

No one goes through life without some disappointments and sad experiences. When unexpectedly faced with such conditions, knowing how depressive thinking works can give you an edge. You can better accept the condition and the accompanying stress sensations by acting to quell the double misery of depressive thinking about the experience.

In chapter 7, you'll learn about a basic ABC technique for addressing irrational forms of thinking that relate to double troubles. For now, here are some questions to put double troubles into perspective:

- Is it possible for you to accept the unpleasant and sometimes painful mood, sensations, and thoughts of depression?

- Is it possible to shift perspective from how badly you feel to how you've managed to operate despite depression?

- What positive information have you gathered about your ability to survive depression?

- What things have you learned from your experience with depression that you think would be helpful for someone else to know who also feels depressed?

> When you take concrete steps to exit depression, you simultaneously take steps to shift perspective to seeing life as evolving, and not as depressively static.

By focusing your attention on positive answers to these four questions, you can shift your attention toward what you can accomplish, rather than on how rotten you might feel.

Daily Gratitude Technique

U.K. counselor Jim Byrne (pers. comm.) suggests an exercise for shifting perspective from inward-directed depressive thoughts to a more balanced perspective. His daily gratitude technique can prove useful to a subgroup of people with depression, where a shift in focus from inner complaints to gratitude can prove helpful in alleviating the pain of depression. Byrne's perspective-shifting exercise divides into two phases, which you can try:

- At the end of each day, write down three things that happened for which you can be genuinely grateful. These can be tiny, almost insignificant events. For example, the sunrise, the sunset, the taste of honey, and the smell of baking bread may all be experiences that can evoke a sense of gratitude. Seeking experiences to feel grateful for can help counteract unhealthy doomsday-type depressive thoughts.

- Identify people who have been kind to you or who have helped you. Tell them of your gratitude. It could be as simple as saying "I appreciated . . . ," "thank you for . . . ," or "I like it when. . . ." Small acts of acknowledgment from you can help shift your focus from what is going wrong in your life to helping others realize that what they do can make a difference.

It is in the nature of depression that attention draws inward; both the inner and outer world seem bleak. Byrne's two-phase daily gratitude technique can help you to shift your focus from negativity toward gratitude for external gifts. By acknowledging events and people to appreciate, you can find that it is harder to maintain extremist depressive thinking views, such as "nothing is worthwhile."

"Just Do It" Technique

Florida psychologist Robert Heller (pers. comm.) suggests a way to block the downward spiral of depression. When in a depressive spiral, people tend to withdraw from others and from many activities of normal daily living. In an often ill-fated hope that they'll get their lives back to normal once depression passes, members of this subgroup tend to allow this downward spiral to go uninterrupted. This wait-for-a-better-day illusion often leads to an increased sense of isolation and loneliness. As an alternative, he suggests a "just do it" technique where you initially act without inspiration.

Heller is initially not concerned about the recognition of depressive thinking and of connecting the dots between events, thoughts, and depressive feelings. He takes the position that by changing your behavior, you can shift your focus from depressive thoughts and premonitions to antidepressant action themes.

As a motivational tool, he suggests keeping an activity log in a notebook. The purpose of the log is to keep track of what you do each day and to gradually and consistently add activities, regardless of how you feel. This record provides a progress measure.

Through reviewing your ongoing record, you can recognize gaps in your activities, say, where you avoid personal contacts that might help curb loneliness. You might then add activities that increase interpersonal contacts. They can include greeting neighbors, asking a clerk in a store for information about a product, or asking where the product may be found. Instead of shopping once a week, you might choose to shop for a different basic item each day.

To benefit from this procedure, you would continue doing this exercise even if you experience no initial benefit or pleasure. After all, a prime feature of depression is a loss of pleasure. Even though you may gain no short-term pleasure through this process, it, nevertheless, represents a viable path up and away from depression.

This "just do it, even if you don't feel like it" technique is consistent with one of this book's main themes, which is to apply procrastination technology to defeat the depressive process. The "just do it" process provides at least five benefits:

1. You are taking steps to avoid becoming overwhelmed. Thus, you'll have fewer things to attend to once past depression.

2. You are showing yourself that you don't have to feel inspired to follow through on what is useful to do.

3. Accepting that some activities will not bring pleasure can counter thoughts that you have to wait to feel inspired before doing better. (The opposite is often true. You act to do better in order to get better.)

4. By looking beyond the moment, you are acting to accept that the side effects from this kind of "medicine" are far less than the effects of the downward spiral of depression. Even with the possible absence of initial pleasure with the change, in the longer term, this process can help break the back of depression.

5. You are acting against procrastination, which will help you avoid a downward spiral of depression.

If the idea of "just doing it" seems overwhelming right now, that's understandable. The next section discusses this dilemma and what to do about it.

Rehearsing the Change

When depressed, there will be a gap between your current experiences and your nondepressed future experiences. At least part of the gap can be filled with activities directed toward disabling the depressive process you experience. But following through with antidepressant activities that you may not feel like doing is asking a lot when you feel depressed. In the probable absence of short-term pleasure for accomplishments, you almost have to act on faith that a "just do it" technique can pay off.

Let's assume you decide that the "just do it" technique can be helpful, but you still experience yourself glued to a seat of depression. To get started, here's a simple time projection technique described by psychologist Arnold Lazarus (1971). Using this method, you project yourself several days to years into the future where you see yourself functioning effectively. Lazarus (pers. comm.) believes that this time projection is helpful when you feel depressed.

To use this technique, you first decide how you would put yourself through the paces at a time in the future. For example, if a "just do it" goal is to initiate social contacts, then, in your mind's eye, put yourself through the paces, where you give yourself instructions and experience how you'd like to feel. Then, imagine yourself going through the paces. Here's my version of how to structure this time projection process:

1. First decide what actions would be in your best long-term interest to take. This can break down into a dichotomy of choices: Do nothing to interrupt a sense of isolation and allow a depressive spiral to play itself out. Or take steps—however small—to help break a sense of isolation.

2. Let's assume that you believe that purposeful, directed, antidepressant social actions can, over the long run, help relieve loneliness and stem the flow of depressive thoughts, feelings, and behaviors. Now, you have a rational basis for looking beyond the moment of depression to a future filled with relief from depression. Next, the question is how can you bridge the gap between now and some point in the future? Mentally rehearsing and taking follow-up actions can help bridge the gap.

3. In mentally rehearsing the behavioral part of this change process, imagine yourself, say, going to a grocery store for a loaf of bread. You first walk to your vehicle (or walk toward the store, if that is what you normally do), get into the vehicle, start the car, drive to the store, park the vehicle, walk into the store, walk to the area where the bread is shelved, pick up the bread, and walk to the check-out counter. Imagine yourself making small talk with the cashier, such as saying "it's a nice day," then leaving and saying "have a nice day."

4. Follow up on your time projection mental rehearsal by taking the steps you rehearsed in your mind.

5. Remind yourself that you don't have to initially feel any pleasure through this type of activity. The idea is to help prevent or curb a downward spiral of depression, where a sense of isolation and loneliness triggers and supports the process.

By mentally rehearsing actions, you prepare your mind, emotions, and muscles for taking action. This preparation can lead to purposeful antidepressant actions that you may have previously thought you were precluded from taking.

Later, you can expand on mental rehearsals to include the type of positive thinking, emotions, and behavior that can override depressive thinking, stress-related sensations, and depressive behaviors.

KEY IDEAS AND ACTION PLAN

At the end of each chapter from now on, you'll find space to sketch notes about the key ideas and exercises that you found most useful. Following that, you'll find space to develop an action plan. This is where you list the actions that you can take to disrupt your depression.

This recording process provides a record for you to refer back to. Human memory is fallible. The notes you take can jog that memory. It also can be useful to periodically refer back to what you thought was important and what you can do. This process of active participation in your evolution from depression can promote positive change. Try it and see!

Key Ideas

What are the key ideas you got from this chapter that you found helpful?

1. _____

_____

2. _____

_____

3. _____

_____

Action Plan

What actions can you take to progress?

1. _____

_____

2. _____

_____

3. _____

_____

When it comes to taking action against depression, if you are like most, you'll likely let the ideas swirl about in your mind. Then, you'll tentatively test a few. That's a normal phase of making constructive changes. However, getting stuck at the level of awareness, without following through with action, is like eating empty calories.

POSTSCRIPT

From time to time, people will inventory their lives to see what is going well, and what is not. This process typically involves a global check to see where to make adjustments, what to drop, and what to continue doing. When depressed, an inventory of your life can look bleak. It may seem that nothing is worth doing. But then, an inventory of your thoughts and signs of depression gives you areas to target that you can progressively change. That's a real form of hope!

There are multiple ways to address depression. Finding a way to develop resiliency from depression is part of the challenge. When depressed, practically any action can seem strenuous. However, forcing yourself into constructive actions can both be challenging and productive. Although any one action may not tip the balance in a direction away from depression, it is the cumulation of actions—even snail-paced actions—that can eventually shift the weight in favor of relief from depression.

CHAPTER 3

A Master Plan to Defeat Depression

If you visit a cognitive behavioral therapist, you may hear these questions: What brings you here? What would you like to accomplish? How might you proceed? The therapist's questions point to what is often a challenging journey with many twists and turns along the way.

When you bought this book, it is likely that the theme attracted your attention because you'd like to get past feeling depressed. This chapter seeks to help answer how you can proceed. It describes how to develop a master system for addressing and defeating depression and thus provides a compass for your journey.

Through developing a self-guidance program to defeat depression, you can boost your effectiveness in overcoming this ancient nemesis. Part of the process involves gathering facts and reliable information about depression, using your mind like a planning room, and mapping out a path to overcome depressive thinking.

In your imaginary planning room, you'll find a chalkboard, chalk, and an eraser. In developing your self-guidance program, you can use information from your depression inventory in chapter 2 and what you now know about the nature of your depression. You can write this information onto your imaginary chalkboard. However, this process is fluid. You are likely to make changes over time. Throughout this workbook, you'll get additional ideas to improve your self-guidance plan. That's why you have an eraser. When you get a better idea, eliminate the older version, and replace it with the new.

> The Greek philosopher Socrates once said that "the unexamined life is not worth living."

METACOGNITIVE THINKING

Psychologist John Flavell (1979) coined the term *metacognitive* to describe a self-monitoring approach that involves thinking about thinking and connecting knowledge, beliefs, and strategies to achieve desired results. Metacognitive approaches have been used in classroom settings and found to increase determination and learning autonomy (Vandergrift 2005). Flexible executives use feedback to adjust their metacognitive thinking and actions so as to better achieve their corporate vision. However, metacognition has a dark side. People who obsess over their thinking can distress themselves and distract themselves from taking constructive forward-looking actions.

Psychologist John Dollard (1942) thought that people could monitor their thoughts and connect them to their emotions and actions. He called this process "self-study." Dollard's approach involved monitoring self-talk, setting goals, working out plans, and putting the plans to the test.

Combining the metacognitive idea of thinking about thinking with self-study is a platform for devising a metacognitive self-guidance plan. By using this approach, you can boost your chances to get past the clouds of depression.

SEVEN SELF-GUIDANCE STEPS

Metacognitive self-guidance is an awareness and action process that includes:

1. Establishing a mission

2. Setting goals

3. Planning to meet the goals

4. Implementing the plan

5. Evaluating your progress

6. Revising the plan

7. Recognizing procrastination impediments

> Self-knowledge is rarely static. Self-study is an organic process.

By setting a mission, you give yourself a direction. Through establishing goals, you identify steps to achieve the mission. Your action plan provides a design for achieving your goals. By executing the plan, you move forward and test its validity. By evaluating the results of your plan, you identify its strengths and what needs improvement. Using your evaluation, you revise your plan. Through this process, you can improve your metacognitive self-guidance system.

Once you overcome the distress of depression, you may find it desirable to expand your range of self-knowledge, build quality relationships, and routinely deal with the inevitable stresses that are part of life. Metacognitive self-guidance can support such desires to get more out of life with fewer needless hassles.

Metacognitive self-guidance has many uses that go beyond depression. Besides using it to get more out of life, you can use it for general health purposes, such as designing and modifying a diet-and-exercise program. But for now, let's see how to use metacognition to address and defeat depression.

Establishing a Self-Development Mission

A self-development mission is a long-term assignment for accomplishing what you desire. A properly articulated mission is important because it describes the direction and key ingredient for change.

The metacognitive mission described here is a two-stage process that involves doing something to gain something. The Indian independence leader Mahatma Gandhi's mission was to free India for self-rule. An example of a counter-depression mission is to defeat depressive thinking in order to free your mind from depressive strain. Missions also can represent a special purpose, such as to develop your personal resources to contribute to the welfare of those who can't care for themselves.

YOUR MISSION STATEMENT

Describe your antidepression mission in the space below:

_____

_____

_____

_____

Setting Goals

Setting goals is one of the most significant steps that you can take in an ongoing process of ridding yourself of depression. To achieve those goals, you need to establish objectives.

Objectives are like stepping-stones on the way to a goal. They describe specific and measurable actions to take to achieve the general goal. A walk in the park thirty minutes a day, rain or shine, is specific and it is measurable. A goal for effectively dealing with depressive thinking can involve the following objectives: recording depressive thoughts in a notebook; evaluating the validity of this thinking you record. A goal to boost your activity level can involve the following objectives: identifying the single-most important activity to accomplish during the day; picking a time to start; deciding on the first step.

SETTING GOALS TO COUNTER DEPRESSION

What are your counter-depression goals? What objectives support the goal?

Goal: _____

_____

Objectives: _____

_____

_____

_____

Goal: _____

_____

Objectives: _____

_____

_____

_____

Goal: _____

_____

Objectives: _____

_____

_____

_____

Setting goals can be one of the most valuable phases in a program to overcome depression. Once you've mapped the steps, your mind may play with the ideas as you get ready to take action. However, one limitation to a self-help book is that the book can't interact with you and say if the goal and objectives represent a reasonable path to achieve the mission. That is something that you have to do for yourself. If you have a willing acquaintance, family member, or counselor, however, who is interested and knowledgeable about setting goals and objectives, sharing ideas about this phase of the process can serve two purposes. You can refine your antidepressant goals and the specifics of the objectives. And by sharing this goal-development process, you are making an announcement to change. You may be more motivated to follow through on the objectives if you know that you have a "buddy in the wings," to whom you've announced that you are setting goals to make a change.

Converting Negativity into Positive Goals

When you look through a veil of pessimism, missions and goals may sound good for the other guy. You may see yourself as too smothered in depression to care much—or do much, even if you did care. Part of a metacognitive self-guidance approach is to think about your thinking and to address self-defeating thoughts and beliefs. This step provides a goal-related opportunity to turn depressive thoughts into positive goals. This process can be surprisingly effective in cutting through the "I don't care" inertia mentality that so often accompanies depression.

Depressive pessimism is seen in such thoughts as "I am lost. No one appreciates me. I can't get through this. I can't stand how I feel. I am useless." These thoughts suggest that you have no way up from the bondage of depression and that you will suffer forever. Although such pessimistic thoughts cast a pall of bleakness, they also suggest positive goals. Flip them around, and you may find a positive goal.

The following chart illustrates this process.

Depressive Pessimistic Thought	Positive Alternative Goal
I am lost.	Find a bearing.
No one appreciates me.	Find exceptions to this statement.
I can't get through this.	Question hopelessness assumptions.
I can't stand how I feel.	Learn to tolerate what I don't like.
I'm useless.	Question worthlessness assumptions.

THINK POSITIVE

Use the following space to translate your negative thinking into positive process goals:

Depressing Pessimistic Thought	Positive Alternative Goal

Planning to Meet the Goals

Missions and goals describe where you'll target your efforts based on what you want to accomplish. Plans represent procedures for turning ideas into actions. The planning phase of metacognitive self-guidance starts with two questions: What do I need to know and do to start? How will I go about achieving my goals?

Articulating your plans can seem like an unnecessary step. After all, if you have goals and objectives, why not just achieve them? The fact is that goals without plans often go nowhere. Depression can get in the way of the best articulated goals, but even those who aren't depressed can have trouble achieving goals. For example, around New Year's, many make resolutions. Few achieve their goals. That is because most people have vague plans or no plans at all. New Year's resolution procrastination is a classic example of how a goal without a plan can fizzle.

In the planning phase of this self-guidance process, you set priorities. The priorities determine what you will do first, second, and so forth. Each priority will have certain steps. The plan describes how you will take them and when you will take them. For example, you can sequence your activities of daily living to achieve a goal of "normalizing your life." The sequence can be your objectives, and the plan can be for when you execute them. A daily routine of showering at 7:00 A.M. each morning, going out to a local breakfast nook at 8:00 A.M., and taking a half hour walk at noon are positive actions that you can do to regularize your life and counteract depression, including seasonal affective disorder, if you suffer from it.

YOUR ACTION PLAN

What is your plan? Use the following space to describe your design:

_____

_____

_____

_____

_____

_____

_____

_____

_____

_____

_____

_____

_____

_____

_____

_____

_____

_____

_____

_____

_____

Implementing the Plan

The execution phase of your metacognitive self-guidance plan involves taking the steps you've outlined in your plan. To aid this process, you can add a step by talking yourself through the paces. For example, you can say the following:

- "I'll record depressive thinking in a notebook."

- "I'll organize this thinking according to logical categories."

- "I'll look at how these thoughts affect how I feel."

- "I'll test their plausibility by assessing their validity." (You'll learn more about plausibility testing in chapter 5.)

Executing a plan involves commanding your muscles to move. It can involve self-expressions and assertions. It can involve getting past impediments such as behavioral procrastination, where you come up with sound goals and a plan to execute them, and then quit at the phase of execution. This is like preparing for a race, running the race, and then stopping before getting to the finish line.

If you prepare yourself for action and bog down at this phase, then some of the techniques for dealing with behavioral procrastination can apply. Later in this chapter, you can look at ways to counteract behavioral procrastination.

Evaluating Your Progress

Few self-guidance plans are flawless from the start. Therefore, revisions are common. This self-guidance evaluation starts with these questions:

- "Did I give myself workable instructions to implement the plan?"

- "Did I follow the process I set for myself?"

- "If I accurately followed the plan, what did I learn?"

- "What unexpected conditions came into play?"

- "If I avoided the plan, where did the breakdown occur?"

YOUR EVALUATION

What did you learn through this evaluative process? Use the following space to describe what you learned:

_____

_____

_____

_____

Revising the Plan

Accomplishments are often preceded by revisions. You don't get to be a skilled accountant by just reading a job description. You have to pay the price to learn the trade. However, in using this metacognitive self-guidance approach, the accomplishment is often found in engaging the process. A potential by-product is that of decreasing depression.

Few things that are complex proceed without a hitch. The history of time is a great example of how we make advances through evolution and revolution. The ancients used various devices to measure the hours of the day, such as the sundial. But how could you measure time at night? The Egyptians devised a mechanism for measuring time that involved water flowing out of a container that had marks inside to designate the hours. Watches, clocks, and other time measurement devices keep us in constant touch with where we are during the day. The whole process is now much simpler than when sundials were common and people read the time from a container dripping water.

YOUR REVISIONS

As with the evolution of measuring time, your self-guidance program can undergo refinements. For example, what modifications or revisions would improve the plan?

_____

_____

In most instances, you can use what you learn from executing your plan to adjust your thinking and future actions to improve your self-guidance metacognitive system.

Recognizing Procrastination Impediments

Depression is an obvious impediment to a metacognitive self-guidance plan. When depressed, you may not feel like going through the drill. However, the act of preparing yourself for action and then taking action can give you a bearing to exit from the woods of depression.

Procrastination is a major impediment to overcoming depression. This habit of delay can be an offshoot of depression, predate depression, and contribute to depression.

What is this process called procrastination? Procrastination is an automatic habit pattern where you needlessly put off, postpone, or delay a timely and relevant activity until another day or time. Procrastination ordinarily starts with a perception that the more important activity is uncomfortable, unpleasant, boring, threatening, or negative. When depressed, you may even view basic activities as not doable.

When you procrastinate, you always substitute a less important activity for the one you put off. These diversionary activities can include daydreaming, sleeping, ruminating, watching TV, cleaning your fingernails, dwelling on your depressive thoughts, or doing something else that you'd typically put off but now find less burdensome. In this procrastination process, you are likely to tell yourself something like "later is better" or that you'll get to it when you feel inspired or energetic.

The Tomorrow Illusion

When procrastination fogs your vision
Tomorrow comes with a hidden division.
Concealed within a twisted hope,
Blinders cloak the way to cope.
Wrapped in the disguise of congeniality,
Procrastination pretends to be reality,
When we know with finality,
Tomorrow is on the run.
We smile, we laugh,
Long lost is our able nature.
We greet strangers with our mask.
Finding it is now the task.

—Bill Knaus, Diane Cleary, Dale Jarvis

Practically everyone will, from time to time, needlessly postpone priority activities until another day or time. Even the most efficient people have procrastination zones in their lives where they put important things off and then feel befuddled by a habit of delay that doesn't go away. When you feel distressed and depressed, you are more likely to postpone timely and relevant activities until another day or time. It doesn't matter if you were an efficiency dynamo before depression descended. You are likely to mimic procrastination thinking and avoidance actions when depressed.

When depressed, most people will find that it is initially easier to put off doing a metacognitive self-development activity than to follow through with it. If you follow through like a dynamo, the chances are that you are not so depressed as you think or more able to address depression than you may have once thought.

APPLYING PROCRASTINATION TECHNOLOGY TO DEPRESSION

A decision to delay until another day offers hope for a brighter tomorrow. However, when procrastination coexists with depression, this false optimism is often replaced by a false pessimism, such as "I'll never be able to do this." In this section, we'll look at how to use procrastination technology to overcome depression.

With *procrastination technology*, you apply your practical knowledge to challenge procrastination and follow through on what's important to do. This technology brings a powerful new awareness and action dimension to combating depression.

The "Do It Now" Exit Plan

Activity is a time-tested remedy for depression, and procrastination can get in the way. When procrastination coexists with depression, addressing procrastination boosts your chances to defeat depression.

The "do it now" prescription is an antidote for addressing both procrastination and depression. This approach involves doing reasonable things in a reasonable way within a reasonable time in order to increase your personal efficiency, effectiveness, and satisfaction. Your "do it now" pace, however, depends upon your energy and circumstance. Plodding along, when depressed, is consistent with the "do it now" view. This plodding can reduce the risk of feeling overwhelmed. With less to feel overwhelmed about, you'll have less to feel depressed about.

Defeating Dead-End Thinking

Procrastination normally involves a justification for the delay and a hope for a better tomorrow. This false hope is the *mañana ploy*.

> Procrastination is an excursion into a diversion where you substitute one activity for another. Part of the solution is to avoid taking the diversionary bait.

In the world of procrastination, the justification and hope for a better tomorrow are false. For example, you put off paying your bills while telling yourself it is too much of a hassle. You'll get to it later when inspired to pay them. But what is inspiring about paying bills? How far off into the future is *later*?

When you are not in a depressive funk, procrastination usually involves an upbeat justification for the delay, such as later is better. In depression, the reason for a needless delay often involves a pessimistic twist. You might think, "Why bother doing anything. I don't have the energy. Whatever I do is meaningless." This dead-end excuse is a version of *Catch 22 procrastination*, so called because you've boxed yourself in where there is no way out. This Catch 22 thinking is the opposite of the typical false optimism of procrastination thinking.

In Catch 22 thinking, you avoid following through because you pessimistically tell yourself that you can do nothing to help yourself. For example, you believe that getting an advanced degree could enable you to escape your current dead-end job, open opportunities for a profitable career, and help you overcome depression. But you don't believe that you have the ability to get the degree. So, you don't apply. Instead, you create a self-fulfilling prophesy and stick with the dead-end job.

You can cut through such self-fulfilling prophesies by looking for Catch 22 procrastination thinking. These excuses can take these forms: "I can't succeed, so why try?" or "I don't have the energy, and never will." By labeling these thoughts "Catch 22 predictions," you can change your perspective. For example, instead of "I can't succeed, so why try?" convert the fatalistic thought into an action goal: "I will write a check to pay my mortgage at 2:00 P.M." This action is definable, purposeful, and measurable.

If you think that discomfort (a depressed mood) is a signal to dodge an activity of daily living, this is a form of diversionary thinking that is similar to the Catch 22 variety. Accepting the discomfort of depression as part of the process of change is a leap forward.

The Sooner-or-Later Approach

Keeping up with your normal daily responsibilities reduces the risk of procrastination in that area of your life. To help yourself build follow-through into your daily routine, consider the "sooner-or-later" question. This question asks whether it makes sense to follow through now, or whether there is a strategic reason to delay until later.

CHOOSING WHEN TO START

If you think later is better because life will someday be easier, you have an interesting dilemma. Will it actually be better to begin later rather than now? Look at the advantages and disadvantages of starting later versus now. Write down your reasons for starting later. Then write down the potential consequences.

1. Reasons for starting later: _____

_____

2. Consequences for starting later in the form of advantages and disadvantages: _____

_____

Now that you've completed this exercise, would it be better to start now or later?

Basic Techniques for Addressing Procrastination

Here are a few basic tactics that people struggling with procrastination find useful. They also apply to depression:

- Identify and stick with your priorities.

- If a challenge is complex, break the priority activity down into subsets. Even the most complex of tasks has simple beginnings. Work in bits and pieces until done.

- Start the first subset using the five-minute method. Here you agree to work at the project for five minutes. At the end of the five minutes, you decide to continue for another five minutes or to come back later at a designated time.

- When you have a pressing priority to be done, refuse to engage in diversions, such as watching TV.

- When you have multiple activities of daily living that command attention, list them in order of their priority. Check off the activities as you finish them. Seeing yourself gain ground in this way can prove encouraging and rewarding. If your depression dulls the effects of a reward, at least you now have fewer things to do. You have taken action steps that illustrate that you are not helpless to act.

At a point when your depression diminishes and your energy starts to return, a new challenge emerges. You might think that you have too much catching up to do. If this frustrating thought arises, it can be followed by one of resignation: "It's useless to try to catch up." But this is a time to start to do what is most pressing and useful to do.

Three Techniques to Master Procrastination

To address procrastination that links with depression, consider the following options:

- Tune into your inner voice of procrastination and listen to what you are telling yourself. Is it something like "I don't have the energy to follow through"? If you hear this voice, then ask yourself what it will take to move one more step. Is it a vision of getting a step closer to wiping out your depression? Is it a sense of personal pride for you to see yourself stretching a bit farther? If the answer is yes to either question, then take the step. If you have no answer, force yourself to take the step and see if an answer arises from this process. If there is no meaningful answer, consider that you are now one step closer to your goal.

- Do you typically work better by project or by schedule? If you work better by schedule, set times to do listed actions. Then make a good-faith effort to follow the schedule. People who work better by schedule typically have several activities organized with designated times to do them. They may take a piecemeal approach to getting things done. If you work better by project, view the exercise as something to get done before moving on to something else. People who work better by project typically focus on the project as a priority and tend to work in longer time clumps. Other activities typically get put on the back burner when the project is in process. However, when depressed, you may have to lighten up on your schedule. Working by project can involve shorter time spans than usual.

- Pace yourself. If you have more energy later in the afternoon, save that time for doing those counter-depression activities that take the most concentration.

By addressing procrastination during times of depression, you evoke an activity remedy that can help disrupt depression. By applying procrastination technology to depression, you can decrease the number of tasks you would ordinarily delay and, thus, will have less to depress yourself over in the future. This efficiency can feel liberating.

KEY IDEAS AND ACTION PLAN

What are the key ideas that you got from this chapter? What actions can you take?

Key Ideas

What are the key ideas that you found helpful?

1. _____

   _____

2. _____

   _____

3. _____

   _____

Action Plan

What actions can you take to progress?

1. _____

   _____

2. _____

   _____

3. _____

   _____

POSTSCRIPT

A metacognitive self-guidance approach takes more than an afternoon of reflection. People develop this skill over several weeks or months. But this is a process that you can continue over a lifetime. This metagognitive self-guidance system can be an ongoing framework for learning and living. So start with a pencil and eraser. The process is likely to change with use and development.

CHAPTER 4

Recognizing Depressive Thinking

Throughout the day, we normally think thousands of thoughts—perhaps tens of thousands. Psychologist William James used the term *stream of consciousness* to describe this uninterrupted flow. But when depressed, this stream churns up more than its share of mud.

Focus on unpleasant experiences, describe yourself as a failure, view the future as hopeless, think of yourself as a burden to others, think that life is not worth living, and the chances are that you are thinking depressively. When active, this form of thinking is a distressing added source of misery.

Depressive thinking is typically automatic and does not represent a conscious choice, such as which shirt you will wear on any given day. I know of no one who chooses to think of the future with pessimism. It is not as though people with depression conspired with Edgar Allen Poe's raven who appeared at midnight above a door to cite the word "nevermore." But there is a real choice hidden here. It is in the decision whether to recognize and deal with this form of oppressive thinking.

IDENTIFYING DEPRESSIVE THOUGHTS

In a depressed state, people typically draw within themselves, ruminate on what plagues them, and reflect upon how bad they feel. Their ruminations typically center on personal problems, self-criticism, self-blame, helplessness, hopelessness, worthlessness, pessimism, and related states such as anxiety, shame, guilt, and anger. Many will tend to catastrophize about their situation, which is to say they exaggerate the situation while minimizing their ability to cope. These depressing thoughts feel real, but they represent a distorted reality. For example, when you tell yourself that you will "never" get better, or you will "always" stay depressed, you make an overgeneralization. That's a distortion. How could anyone possibly know the future with such a high degree of certainty?

If you feel depressed, it can seem like a forever proposition. But what happens when you break from depression, or go through a nondepressed period? How does "never" or "always" work then?

Your thinking can affect the degree to which you experience depression, but depressive sensations and mood can trigger depressive thinking. From whatever direction these thoughts arrive, when activated, they can come to influence your outlook and your mood.

How do you know if a thought is depressive? Here are several clues:

- A simple way to tell if a thought is depressive is by its results. Depressive thoughts have surplus negative meaning, which serves as a catalyst for the unpleasant and oft painful sensations of depression. They can and typically do deepen your sense of misery.

- You can take a common sense approach. If it sounds depressive, the chances are that the thought is depressive. Thoughts like "I'll never get over my loss, poor me" sound depressive.

- Depressive thoughts tend to occur repetitively. You are likely to recycle the same and similar thoughts again and again.

- Depressive thoughts have a distinctively pessimistic flavor.

- Although there is great variability in the content of these thoughts, they typically boil down to themes such as helplessness, hopelessness, worthlessness, and self-blame.

- Depressive thoughts represent a form of all-or-nothing overgeneralized thinking, where you see life in only one way—miserable—until you come to see things more pluralistically.

- Depressive thoughts can reflect a demanding tone translated through "should," "ought," or "must" thinking.

- Depressive thoughts can include a morphing of catastrophic expectations with a crashed mood punctuated by pessimism.

- Depressive thinking is typically circular, where a depressive mood reflects depressive thinking and vice versa.

- Depressive thoughts tend to be automatic and continue until recognized and overcome.

- Intrusive, negative, and unnecessary depressive thoughts are typically absent when your mood is neutral or positive.

As you proceed through this workbook, you will discover many examples of depressive thoughts. The examples provide additional ways to recognize depressive thinking. Chapter 5 gives examples of depressive thoughts that can be addressed through critical thinking and logic. Chapter 6 identifies various distortions of thought that link with depression. Chapter 7 provides guidelines for separating rational from nonrational thinking that is likely to accompany depression. These chapters will also give you some techniques to gain freedom from this form of oppression.

Other forms of distressful thinking that are not necessarily depressive can nevertheless support and exaggerate the distress of depression. For example, anxious and angry thoughts commonly accompany depression. Later chapters in this book describe such thought themes and how to address them.

THE INNER WORLD OF DEPRESSIVE THINKING

People with depression can have different depressive themes running through their minds (Alloy et al. 2000). Despite these differences and complexities, persistent pessimistic depressive thoughts are changeable (Riso et al. 2003). Knowing the distinctive depressive thinking themes and how to deal with them gives you an advantage in defusing them, getting relief from depression, and preventing a relapse. To start, let's look into the thoughts of five people who suffer from depression.

■ Ken's Story

Ken lost an important sale. He immediately thought, "This should not have happened." Then, he heard a chant of negative ideas echoing through his mind: "It's unfair. I can never face my family. This is horrible. I can't stand it." In concert with these sour mental notes, Ken felt a wave of distress and depression sweep over his body. For Ken, a lost sale—or anything that went wrong—was catastrophic, and such catastrophic thinking was a prelude to hopelessness thinking and dull, depressive sensations that sometimes lingered for days to months.

Ken's depression grew and lingered as his depressive thoughts swelled to include "I can't do anything right. I'm a failure as a salesperson. I'm a complete fool. I'm no good. My family would be better off without me." This depressive flow of thought strongly influenced how he felt.

Once he cued himself to these depressive thoughts, Ken began to counteract them through shifting his sense of perspective from catastrophe to reality. For example, he came to see sales as a "percentage game." Although it was a measure of his performance, it was not a measure of his global self-worth. He came to believe that while his sales performance can affect his income and standard of living, one lost sale here and there was not his whole life. His wife and family were far more important. What he thought of himself was more significant than his level of income. Within a year, Ken felt significantly less pressured and less depressed. His sales percentage improved, partially because he wasn't so uptight about succeeding.

■ Sandra's Story

A significant depression can signal that something has gone wrong in your life. Sandra suffered a financial setback on the stock market. The market was depressed, and so was she. She told herself, "I've lost a fortune. I cannot retire. This shouldn't be. I ought to have seen it coming. I'm such a fool. I need the money. This is awful. I can't stand the loss." Her catastrophic thinking morphed into depressive thoughts such as, "It's hopeless. I'll never recover. I'll die poor and alone." This distressful thinking added a burden on top of her negative financial situation. Because she felt depressed, she thought her feelings of depression validated her prediction that she would never emotionally recover. And because she believed that she could never recover, she simultaneously believed she would stay depressed forever. Sandra was not unique. When people get into distressful self-talk, they typically believe that the distress they experience validates their thoughts and vice versa.

Sandra started to make significant progress when she recognized that the meaning she gave to her financial loss overshadowed another value, which was to act kindly toward others, including herself. That helped break the circular loop of depressive thoughts and depressed mood. This was the start of her journey up from depression.

■ Donna's Story

Depression may bear little relationship to the events presumed to evoke them. Donna, for example, sobbed that she married too soon, and that was why she felt so depressed. She wanted to divorce her husband. She said she had been feeling this way for the past year, and she was feeling a more urgent need to end the relationship.

The event of "marrying too soon" had nothing to do with Donna's depression. It was a desperate attempt to find a reason for her misery.

Donna was thirty when she married. She dated her husband for over a year before their engagement. Prior to that, she believed that she was getting too old to find a suitable mate. She paused, confused when asked, "If you once saw yourself as too old to get married but now see yourself as having married too soon, how is this to be explained?"

Donna quickly saw the incongruity between these thoughts. She understood both could not be true. This was a start in her journey to shed herself of her depression.

When Donna overcame her depression, she viewed her marriage as solid and her husband as loving. She later mused, "I can't believe I once thought that my marriage was the cause of my depression."

Donna is now diligent about detecting depressive thoughts, and debunking them as they arise. She sees this as her "mental workout exercise." She describes it as a discipline, like jumping rope every day to stay in shape.

■ Tim's Story

Tim works at a job where he feels continually under pressure and stress. He lives in a dangerous neighborhood. He is close to poverty. He lives alone. He drinks too much. He blames the "world" for his problems. These combined conditions are typical risk factors for depression. Tim was depressed.

It took Tim over a year to stop drinking, work out of his depression, go back to school, establish friendships to replace loneliness, and engage a passion that was likely to last a lifetime. Once past the fog of depression, he discovered an interest in exploring and writing about the history of Native American tribes.

■ Sally's Story

For most of her life, Sally would have described herself as a happy person. In the days before her depression, she looked forward to coming home from work and seeing her children at play. If the children were not doing homework, she would tell them they could play after they finished. She would do this in good humor, but with a quiet determination that got her message across.

Following an unwanted divorce and unusual job pressures, Sally found herself slogging through her day. She felt cranky, irritable, and moody. As her depression deepened, her tolerance for frustration decreased.

One day Sally came home from work, walked into her living room, and went wild when she saw "the mess." Her children were running and playing in the living room. She saw toys strewn everywhere. She saw their backpacks by the door. She knew they had not done their homework. She experienced a strong wave of tension as a rush of negative thoughts went off like firecrackers in her head. She described herself emotionally unraveling, screaming, and finally collapsing into a corner sobbing uncontrollably.

Her outburst frightened her. She decided she needed to get help before her children came to hate her.

When Sally first went to counseling for her depression, she worked on what she was thinking. Negative emotive thoughts can sometimes seem like a mishmash. Separating and reviewing them can have a calming effect. When you know the types of thoughts that you are dealing with, a big part of depression can come under scrutiny.

By writing down her depressive thinking, Sally turned a chaotic process into an orderly sequence of thoughts:

1. "I've had a difficult day."

2. "The kids should be quiet."

3. "They should have picked up before I came home."

4. "They should have done their homework."

5. "They're little monsters."

6. "I can't control them."

7. "I'm a bad mother."

8. "I can't control anything in my life."

9. "I'm doomed."

With her thoughts described in this sequence, she was better positioned to evaluate them. To start, Sally separated the realistic thinking from her depressive reasoning. She found the idea "I've had a difficult day" valid. The rest she saw as far-fetched.

Sally discovered that her kids' behavior was not the main issue. The key issue was her depressed thinking and mood. As Sally saw through her pessimism, she came to understand why her depressive thoughts were too general to be credible. Like sieves, they didn't hold much water.

Left unchecked, depressive thinking clutters the thoroughfares of thought with gridlock such as: "Nobody cares about me." "What's the use?" "I'm such a failure." "My life sucks." "I'm weak and worthless." "I don't know what to do." "Nothing will help." "Life is like hell." Breaking the gridlock allows you greater freedom of choice. Can you break the gridlock? You bet! Depressive thinking can be examined, questioned, and effectively challenged.

LOGGING DEPRESSIVE THOUGHTS

Keeping a journal of depressive thoughts and feelings can enable you to evaluate them and see their flaws. Though challenging to do at any time, this can also prove challenging when you feel depressed. However, recognizing and demystifying your depressive thoughts can prove highly beneficial. Recognition can lead to a sense of control and hope.

In culling out and recording depressive thoughts, the first challenge is to recognize them. Although these thoughts can fly below your mental radar, by knowing what to look for and by monitoring your thinking, you can identify the links between negative ideas. For example, you might first think that you are useless. This idea can link to the idea that you are powerless to change, which can link to a sense of hopelessness. You may then blame yourself for feeling as you do, which can link back to uselessness. Once a depressive circle of thought is seen, you can defuse it.

Depressive thoughts typically go unnoticed, unmonitored, and unquestioned until you recognize how they sound and their abusive nature. Addressing this self-defeating thinking then involves pulling them from your stream of consciousness. How do you record a stream of consciousness and pick out the distressful thoughts? A pocket-sized notebook, tape recorder, or computerized device, such as a personal digital assistant, will do.

> Dealing with depressive thinking involves recognition, acceptance of the thinking, and debunking the thinking through cognitive and behavioral methods.

YOUR THOUGHT LOG

There are many ways to log thoughts that you know or suspect are depressive. The following method is simple to use. Divide a page into three columns. Then record ongoing examples of experience that exacerbate or evoke a depressed mood, record your thoughts about the event, and describe your thought-related reactions, such as how you feel and what you do. The following log includes some examples of how to use this three-step method. As occasions arise, when you know or you suspect that your thinking is depressive, fill in the blanks. You can expand this log in a notebook.

Experience	Thoughts About the Experience	Thought-related Reactions
"A depressed mood."	"This will never end. I can't stand it."	"A sense of futility. Intolerance for the mood. Frustration."
"A setback at work."	"I can't do anything right. I'll lose my job."	"Worthlessness. Panic. Hopelessness."

This logging approach involves thinking about your thinking and then linking it to your experiences and to your subsequent reactions. By practicing this approach, you can separate depressive thoughts from your stream of consciousness. This begins the process of disconnecting your thoughts from the sensations of depression. When you no longer believe your depressive thoughts, you've broken the depressive thoughts $\Rightarrow$ depressive sensations loop.

Feelings-to-Thoughts Technique

Sometimes depressive thoughts are described as feelings. Tammy feels hopeless. Andy feels helpless. When these "feelings" are viewed as part of the self, they can seem permanent. But if the feelings were to speak, they would represent depressive thoughts. If you feel hopeless or helpless, start by translating the feelings into thoughts. The following chart describes how.

Depressive Feelings	Translations into Depressive Thoughts
"I feel hopeless."	"I tell myself that my situation (life) is hopeless when I experience depression."
"I feel helpless."	"I tell myself that there is nothing I can do to make positive changes."
"I feel worthless."	"I tell myself I have no value, and, therefore, there is nothing to do to change this outlook."

By translating feelings into thoughts, you can come to identify thoughts that link to depression. By saying "I tell myself . . . ," you rightly assume the ownership of the thought. The thoughts are then no longer some tormenting entity over which you have no control. You can change them.

TRANSLATE YOUR FEELINGS INTO THOUGHTS

Use the following chart to translate your depressive feelings into depressive thoughts:

Depressive Feelings	Translations into Depressive Thoughts

When you think depressively, this is like looking through a distorted lens. The lens stays in place until you change it.

CATEGORIZING DEPRESSIVE THINKING

It is important to be aware of the context for and the content of depressive thoughts. However, the thoughts may bind to combinations of underlying concepts, which is the target for this review. Self-statements such as "I can't do anything right" can represent a combination of underlying concepts such as a negative self-view, helplessness, futility, and low frustration tolerance. To address these underlying depressive concepts, you must first be able to recognize them.

There are many ways to categorize and organize depressive thinking, and you will find different methods throughout this book. As one example, you can match potentially depressive thoughts against six general depressive thought themes to see if you can find a fit. These often overlapping themes include negative self-perception, pessimism, powerlessness, negative bias, demandingness, and distortions.

Negative self-perception.   This thinking typically includes self-doubts and self-downing. For example, you may routinely describe yourself as confused and you think ill of yourself.

Pessimism.   This thinking projects an ominous belief that the future, others, and situations will be bleak. Expecting to remain depressed forever is a harmful, pessimistic, hopelessness thought. (Although pessimism may not cause depression, this thinking typically accompanies depression.) An example of this form of depressive thought is "I am doomed."

Powerlessness.   This is a classic form of depressive thought. When you think that you can't control events that matter and view yourself as helpless, you will likely experience your future as hopeless. This form of thought can include viewing yourself as overwhelmed and unable to act. It can include a belief that you can't help yourself.

Negative bias.   People with depression tend to have a selective bias where they zero in on the negatives in their lives. This shows up in selective memory, such as focusing on negative experiences. Since we can think associatively, remembering a humiliation can trigger other examples of feeling humiliated. Here, omissions are important. How many positive experiences can be counted? Do they outnumber the "negative" experiences?

Demandingness.   This black-and-white thinking relates to how you, others, or the world ought to be. When your expectations spark demands for compliance to inflexible personal standards, this distorted pseudo need can lead to frustration, self-blame, and anger. The words that typically accompany this state of mind include "should," "ought," "must," "require," "need," "demand," and "expect."

> You can tell a depressive thought by its results. You feel worse.

Distortions.   This is like looking through a warped lens. A common distortion is that of overgeneralizing from negatives. For example, after making an error, you think you can't do anything right. Distortions include reading too much into situations, such as thinking that if someone doesn't greet you, they must hate you. This state of mind is often linked to catastrophic thinking, where molehills become mountains.

The following chart illustrates the common depressive themes of negative self-perception, pessimism, powerlessness, negative bias, demandingness, and distortions.

Negative Self-Perception	Pessimism	Powerlessness	Negative Bias	Demanding-ness	Distortions
"I don't think I can solve my own problems."	"My future looks bleak."	"I can't control the events around me."	"Life sucks."	"It shouldn't have happened. It must not be."	"If I lose my job, I'll never get another."
"I'm a real loser."	"I can't change."	"I'm weak and can't cope."	"I always mess up."	"I must pull myself up by the bootstraps."	"Everyone hates me."
"There is nothing about me that is useful."	"I'll never get better."	"I feel overwhelmed."	"People will find out that I'm a faker."	"You must give me what I want, or I'll make your life miserable."	"That C grade proves that I'm dumb."
"I have weakness and flaws that others can see."	"I can never do anything right."	"I'm helpless."	"Good things happen to other people."	"I must be the best or I'm nothing."	"I feel depressed because I'm inherently bad."

GATHER YOUR DEPRESSIVE THOUGHTS

You can organize your depressive thoughts using these common depressive themes or others that you find suitable. Using the following blank chart or create your own in a notebook.

Negative Self-Perception	Pessimism	Powerlessness	Negative Bias	Demanding-ness	Distortions

You can group depressive thinking around classifications such as *cognitive signatures*. These signatures are the distinctive patterns of thought associated with a distressful state. Cognitive signatures of depression include hopelessness, helplessness, worthlessness, and blame. Following the examples, you can use the rest of the chart to record cognitive signature themes.

Helplessness	Hopelessness	Worthlessness	Blame
"I can't cope."	"I'm destined to suffer forever."	"I'm an idiot. I can't do anything right."	"It's all my fault. Everything is always my fault."

When you monitor, recognize, and label depressive thought themes, you have taken a step in the direction of controlling them. Once they are visible, you can question the assumptions behind the ideas and exile them to a junkyard of broken ideas.

Thoughts are far more changeable than the color of your eyes, your height, and a primary emotion. They are more like the clothing you wear. You can shed them and replace them with something more suitable.

Depressive thoughts can and often do have multiple meanings. What do you do if you believe that the content of your depressive thoughts fit many categories? The "I can't do anything right" type thought can link to different depressive concepts, such as worthlessness and helplessness. This multiple concept recognition can prove advantageous. By distinguishing the different meanings and addressing each, you can do yourself considerable good as you work to break the linkage between one thought and several negative and depressing concepts.

By breaking one of the links, you can weaken—perhaps vanquish—the others. This process can prove simpler and easier than it first appears:

1. Define the context (evocative situation) for the thought.

2. Isolate the depressive thought that you suspect has multiple meanings, such as "I can't do anything right."

3. List the different concepts that you suspect underlie the thought, such as worthlessness and helplessness. Then address each concept using the following process.

To weaken a sense of worthlessness, ask yourself whether the depressive thought defines you or reflects what you think of yourself. Extremist thoughts such as "I can't do anything right" are hopelessly flawed from the start, so they can't realistically represent you. These thoughts can only reflect what you think about yourself at that moment in time. This presents an opportunity to think about yourself in other contexts. What are the exceptions where you have experienced a sense of worth and your actions are congruent with that sense? This thought can serve as a helpful signal to say that it is important to broaden your perspective on yourself.

To weaken a sense of helplessness, ask yourself whether your performance proves that you are only one way: helpless. Since extremist thoughts are hopelessly flawed from the start, the present one can't realistically represent your competencies and capabilities. Prove this to yourself by looking for exceptions that deviate from the "I can do nothing right" idea. Does that mean you don't know how to blow your nose or read a newspaper headline? The helplessness thought can represent what you *think* about your capabilities in the context in which it occurs but can be factually incorrect.

THEORIES OF DEPRESSIVE THINKING

Cognitive approaches involve the application of critical thinking techniques to depressive thoughts. The idea is that by changing your thinking, you can subdue depression and establish a buffer against depression.

> Whether the chicken or egg of depressive thinking came first, cognitive interventions are effective in reducing the negative impact of this thinking. Reductions in depressive thoughts correlate with improvements in mood.

There are many psychological systems with techniques for defusing depressive thinking. We'll look at Aaron Beck's theory followed by that of Albert Ellis.

Cognitive therapist Aaron Beck's theory of depression is that people with depression engage in recognizable patterns of negative thinking, such as hopelessness (Beck and Shaw 1977). These beliefs predate the depression.

Beck thinks that in order for you to get depressed, you have to have a preexisting vulnerability. This vulnerability can come from many sources, including a genetic predisposition. Depression can link to childhood adversity, which promotes vulnerability for depression. Adverse events are encoded in memory to predispose the individual to relatively stable cognitive p atterns of thought which can be activated by sets of situations that remind the person of the earlier event(s). These *schemas*, or embedded mental patterns, include depressive ideas, such as "I am worthless." Three core schemas (beliefs) form the cognitive triad of self-downing, helplessness, and hopelessness that typically appear during periods of depression.

Some authorities question Beck's view that depressive thinking predates depression (Teasdale et al. 2002). For example, depression can come out of the blue. Depressive thinking can follow a tragic loss and deeply saddened mood.

The activation of depressive thinking may not be a matter of what came first, the chicken or the egg. It appears that depressive thinking can work either way. It can activate a depression as well as come about through association with a depressed mood.

> A Buddhist view is that human thought arises from perceptions and sensations. Depressive perceptions and sensations can trigger depressive thoughts.

Whether depressive thinking precedes or reflects a depressed mood, depressive thinking is a surplus stress. Whatever the source of this thinking, the solution is the same. By defeating depressive thinking, you can overcome a depressed mood (Hollon, Thase, and Markowitz 2002).

Regardless of whether Beck's theory of depression is correct, his cognitive approach enjoys rich research support as a prime way to alleviate depression. It is the gold standard for this purpose.

New York psychologist Albert Ellis's rational emotive behavior therapy (REBT) system is based on the Stoic philosopher Epictetus's idea that you feel the way you think. Epictetus held that we are not moved by events as much as by our interpretations of them. Ellis (1962) views people as having biological tendencies to think irrationally and to disturb themselves. When they inflict themselves with irrational ideas, this can prove distressing and promote depression.

Ellis (1987) thinks that expecting, then demanding that reality conform to your requirements, and self-downing are core conditions of depression. For example, if you think you should be able to vanquish depression on command, you are likely to doubly upset yourself when depression persists. If you expect that life should be pleasant, you set yourself up for many needless disappointments. Self-downing refers to demeaning yourself for real or imagined deficiencies. This form of worthlessness thinking can be the offshoot of perfectionist expectations. Perfectionist beliefs carry this type of message: "If I'm not as I should be, I'm worthless."

Ellis's theory of depression has encouraging empirical support (Solomon et al. 2003; Ziegler and Hawley 2001).

DEPRESSION AND INTENTION

In nature, storms come and go. And so it can be with depression. Unlike weather, which you wait out, you can immediately start to act against depression.

If you look for an easy, quick, and painless solution to depression, you are likely to be disappointed, however. Beating depression easily is as easy as flying by flapping wings of lead.

Curbing depression involves intent. How do you know if you have the intent to curb your depression? Suppose you think, "I may not know how to defeat depression now, but I'm going to find a way to do it!" That's intent.

Intent means that you will start to take steps to defeat depression. Does intent mean that you move like a rocket through space? Hardly. Intent can mean first moving like a snail.

Moving at a snail's pace can seem discouraging. Still, you have good reasons for keeping your expectations modest. Depression normally brings fatigue. Depression interferes with attention and concentration. Depressive thinking interferes with progress.

Breaking the oppressive restraints of depression ordinarily involves doing something else first:

- Believing that a self-directed approach is worth trying.

- Accepting that the unpleasant thoughts, mood, and sensations of depression are temporary.

- Recognizing the value of identifying and challenging depressive thinking, then doing it.

- Pushing yourself to keep up with basic activities of daily living.

- Starting and maintaining an exercise program. (Exercise correlates with reductions in depressive symptoms.)

When depressed, your resources are likely to be diminished. But moving at a slower pace is still moving forward. It takes time to vanquish depression, even when you do all the right things. Nevertheless, it sometimes happens that when working to defeat depressive thinking, you make sudden gains (Tang et al. 2005). People with depression also spontaneously recover. Still, progressing slowly over a twelve week or longer period is more the norm. In that sense, the process of defeating depression is more like training for a long distance race than for a 100-meter dash. To get into condition, you have to start somewhere.

Sixth century BC Chinese Taoist philosopher Lao Tzu's proverb points to the trail of change: "The journey of a thousand miles begins with a single step." Through this journey, you can find a combination of actions to take that can work for you in your efforts to defend depression.

A DUAL THEORY OF CHANGE

When you effectively use cognitive and behavioral principles to break a sequence of depressive thoughts, why might positive changes take place in your mood and behavior? Here is a compound answer.

- You have altered your thinking and no longer believe that your situation is hopeless.

- You have come to believe that you can do something to help yourself and, therefore, you can't be helpless to act.

- You come to see that you have the skills to make constructive behavioral changes.

- You rediscover your ability to solve your problems and view yourself as capable of exercising this ability.

- You start to believe in yourself again.

- You increasingly feel a sense of well-being.

According to this dual theory for defeating depressive thinking, when you take effective action to address depressive thinking, your mind changes to a more optimistic or calmer outlook, and your body simultaneously recalibrates itself in rhythm with these changes, thus reducing sensations that can activate depressive thinking. You are also more likely to feel energized and accomplish more with less strain and effort. These changes may be noted in brain wave patterns associated with neurotransmitter efficiencies such as serotonin and GABA, which are associated with relaxation and calm, and dopamine and acetylcholine, which are associated with higher energy and accomplishment. They will also be noted in brain imaging that shows the color of the depressed brain changing to the color of a nondepressed brain. But whatever the brain measures of the brain hardware may be, the mind and body will have a calmer feel.

By refining and using your reasoning skills and by engaging in problem-solving actions, you can recalibrate your biology until you experience a more general sense of well-being. By taking problem-solving actions, you can achieve these positive effects over time:

- You can change your thinking from depressive to progressive.

- This process is like a feedback loop. When your body is in a state of positive equilibrium, your thinking is likely to be clear.

- When your thinking is clear, you are likely to feel free of distress.

- When you are in control of your actions, you are likely to have better command over your thoughts and emotions.

- As you engage in positive problem-solving actions, you will tend to strengthen and expand your positive resources.

Throughout this process, you will face many frustrations. As you face frustrations, you can boost your tolerance for frustration. Your ability to withstand discomfort and distress predictably rises. With this resilience comes a greater sense of inner command and confidence and a decreasing tendency to think depressively. At different times through this process, your body recalibrates itself to reflect clear thinking, a higher frustration tolerance, resiliency, and "can do" mentality.

Exiting from depression involves patience. When you do all the right things to overcome this state of mind and body, you are likely to find that you can control your thoughts and actions more directly than you can your biology. The body has its own rhythms. It normally takes time to get back into sync. For example, flying from New York City to Honolulu leads to jet lag. Within several days, your sleep cycle will normally adjust to the change. Still, your adrenal hormones can take several weeks to reset to the new schedule. In a similar sense, it normally takes time for positive thoughts and actions to recalibrate and stabilize your biological processes.

When you follow a self-help approach and your depression lifts, what does this say? Your outlook has changed for the better. You've come to believe that you can turn your life around. Then, where did the depressed ideas and sensations go?

KEY IDEAS AND ACTION PLAN

What are the key ideas that you got from this chapter? What actions can you take?

Key Ideas

What are the key ideas that you found helpful?

1. _____

_____

2. _____

_____

3. _____

_____

Action Plan

What actions can you take to progress?

1. _____

_____

2. _____

_____

3. _____

_____

POSTSCRIPT

You can't always choose what you'll think. That is because events can evoke thoughts that associate with and link to unpleasant events. You can, however, choose to monitor your thoughts to find those that negatively exaggerate the event, and that can add surplus misery to an already unpleasant depressive state. By coping with such thoughts, you can help yourself make changes in your outlook and mood. We'll next turn to examine techniques to defeat depressive thinking that you uncover.

CHAPTER 5

Using Reason Against Depressive Thinking

Socrates (470–399 BC), an early Greek philosopher and teacher, was renowned for his ability to ask pointed questions to get to the "truth." Through his clear-thinking method, Socrates invited his students to examine their premises and opinions in order to gain knowledge about their thinking and about themselves. His approach represented a search for truth through reason.

A form of Socratic reasoning that applies to defeating depressive thinking includes obtaining definitions for a specific thought, obtaining examples that support the definitions, and obtaining examples of exceptions. For example, if you said you were helpless to free yourself from depression, Socrates might ask, "Could you tell me what you mean by 'helpless'?" He might hear you respond, "I can't change." He might then ask for examples to show that you can't change. You might respond, "Whatever I do, I stay depressed." He might ask you to give examples of when depression has lifted and why this might have occurred. You might respond, "When I take a fast walk." He might then ask, "If you can't change, then how do you explain changing when you walk?"

To use a modified Socratic method to defeat depressive thinking, you can start by defining the meaning of the words you use to describe your depressive experience. Then, you can give yourself examples that fit the definition followed by exceptions that can contradict the definition. Through this self-questioning process, you can discover weak points in depressive thinking. Here's how:

Start with a definition of the depressive belief. If you think you are helpless, what does "helpless" mean? Does the word refer to a specific situation or to your entire being? Does it mean that you can't do anything right? Does it mean that you can do somethings right but not all things right? Does helplessness refer to feeling fatigued or apathetic?

Look for examples that support the definition. Do they represent a pattern of repeated thoughts about the same events?

> **Building Reasoning Skills**
> - Obtain and question definitions.
> - Look for supporting examples.
> - Check for exceptions that make for contradictions.

Look for exceptions to the definition. Finding contradictions raises questions about the legitimacy of a depressive belief. For example, if you think you can't do anything right, contrast this idea against what you *have* done right. It is possible to contrast having misplaced your keys, say, with what you can do well right now, such as open a door, count to 1,000, or write a poem.

If you define "helpless" as an inability to change a past loss, this is legitimate. But you still have a choice. You can lament the unchangeable or accept that you can't go back. However, if you defined "helpless" as an inability to do anything right, what is "anything?" What is "right?"

SOCRATIC EXERCISE

Following basic Socratic review, first define, then separately examine each suspected depressive idea, such as "I can't do anything right."

1. Start with your definition of the "can't do anything right" statement. What does it mean? Does it mean that you are less effective than you'd prefer to be in the context of where the thought erupted?

2. Provide examples that support your definition. For example, if it narrows down to a specific event and your memory of past associated events, then how do these experiences justify an extreme view that implies that everything you always do in these contexts is wrong?

3. Look for exceptions. Can you think? Can you add one and one to get two? Can you open a door? Can you recognize a squirrel? Can you pronounce your name? Can you think of steps you can take to eat a bowl of cereal?

Depressive idea:	
Meaning of the idea:	
Examples that support the idea:	
Examples that contradict the idea:	

This variation on the Socratic method is a tool to help break the links between depression and its associated thoughts. Breaking such linkages is like shedding an unwanted weight.

Through following this modified Socratic method, you can identify potential contradictions and gain an improved sense of clarity. With this clarity, you can find that you have one less thought burden to contend with. That can feel like a weight off your mind.

CRITICAL THINKING

Critical thinking researcher Richard Paul (1990) developed a Socratic questioning approach that can be adapted to defeat depressive thinking. This six-point process includes asking and answering clarifying questions, questions about assumptions, questions about evidence, questions about other viewpoints and perspectives, questions about implications and consequences, and questions about questions.

These six questions can apply to practically any form of depressive thinking, such as hopelessness thinking. The following chart illustrates how to use these questions to address hopelessness thinking. The chart gives sample questions, sample responses, and sample conclusions.

Depressive thought: Hopelessness

Clarifying Questions	Questions About Assumptions	Questions About Facts and Evidence	Questions About Viewpoints	Questions About Consequences	Questions About Questions
Question 1 "What do I mean when I tell myself that I have no hope?"	**Question 2** "What am I assuming about the future?"	**Question 3** "Does hopelessness thinking reflect a factual reality?"	**Question 4** "What could disprove a hopelessness outcome?"	**Question 5** "What are the consequences of pessimistic thinking?"	**Question 6** "Do the previous five questions refocus my thinking?"
Response 1 "Nothing changes."	**Response 2** "I have a crystal ball that tells all."	**Response 3** "There is no evidence."	**Response 4** "Defeating hopelessness thinking."	**Response 5** "Doom thinking is depressing."	**Response 6** "The questions can restructure thinking."
Conclusion 1 "That's implausible."	**Conclusion 2** "That's implausible."	**Conclusion 3** "Hopelessness depressive thinking reflects a subjective impression, not a factual reality."	**Conclusion 4** "Defeating hopelessness thinking is plausible."	**Conclusion 5** "Pessimistic thinking does not necessarily predict the future."	**Conclusion 6** "It is possible to shift thoughts from a narrow pessimism to a broader perspective."

USING CRITICAL THINKING

Following the above example, test Paul's critical thinking system against one of your depressive thinking themes:

Depressive thought: _____

Clarifying Questions	Questions About Assumptions	Questions About Facts and Evidence	Questions About Viewpoints	Questions About Consequences	Questions About Questions
Question 1	Question 2	Question 3	Question 4	Question 5	Question 6
Response 1	Response 2	Response 3	Response 4	Response 5	Response 6
Conclusion 1	Conclusion 2	Conclusion 3	Conclusion 4	Conclusion 5	Conclusion 6

Critical thinking does not make up for a lack of knowledge. Rather it provides a means to acquire knowledge and wisdom. By using this method, you can recognize gaps in your knowledge, and you can take steps to fill them. Well-articulated questions can point to gaps in knowledge, which leads to an examination of that knowledge and possibly to wisdom in an area where once there were gaps.

Using Socratic reasoning techniques to defeat depressive thinking has a hidden benefit. You will have practiced the use of a thinking tool that you can use in other situations where it is important to separate truth from fallacy.

APPLYING LOGIC TO DEPRESSIVE THINKING

Logic refers to a process for making reasoned and reliable inferences. When you are described as logical, this suggests that your thinking is largely clear of fuzziness, irrationalities, and fallacies. It is likely to be more fact-based and backed by common sense.

Deductive logic is a common logical process that includes a primary (major) premise, a secondary premise (minor premise or inference), and a conclusion. The following is an example of deductive logic:

- Depression typically includes pessimistic thinking.

- Depressive pessimistic thinking is changeable.

- You can progressively gain relief from depression that involves this thinking by uncoupling it from depression.

Sometimes inferences and conclusions involve probability statements:

- Past behavior predicts future behavior.

- James has and currently feels depressed.

- In the future, James will probably feel more depressed more often than the average person.

> To advance a logical argument, you typically start by stating your proposition, including your premises and assumptions.

The validity of the argument is found in the future. Since the statement is based upon a probability, it automatically involves elements of uncertainty. It also doesn't take into account the fact that you can act to change aspects of your future. For example, awareness and action interventions can disrupt and diminish the impact of depressive thinking. Through awareness and action methods, you can falsify a belief such as "depression is forever."

IS DEPRESSIVE LOGIC ILLOGICAL?

Ideas can logically follow each other and still be false and thus illogical. Polytheism flourished in many early civilizations, where the people believed that different gods were responsible for human benefits or adversity. In ancient Greece, a primary premise was that gods control human destiny. A secondary premise was that Zeus was the father of all gods. A logical conclusion was that Zeus controls human destiny, and that appeasing Zeus was paramount to survival. However, the primary and secondary premises and conclusions were all false.

You could say that there is hysteria in the town of Salem, Massachusetts (primary premise); the hysteria is caused by witches (secondary premise); to stop the hysteria, the witches must die (conclusion). This logical process formed the basis for the Salem witch trials. Although the primary premise was based on observation, the secondary premise and conclusion were false.

The ultimate test of a logical argument is that it is consistent with scientific findings. However, science is based upon the proposition that tested theories and laws are tentative and can be overturned by evidence. If you can assume that depressive thinking and philosophies are tentative, and you seek ways to disconfirm them, you are on your way to expose their fallacies to defuse their impact.

Depressive thinking has its own logic. Some depressive logic contains verifiable statements. It also can involve a false conclusion as follows:

- Depressive thinking provokes or adds to the misery of depression.

- Depressive thinking takes time and skill to challenge.

- "I don't have the time and lack the skill to challenge depressive thinking, therefore, I'll stay depressed forever."

The primary and secondary premises have a basis in fact. The conclusion is a rash speculation that does not logically follow.

CONFRONTING DEPRESSIVE THINKING

When depressive thinking is active, you can find yourself associating one negative thought with another. Suppose you believe: "I am a failure." "I can't do anything right." "I will stay miserable and depressed forever. " You can order these thought associations according to a primary premise, secondary premise, and conclusion. To establish this ordering, all you need to do is to put the beliefs into a sequence that flows logically. This ordering sets the stage for examining each phase.

Let's assume that "I am a failure" is your primary premise. You can attack that premise right away. The simplest approach is to recognize that this premise is an overgeneralization. It is irrational to assume that you can be only one way, now and forever. If you can tie your shoes, read this paragraph, or answer the phone, you clearly succeed in some aspects of your life; how then can you be a failure? Even though you will periodically operate below standards, as is true of practically every other human being, it is irrational to describe yourself as an incompetent failure in the present moment and then to extend this idea to the future. The fact that you can read this page may seem trivial. Nevertheless, reading this page means that you can't be a total failure. When the depressive premise is flawed, the other parts of the proposition typically go down the tubes with it.

You can attack the primary premise from another angle. Start with defining what you mean by failure. For example, does failure mean that there is a gap in your knowledge? That your skill level is less than you wish in a particular area? Or that you don't have something specific that you want? You can take each part of the definition and convert it into a proposition for action. For example, if there is a gap in your knowledge, what can you do to fill it?

An overgeneralized failure view can incorporate another overgeneralized view, which is that you can do nothing right. You can view the "I can't do anything right" self-statement as a secondary premise. You can then attack this secondary premise by asking yourself for a definition, examples, and exceptions. For example, "What does it mean when I tell myself I can't do anything right? What have I not done 'right' in the past year that supports this idea? What have I done in the past year that I or others might consider right?" Your answers to these questions can reveal the flaws in the secondary premise. The chief flaw, however, is that the premise is an overgeneralization.

Following a defeat of the primary and secondary premises, a conclusion such as "I will stay miserable and depressed forever" can collapse because it is an absurd overgeneralization. Nevertheless, it is still useful to address the conclusion. By matching the conclusion against contradictory information, you can destabilize this end product of depressive logic.

The "I will stay miserable and depressed forever" belief suggests you have a *foresight paradox* to resolve. You can take advantage of this paradox by asking yourself, "If I believe I have the foresight to accurately predict the future, then can I not act now to start to change a bleak future to one filled with opportunities and choices?"

The following chart shows how to logically organize the "I am a failure" example. It describes how to break this down into primary and secondary premises and a conclusion. It provides a sample way to question each phase of this "fuzzy" logic to uncouple this thought process from depression.

Primary premise: "I am a failure."	Self-help questions: "Where is the proof that my future is foretold, and that I will forever be only one way, a 'failure?'"	Results: "There is no absolute evidence. The belief is unprovable. It is more likely that I'll continue to learn and make changes."
Secondary premise: "I can't do anything right."	Self-help questions: "Can I tie my shoes? Can I read this book? Can I recognize and question a faulty belief?"	Results: "This belief is an example of an overgeneralization with more holes in it than a piece of Swiss cheese."
Conclusion: "I'll stay miserable and depressed forever."	Self-help questions: "Do I have a precognitive ability that allows me to foretell the future? What steps can I take to contest this depressive thinking?"	Results: "The conclusion involves a prediction that is absolute. It eliminates alterations in thinking and life situation. This is such an extreme prediction that it sinks on the basis of its own absurdity. A primary step away from this belief is to disprove the conclusion by showing that altering my thinking about my future is not only possible but probable."

CONFRONTING YOUR DEPRESSIVE THOUGHTS

Now, it is your turn to tackle the logic of an associated series of depressive thoughts. Use the following space to organize what you believe is a depressive sequence of thoughts into a primary premise, secondary premise, and conclusion. Construct questions that can help you to change your perspective on each. Answer the questions and record the results.

Primary premise:	Self-help questions:	Results:
Secondary premise:	Self-help questions:	Results:
Conclusion:	Self-help questions:	Results:

What does it mean when you see the fallacies in your depressive thinking yet continue to feel depressed? Depressive thinking is one of many complications of depression, and depression can continue beyond the time that you disengage from a depressive belief. However, freed of negative depressive thinking, you will have relieved yourself of one significant source of stress that can fuel a worsened sense of depression. Changes in thinking from depressive to nondepressive thoughts are often a prelude for a fading away of the unpleasant mood and physical sensations of depression. A positive change in mood can also lead to a positive change in thought.

DETECTING SELF-DECEPTIONS

People normally don't consciously go out of their way to fool themselves. Rather, they have certain habits of mind, or belief, that are self-deceiving.

We all have the capability to deceive ourselves. Most people believe that their memory is fallible and that they can be forgetful. At the same time, if you forget where you put your keys, you may think someone else put them in an unknown place. In that sense, you are denying that your memory is fallible.

When depressed, how do you know when you are deceiving yourself? Deception can be put to a plausibility test. Here are some guidelines to uncover depressive self-deceptions:

- Does the idea sound plausible? (That is, can you buy the Brooklyn Bridge with a small investment, and make a fortune charging tolls?)

- Is the statement verifiable?

- Does the statement fit with everyday experience?

- Is the statement consistent with known facts?

- What do you gain by believing or disbelieving the statement?

- Would a reasonable person believe the statement?

USING A PLAUSIBILITY CHECKLIST

You can use the following plausibility checklist to gain clarity about a depressive idea. The process involves citing the suspected depressive idea and asking six plausibility questions, determining if the question warrants a yes or no answer, and citing why you came to that conclusion.

Depressive idea: _____

Clarifying Question	Response		Why
1. Does the statement seem plausible?	Yes	No	
2. Is the statement verifiable?	Yes	No	
3. Does the thought fit with ordinary life experience?	Yes	No	
4. Is it consistent with known facts?	Yes	No	
5. Is there an advantage to believing the statement?	Yes	No	
6. Would knowledgeable people agree?	Yes	No	

What does it mean if you deceive yourself with depressive thinking? It means that you share this form of self-deception with countless millions of others.

STATEMENTS IN DISGUISE

Some questions that people ask themselves are statements in disguise. A question like "what's wrong with me?" is a statement in disguise. "Why can't I do anything right" suggests that you can't do anything right and is a statement in disguise. This close-ended rhetorical type question is really a statement that something is wrong.

If the question is not intended to promote an open, fair-minded inquiry and has its own conclusion built into it, it is a statement in disguise. Open-ended questions involve questions such as, "How might I approach depressive thinking in order to increase my chances for recognizing and defeating this form of thought?" This open-ended question promotes inquiry and discovery.

When statements in disguise arise, it is useful to recognize and question them. But first, how do you recognize statements in disguise?

■ Statements in disguise represent a form of one-way thinking that suggests its own answer.

■ The question reflects a *confirmation bias*. A confirmation bias refers to a tendency to accept certain ideas and assumptions that confirm the bias and dismiss those that contradict it.

When depressed, and you ask the question, "Why is this happening to me?" you could be experiencing a statement in disguise if it means "I deserve punishment." By translating the question into a statement, you have already taken a solid step forward in identifying potential depressive core beliefs. By questioning the core belief, you can defuse its impact. For example, in what ways and for what reasons do you deserve punishment? In what ways and for what reasons do you deserve to give yourself self-acceptance?

After answering open-ended questions such as, "In what ways and for what reasons do I deserve to give myself self-acceptance?" you've shifted from the false certainty of a false core belief to one of a more open-ended inquiry.

A PHILOSOPHICAL PERSPECTIVE ON DEPRESSION

The French philosopher Charles Renouvier (1842) thought that people don't knowingly bring bad things upon themselves. Still, he saw that some people act like they are blind to the power of their negative habits. He saw freedom from negative patterns as a by-product of reflection. He believed that the mind was endowed with the power to refuse to capitulate to determinism, or the belief that our patterns are fixed.

Renouvier would probably see helplessness in depression as a determinist belief. He would predict that freedom (free will) surfaces when individuals see that they can make different choices in thinking and are not bound to the habitual depressive thoughts they previously had. For example, when you see that hopelessness is a choice, you can exercise free will by making one choice when you could have made another. You can choose to believe that you can act to improve your conditions of thought by freeing yourself of the burden of hopelessness thinking.

The eighteenth-century founder of American psychology, William James, suffered from repeated bouts of severe depression. He found the behavioral techniques of his time lacking. James found relief from depression through using Renouvier's philosophy of free choice.

Renouvier admits that freedom of choice may be an illusion. It could, for example, involve choices between fictions of optimism and fictions of pessimism. But freedom also may represent the ability to make legitimate choices. James, for his part, accepted that any free act was a choice.

When depressed and pessimistic, you believe in a bleak future in advance of its occurrence. But what if you decide to act as though free? Can this choice lead to the process of rationally disrupting depressive thinking and reshaping the future through clear thinking?

> Free will is doing one thing when you could have chosen to do another.

An act of free will that involves the choice of disengaging from depressive thinking can involve secondary choices. These choices can include the following:

- A conscious recognition of an oppressive flow of thought. This choice involves learning examples and criteria for depressive thinking, monitoring mood-related thinking, and extracting thoughts that fit the criteria and "feel" depressing.

- A conscious acceptance that you have a choice to accept the overgeneralized nature of depressive thoughts or to examine the meaning and significance of the thoughts. Helplessness, for example, typically represents an overly general idea that can be true in specific situations but not all the time. A choice is to look for exceptions to the helplessness proposition.

- Exercising the choice to accept depressive thoughts as a given or to question and defuse them. Blaming yourself for being depressed, for example, can be viewed as a choice. An alternative choice is accepting responsibility for your errors in thought, accepting yourself despite the errors, and acting to correct the errors.

By accepting that depressive thinking is something other than an immovable mountain, you are free to entertain the idea that you can exercise choices that will shape the direction of your efforts. For example, you can accept that depressive ideas will forever stampede like a herd of cattle through your mind, or you can exercise the choice of turning the herd. An understanding that you have choices makes it possible to deal with depressive thinking.

LOGICAL-THINKING HOMEWORK ASSIGNMENTS

Developing your reasoning skills can lead to structural changes in the brain that relate to the refinement and expansion of these skills. Through developing your Socratic reasoning skills, you can more quickly and thoroughly apply critical thinking and logical ways of knowing and doing to solve personal problems, such as those reflected in depressive thoughts. If you want to refine your clear thinking skills, the following exercises can assist this process.

- Most advertisements contain logical flaws and omissions. Some provide great opportunities to practice logical thinking. Weight-loss advertisements can prove especially interesting. When you see an advertisement for a weight-loss product, you'll likely hear multiple testimonials attesting to the value of the program. You'll see before-and-after photographs. You can use these advertisements to practice your reasoning skills. First, look for the omissions (exceptions) in the ad: Does the advertiser show people who gained weight following the use of the diet? Does the advertiser show people who started the diet and then stopped using it? Does the advertiser cite relapse rate statistics?

- News channels that favor extreme political positions are a wonderful opportunity for practicing your reasoning skills. Whenever an ideologically driven group presents a slanted point of view, you can properly ask questions about definitions, omissions, and exceptions.

- The human tendency to label other people provides a rich avenue for sharpening your critical thinking skills. People apply labels to other people with an unwavering frequency such as, "Jack's a wimp." Such negative labels are an obvious target for practicing critical thinking skills. What is meant by "wimp"? What examples apply to Jack? What are the exceptions? This simple three-phase exercise is likely to show that Jack isn't totally one way or another.

- Positive labels provide yet other opportunities for developing critical thinking skills. Suppose a friend tells you, "Jane is a wonderful person." But Jane is no more likely to be 100-percent wonderful than Jack is likely to be a 100-percent wimp. Here are some sample questions: What is the definition of "wonderful"? What examples apply to Jane? What other views about Jane are possible?

Through taking on such assignments, you can refine your skill for separating sense from nonsense. This skill can serve you well throughout your life.

KEY IDEAS AND ACTION PLAN

What are the key ideas that you got from this chapter? What actions can you take?

Key Ideas

What are the key ideas that you found helpful?

1. _____

_____

2. _____

_____

3. _____

_____

Action Plan

What actions can you take to progress?

1. _____

_____

2. _____

_____

3. _____

_____

POSTSCRIPT

General semantics expert Wendell Johnson (1946) asserted that when we are "unschooled in the techniques of inquiry, we tend to flounder in a fog of obfuscation and error." He asserted that many go through life without recognizing the fables in their thoughts, but could educate themselves to think clearly and distress themselves less.

If depressive thinking fogs rational thought, and threatens to deepen and extend depression, effectively addressing this thinking will take away its sting. Of equal importance, clearing the fog of depressive thinking predictably reduces the intensity and duration of the physical factors in depression. Properly framed questions and reality-based answers help clear this fog.

CHAPTER 6

Shedding a Cloak
of Mental Misery

A typical nightmare consists of distorted images that we give order to upon awakening. The master of depressive nightmares has a knack for drafting unhappy scenes and giving them a gloomy twist.

Let's enter the world of the master of depressive scripts. Told through a play called "Tales of Depression," the master reveals a dramatic, dysphoric plot conducted in the theater of the mind.

In a blink, the master disburses the dust of desolation to fill the mind with dull desperation. Then, upon a darkened stage, the master's actors fly to the scene on bleakness wings. The Duke of Dreams brings dreads. The Lord of Lead brings weight. The Baron of Burdens brings bushels of troubles. Gloom comes with Lament. Irritability arrives to play its part.

With a mawkish grin, the Demon of Blame arrives and says, "There must be something you did to deserve your shroud of gloom. You brought it all down upon yourself. Or, perhaps, it is the fault of someone else. Your family did it to you." With Blame in full array, positive opportunities pass unnoticed.

To keep the play going, the play master passes out scripts about hopelessness, loneliness, helplessness, worthlessness, catastrophe, rejection, blame, and more. When you think you can do something to change the script, the master adds a new character, Procrastination. Finally the master scribes a punch line to weaken your resolve: "Depression taints all, and so you shall fall." In this dreamlike theater of thought, your life feels like it's in shambles.

In this theater of the mind, Gloom distorts Reality. But the battle has just begun. The distortions occur during wakeful hours. Untarnished Reality unexpectedly enters the scene to help clear the distortions and rewrite the script. Reality brings good news. The distortions in these waking nightmares can be examined, hit hard, and then abandoned.

RECOGNIZING AND DEFEATING COGNITIVE DISTORTIONS

To defeat depression, Aaron Beck uses a present-focused, active, educational approach. Following this approach, you learn to recognize and reevaluate your depressive thoughts.

According to Beck, people feel depressed because of the negative and distorted meaning they give to events. This triggers emotional troubles that can culminate in depression.

Depressive thoughts represent irrational misconceptions and other cognitive distortions. In a sense, they are like the play master's scripts. These false and misleading ideas or beliefs seem real and true, but they are not that way at all. They negatively magnify the significance of events and overgeneralize to where gloom and bleakness trump common sense and reason. For example, you get a flat tire during rush hour in a rainstorm. Days later you continue to lament the horrors of the incident as you keep telling yourself, "Nothing ever goes right for me in life. Poor me. Life sucks."

Beck saw that depression involved distorted thinking about the self, future, and the environment. He called these three distortions (errors in thinking) the *cognitive triad* (Beck 1976). Cognitive triad themes are automatically stimulated following a triggering event. Thus, the thoughts flow beneath the radar of awareness. Yet they can wreak havoc on the mind and body much like a dramatic drop in barometric pressure can create an atmosphere that is ripe for a storm.

Beck thought that this triad of underlying beliefs stays latent until triggered. The triggers include, but are not limited to, personally relevant events that remind the person of a painful past experience. Unless recognized and challenged, the triad can extend into depression.

Beck's view of depression involves a nonblame view of depressive thinking. You're not responsible for habits of the mind. However, choice comes into play when you see that you can either passively let depressive mental themes go into and out of hibernation, or you can learn how to actively uncouple triad themes from events that typically trigger these depressive thoughts.

Suppose you make a mistake (a personally relevant triggering event). You have a core belief that unless you do things perfectly well, you are worthless. When you don't act perfectly, as you think you should, you simultaneously activate the worthlessness mental theme. Following this activation, your thoughts are likely to reflect a despondent theme. The following describes this depression process:

personally relevant event

⇩

maladaptive automatic cognitive triad themes (errors in thinking)

⇩

depressed emotions and behaviors

Identifying and correcting distortions associated with depression is a tested path for alleviating depressive stresses and for simultaneously reducing the degree and frequency of physical sensations that are associated with depression.

As with other forms of cognitive and behavioral therapies, cognitive therapy (CT) is not about substituting positive words for depressive themes or telling yourself Pollyannish statements such as "things are getting better in every way every day." Things may not be getting better every day. Instead, the cognitive change process involves identifying distorted thinking such as depressive beliefs, challenging it, and practicing new cognitive and new behavioral responses. This cognitive reevaluation phase of change involves thinking about your thinking, and then recognizing and counteracting cognitive distortions through applying knowledge and reason.

CT works on the principle that cognitive distortions associated with depression are best recognized, then questioned to determine whether they are accurate or fallacious. Since cognitive distortions in depression represent a stressful and unhelpful set of beliefs, you may be hard-pressed to validate them objectively. Nevertheless, when present and unchecked, these thoughts can divert your attention from examining healthy alternative views. By engaging in rational problem-solving activities, however, you can destabilize depressive thinking and feel better for the effort. Here is a preliminary framework for using the CT system:

Thought identification: What am I telling myself?
Thought categorization: Do I have negative thoughts about myself, experiences, and the future? If so, what are they?
Thought analysis: What is the evidence for and against the thought?

Dumping a Collection of Cognitive Distortions

Beck suggests that unhealthy cognitive distortions and beliefs strongly contribute to the development of troublesome emotional states and self-defeating behaviors. Identifying and clearing up depression associated distortions can lead to a reduction in distress. The actions you take to clear up these distortions can enhance your coping capabilities. Once seen, the distortions may no longer hold the power to negatively affect your judgment.

Psychiatrist David Burns (1999) popularized a list of cognitive distortions that coexist with depression. As you read through this list, you may note that the distortions have overlapping features. In fact, as you cope with different distortions, you may primarily be dealing with multiple conditions that spin off from a few basic themes, such as overgeneralization and magnification. If you reduce overgeneralization and magnification, then you will have reduced a common source of needless distress.

Overgeneralizing

When you overgeneralize, you draw a general conclusion on the basis of one or a few factors and ignore all disconfirming evidence. Because you see a flying squirrel doesn't mean that all squirrels can fly.

In depression, overgeneralizations take on a reality of their own. For example, you temporarily forget the name of an acquaintance. You tell yourself that you're losing your mind. You try to start a conversation, and someone brushes you off. You take this to mean that you will never be an able conversationalist. When this mind-set is activated, you may think, "Everything is bleak and won't improve."

Although the overgeneralization concept stays the same, the context and content for this response can widely vary. Let's take a context where your lover ditches you and you negatively overgeneralize. Different people can overgeneralize the loss in different ways. One person might think, "I'll never be able to find anybody to love me." Someone else might think, "My life is a total mess. I screwed everything up." Someone else might think, "I'm always making stupid choices in life."

If you catch yourself falling into the depression overgeneralization trap, look for exceptions to the overgeneralization. What are the satisfying, positive parts of your life? What do you value that you can still achieve? What conditions are improving or can improve?

Magnetizing and Minimizing

Have you ever met anyone who does not, from time to time, make a mountain out of a molehill and dwell negatively on a situation long after it has passed? It is in human nature to fall into this magnification trap. However, those who are primed to exaggerate are likely to suffer longer than those who tend to take most matters in stride.

If you tend to magnify the negative, you are likely to blow unpleasant events out of proportion and dwell upon them. You misuse a word, for example, and think that all listeners will view you as unintelligent and inarticulate. You can't let this thought go. You keep replaying the event in your head. That's magnification.

People have known about magnification for centuries. For example, Chicken Little thought the sky was falling after being hit by a branch. Panicked, the fabled character ran through the barnyard, yelling that the sky was falling and panicked the other barnyard animals. The expression "making a mountain out of a molehill" also captures the spirit of this experience.

The first step in a process of defusing magnification involves recognizing when this is happening. Next, you act to strip the magnification of emotionally charged words and phrases. Take the thought "It's horrible that I made a mistake." The loaded word, "horrible," can exaggerate the unpleasantness of making a public error and stressfully captivate the attention of the mind, fixating it on the error and the ensuing emotions. A more realistic substitute phrase, coupled with a coping statement might be, "I misused a word and prefer not to make errors of that sort. But that was as it was. That's the price of being human."

Some people are masters of the understatement and minimize the significance of their accomplishments. This can be seen as a form of humbleness. Depression minimization is different. You take negative happenings and make them seem unimportant. Thus, if you have a stressful job, you minimize the role stress plays in your depression. You do nothing about the situation because "it is not that important." A cost-benefit analysis can yield a different perspective. What are the short- and long-term advantages and disadvantages of dealing with the situation? What is a reasonable first step to take?

Catastrophizing

Catastrophizing is psychologist Albert Ellis's term for describing how people exaggerate the negatives in a real or imagined situation. This process combines magnification with overgeneralizing. People who routinely engage in catastrophic thinking typically feel helpless and overwhelmed. Although practically everyone engages in this thinking from time to time, some catastrophize more than others. Excesses in this area can pave a path to depression.

Here is an example of catastrophizing: You don't get a phone call about a job you applied for. You think that you're going to get turned down for the job. You think that this is your last chance to pull yourself up by your bootstraps. You start thinking that your life is ruined. You envision yourself forever destitute and living on food stamps.

Here's another example of catastrophizing: A friend sounds short with you. You tell yourself, "My friend hates me. I can't maintain my relationships. I'll die old and alone." However, what would it then mean if you discovered your friend was coming down with the flu when you spoke with him or her and later acted as friendly as usual? What would happen to the catastrophe?

Catastrophizing typically involves a chain of increasingly alarming associations. To help yourself break the chain, seek alternative explanations that suggest different results. Separate facts from exaggerations. Label exaggerations as "exaggerations." Focus on what you can do. Make a plan. Take the steps.

Dichotomous Thinking

There are many things in life that are one way or another. If the color is black, it can't be white. If it is an oak tree, it can't be a fox. If you are elderly, you can't be an infant. If you are human, you are complex, not simple.

As a student in a basic statistics course, one of the first things you learn is about variability and probability. In an all-or-nothing world of depression, the matter of variability can be trumped by dichotomous thinking. This distortion reflects on-off, good-bad, right-wrong, black-white forms of thought. There is no middle ground. For example, if you believe that your friends should be totally honest with you, any deviation from that formula can make a person a nonfriend. However, this type of either-or reasoning is discretionary. It differs from "a fox cannot be a tree."

In dichotomous thinking, an overgeneralized and magnified tone is unmistakable. You are either good or bad, worthy or unworthy, intelligent or stupid. The fallacy in dichotomous thinking lies in its lack of variability. To combat this line of thinking, look for exceptions and look for shades of gray. (See chapter 12 for dealing with perfectionist dichotomous thinking dilemmas.)

A Web of Depressing Distortions

In the world of depressive thinking, one distortion can support another to form a depressive web. Here are some other forms of cognitive distortion that can interactively form the threads of the web.

Mental filtering.   You tend automatically to separate out ideas and observations that don't conform to your depressive philosophy. Through this process of selective perception, you magnify the significance of your flaws, faults, and weaknesses. For example, Kathy complimented Ben by saying, "You work so well with your hands. You do exquisite carpentry work." Ben replied, "But I have calluses on my hands." It's typical of mental filtering to look for the one negative. A balancing exercise can help restore perspective. In a given situation where you discount whatever is inconsistent with a depressive view, start adding some contrasting views. For example, cite in writing as many factors as you can—good, bad, and neutral—that relate to the situation. This approach counters the automatic filtering process. Although you may still give disproportionate weight to the negative, you have set your mental wheels in motion to balance your view.

Jumping to conclusions.   This is an inclination to predict the worst without any meaningful evidence to support the belief. When depressed, you are likely to be primed to judge situations based upon depression-related expectations. When depressed, for example, you can jump to the conclusion that you are helpless to do any better and thus you'll never get better. Such a conclusion about depression feeds depression. To blunt this tendency, you can look for alternative explanations for depression and alternative strategies to break free. With increased mental flexibility, you increase your chances to draw wiser conclusions.

Fortune telling.   In a pessimistic, depressive state of mind, you look into the future and only see gloom and doom. You might tell yourself, "My future is hopeless. My life is over." This projection involves a tarot-card type prediction. Despite the hype around magical ways of predicting the future, such as tarot card readings, there is no evidence beyond suggestion and chance that any long-term prediction of that sort is valid, and much evidence to contradict the validity of this type of scam. Withholding judgment until the facts are clear can reduce needless pessimism due to this type of projection. For every negative future possibility, consider a positive alternative.

Mind reading.   Mind reading typically involves reading into a situation more than is actually there. Some people make a studied habit of trying to read other people's motives, temperament, intentions, and even what they are thinking. Few are always right or wrong in such efforts. The risks involved in assuming things about human motives include projecting too much of yourself into the situation. For example, you are at a restaurant with a new date. The person appears distracted. You think that your date thinks that you are a dull date. Then, you learn that the person is having difficulty deciding between fish and steak. The risks of mind reading can dramatically escalate when you are depressed. When faced with a situation where you speculate on what someone is thinking about, consider suspending judgment until you get some credible verification.

Emotional reasoning.   In this classical circular form of reasoning, you act as though your emotions were evidence for your thoughts, beliefs, and perceptions. If you feel like a failure, you may conclude that you are a failure, since that is how you feel. But you may feel anxious and therefore think failure thoughts. If you feel inadequate, and you believe that the feeling validates who you are, this is another circular thinking trap. The emotions you experience are real enough. The thoughts behind the emotion can be phony. Helplessness feelings do not prove the validity of helplessness thinking. To break the cycle, examine the thoughts you associate with the emotions and cull out the thoughts that feed the emotional part of the circle. Then, separate facts that you can objectively verify from subjective impressions.

Using "should statements."   You can tell yourself that you should plan to get up early tomorrow. This is a conditional statement that can serve as a reminder. The "should" statements in depression are a horse of a different color. Representing expectations and requirements, these "should" statements can both precipitate depression and make it worse. For example, depressive tensions can increase among those who believe "I should not feel depressed. I should be over this already." When such "should" statements are persistent, they can feel painfully pressuring and lead to added frustration as the gap between expectation and reality widens. A preliminary solution is to train yourself to think in terms of what you'd prefer to do, what you'd desire to experience, and what you can and could do to help shape that outcome. (Chapter 12 will expand upon how to abandon a "should" philosophy by adopting and spreading a preferential philosophy.)

Labeling.   By affixing a belittling label on yourself, you strip away many positive aspects of your humanity. These pejorative labels include "failure," "idiot," "jerk," "knucklehead," "worthless," "loser," and "useless." This self-marginalizing can lead you to conclude that you are in a hopeless fix. But, this simplification process makes about as much sense as thinking that you can stuff a complex person—yourself—into a small bottle, then label it and cap it forever. To confront this cognitive distortion, define what you mean by the label. Ask yourself how that label, and only that label, applies 100 percent to you. Next, think of ten ordinary things you do that do not fit the definition. Can you see why one label doesn't tell the tale?

Personalizing.   If you think that you are completely or primarily responsible for everything bad that happens, take a second look. Believing you are responsible for a mate's alcohol or drug habit suggests that you have another belief: you can assert control over your mate's pressuring, compulsive, relapsing, addictive process, but you didn't do so as well as you should. This guilt formula is typically based upon the assumption that you have extraordinary powers and did not use them. Blaming yourself for conditions that extend beyond your control is a formula for extending blame into helplessness and hopelessness thinking. If you find yourself in a personalization trap, begin your exit by asking and answering the questions, "Do I think it is a bit grandiose to think that what goes wrong is always my fault? Do I really have that kind of power?"

Coping with Cognitive Distortions

Cognitive distortions alter perception and perspective and typically intensify and extend the experience of depression. At least a few of the twelve distortions just listed are likely to be present when you are thinking depressively. For example, hopelessness depressive thinking is a form of fortune-telling overgeneralization that is pretty common among people who feel depressed.

Deflating the impact of depressive cognitive distortions can start if you boost your awareness of distortions that are part of your depressive views. The definitions can help you decide which fit and which don't. This awareness exercise can prove especially useful. When you can define and articulate a problem, you have taken a big step in the direction of controlling the problem process. The following provides an example for how to deal with cognitive distortions:

Overgeneralization:	Distortion disputation:
"My life is going nowhere."	"Here are three ways to change the direction of the statement: 1. Accept that feeling depressed is undesirable but may persist. 2. Question the meaning of the "my life is going nowhere" statement. 3. Look for exceptions to the belief to expose and override the overgeneralization."

COGNITIVE AWARENESS EXERCISE

Use the following outline to list any distortions you recognize in yourself and to list questions that you can raise with yourself about their validity:

Overgeneralization:	Distortion disputation:
Magnifying and minimizing:	Distortion disputation:
Catastrophizing:	Distortion disputation:
Dichotomous thinking:	Distortion disputation:
Mental filtering:	Distortion disputation:
Jumping to conclusions:	Distortion disputation:

Fortune telling:	Distortion disputation:
Mind reading:	Distortion disputation:
Emotional reasoning:	Distortion disputation:
"Should" statements:	Distortion disputation:
Labeling:	Distortion disputation:
Personalizing:	Distortion disputation:

USING PURRRRS TO DEFEAT DEPRESSIVE THINKING

Computers have many default functions that are intentionally set for automatic reactions. If you don't like the default, you can change it. A depressive thinking decision normally involves a default line of thought. Although this is automatic, it is not intentionally set. These default ideas can include beliefs, such as "nothing can be done to stop feeling depressed." As with the computer, if you don't like the default, you can reset it. Unlike the computer, you may have to reset the new default many times until it starts automatically.

What can you do when you automatically engage default depressive thoughts? Upon discovering a default depressive thought, you can put it into slow motion. Think about its significance. Through this reflective process, you can start to make that which is automatic subject to the powers of reason. The following describes a problem-solving default system. You can take a bold step up from depression by examining and challenging depressive thinking using the PURRRRS method.

The PURRRRS acronym describes a seven-step process: pause, use, reflect, reason, respond, revise, and stabilize. Through PURRRRS, you slow automatic depressive thinking, disrupt the process, and build thinking skills that oppose default depressive thinking processes.

Pause.   Put depressive thinking on pause. That means you stop to think about your thinking. By taking this basic self-monitoring step, you can slow the depressive thinking process and subject it to a more critical evaluation. But what if you routinely forget to pause? A reminder system can help. You can use a felt-tipped pen to mark a small green dot on your watch or the fingernail of your thumb to symbolize "pause." You can put an elastic band on your wrist. You can wear a special ring. When thinking negatively, seeing the dot, elastic band, or ring can remind you to pause.

Use.   The second step involves using your resources to resist letting your depressive thoughts flow unchecked. For example, put your thinking into slow motion by writing out the thoughts and reviewing what you just told yourself. This thought log method makes the thoughts visual and accessible to examination. You can also refuse to accept depressive thoughts at face value. This refusal opens opportunities to review the thoughts that you refuse to accept.

Reflect.   The first and second steps set the stage for reflecting on what you are imagining, telling yourself, or picturing in your mind's eye when you feel depressed. In this reflective phase, you gather information. You reflect on how you feel, what you first tell yourself, and what you continue to tell yourself when you feel trapped within your depressive thoughts. This helps to extend the mapping of a depressive thinking process.

Reason.   Through pausing, utilizing, and reflecting, you may already have started to think about your thinking. In the reasoning phase, you take this a step further. You evaluate your depression self-talk. For example, helplessness, worthlessness, and hopelessness thinking, when fixed in a depressed mood, are depressive thinking, but you can use four questions to put the thinking into perspective: Does the thinking cause you to feel uplifted? Are the thoughts toned with optimism? Do the thoughts lead to improvements in your relationships with others? Is your thinking purposeful in the sense that your thoughts outline prescriptions for engaging in constructive actions?

Respond.   Once you've reflected and reasoned things out, respond by mapping steps to crack through your depressive thinking barriers. Think about the steps that you can take now. There is practically always something that you can do. Give yourself instructions about how to proceed. Follow your plan by talking and walking yourself through the paces.

Revise. Reflecting, reasoning, and responding are like sighting a target, pulling a bow, and releasing an arrow. Reflecting, reasoning, and responding are rarely perfect at the start, so you might miss the center of your target. In looking at what happened, you can get new ideas. Something you hadn't thought about could yield an insight or two. In the revising phase, you readjust your aim. If you've overlooked a step, revision involves adding the missing step.

Stabilize. Stabilizing normally occurs following repeated practice to the point where you have developed a habit for recognizing, evaluating, and replacing depressive thinking with neutral to rational thoughts. As you tend to be more reflective about the relationship between mood and depressive thinking and act to boost your clear-thinking skills, you can better

> **PURRRRS Plan**
> 1. Pause.
> 2. Use resources to slow negative process.
> 3. Reflect on thinking.
> 4. Reason it out.
> 5. Respond through positive actions.
> 6. Revise plan based on feedback.
> 7. Stabilize new learning.

regulate your actions and more often see yourself in charge of what you do. This is a formula for feeling more like a confident, capable person in those areas where you previously felt helpless and hopeless.

Although originally designed to help people overcome procrastination, the PURRRRS mapping process is an important tool for putting a depressive default decision into perspective, positioning yourself for taking action, taking action, and making adjustments to free yourself from the impact of depressive thinking. Through practicing this process, you can stabilize your gains.

Tina's PURRRRS Plan

Let's look at how Tina used PURRRRS to attack her depression. Tina felt burdened by thoughts that her life was one big hassle and wouldn't get better. Here is how Tina used PURRRRS:

1. She *paused* and reminded herself that her first goal was to monitor her thinking by putting it into slow motion.

2. Tina *used* her capability to subdue her automatic depressive thought flow. This suppression was an act of free will, supporting a choice to develop a healthy sense of perspective.

3. She *reflected* on the content of what she was telling herself. She heard herself say that "life is a hassle and will never get better."

4. No longer willing to accept that hogwash, Tina *reasoned* it out. She judged that what she told herself was an overgeneralization. She realized that whenever she thought the word "never" in a variable and changing situation, she fooled herself. She reminded herself that avoiding hassles was not her prime goal. Rather, her prime goal was to get something important done, such as defeat her depressive thinking. Following this insight, she found her thoughts became more fluid and flexible.

5. Tina *responded* by mapping out the steps to separate her overgeneralized thinking from her depressive feelings. She expanded on the *never* issue by showing herself exceptions to the never rule. Tina extended her *response* by giving herself verbal instructions to recognize and challenge her depressive thinking. Because she showed herself she could pause, use her resources to expose an automatic depressive thinking sequence, and start to figure things out, she realized that she couldn't be as helpless as she previously thought. She found herself feeling more tolerant about hassles, and more likely to promptly address them. She also found that she could counter the extremes in her thinking with tolerance.

6. *Revision* came into play as Tina learned more about her depressive thinking and got better at detecting it. She stuck with techniques she found effective, but also modified methods to suit her unique situation. These revisions came about as a result of experimenting with different ways of recognizing and debunking depressive thinking.

7. Tina *stabilized* what she learned through practice. She applied her growing knowledge to emerging situations where she would previously have overreacted and overgeneralized. She got better at cuing her attention to the presence of depressive thinking. She advanced the PURRRRS skills she developed by applying them to boost her tolerance for frustration. By boosting her tolerance for frustration, she helped innoculate herself against overreactions to hassle. She found that she was typically able to address hassles without procrastinating. (See chapter 13 for techniques to boost frustration tolerance and reduce procrastination.)

YOUR PERSONAL PURRRRS PLAN

When you use PURRRRS, you are less likely to go on automatic pilot with a pessimistic idea. Try PURRRRS the next time you recognize that you are sliding into a circle of negative depressing thinking.

Use the following outline to construct your PURRRRS plan for defeating depressive thinking. For example, cite what you might do to pause, use, reflect, reason, respond, revise, and stabilize your approach for dealing with your current depression-evoking condition.

Depressive thinking condition: _____

Pause	Use	Reflect	Reason	Respond	Revise	Stabilize
Stop.	Resist.	Think about what's happening.	Think it through.	Put yourself through the paces.	Make adjustments.	Persist and repeat.

KEY IDEAS AND ACTION PLAN

What are the key ideas that you got from this chapter? What actions can you take?

Key Ideas

What are the key ideas that you found helpful?

1. _____

   _____

2. _____

   _____

3. _____

   _____

Action Plan

What actions can you take to progress?

1. _____

   _____

2. _____

   _____

3. _____

   _____

POSTSCRIPT

Eighteenth-century physician Thomas Fuller said, "A disease known is half cured." In the world of psychology, the way you explain depression to yourself can make a big difference. Once you know and understand the cognitive distortions associated with depressive thinking, you are in a good position to take the next step, to refuse to be bullied by the thought(s). In this way, you help rid yourself of the nightmare of depression and replace the dream master's work, possibly with thoughts of pleasant horizons.

CHAPTER 7

Defeating Depressive Beliefs

You live with a primitive nomadic tribe in a world where there is no written history. There came a time when your mood dropped and stayed down. Your movements slowed. You no longer helped gather food or participated in the hunt. Your appetite was lost. Your sleep was fitful. You looked at life through a heavy gray cloud.

Your family brought you before the tribe's shaman. The shaman recognized a drained look on your face, sensed your lethargy, and saw this as the work of a dark demon called Kazzze, who entered your body to drain life from you to strengthen itself. The shaman had seen this demon before and recognized its power.

With knowledge passed down through the ages by other shamans, this person of the spirit world knew how to fight the demon. Leading you to a circle of stones, the shaman bid you to sit in the middle, then called for the tribe to come and join the ritual. Then, in a frenzied dance, while shaking a rattle, the shaman chanted, "Kazzze, be gone."

The shaman believed that Kazzze was a powerful demon. The dance to vanquish the demon continued with tribe members shrieking and hissing, with some fainting. Then, the shaman raised both of his arms. The dancing stopped. The tribe moved quietly backwards. Then, in a silent dance, so as to go unobserved by the now distracted demon, the shaman spread a powder over the stones. With a menacing glare, the shaman lit the powder and red, yellow, and purple flames streaked skyward. As the flames crackled, you found yourself cloaked by smoke with a heavy sweet smell. You coughed. Your eyes smarted and filled with tears. Then, grabbing a feathered staff, the shaman commanded Kazzze to vanish into the darkness from whence it came. The members of the tribe rushed to the middle of the circle, screaming war screams. The ritual ended. The shaman said the demon was gone, but it would take time for you to regain your strength.

Since the demon was bound to the land on which the tribe camped, it was tribal tradition to migrate to a different place after such ceremonies. With a handful of thirty pebbles, the shaman moved one pebble each night from one pouch to another until the first pouch was empty and the other was full. Each pebble represented a day's journey. It was then that the tribe made permanent camp until the time came to move again.

The mystery was solved. You understood that the demon of darkness possessed you and was draining your life from you. As the tribe moved on, the shaman said your strength would return. And so it was. You returned to the hunt. A smile returned to your face as you watched the children at play. Kazzze was gone.

Magical rituals were once part of the magical world of primitive people. Beliefs in wood demons, gods, and spiritual forces were part of everyday experiences. They were a way for people to explain and to understand reality. Beliefs were and still are part of our human heritage.

Although in the example above, the shaman started with a faulty belief, the processes that he followed could be logical, organized, consistent, and lead to desired results. From a modern perspective, the demon possession belief is false. However, we now know that physical exercise is a powerful antidepressant. Thus, a long journey on foot, from one location to another, could lead to a lifting of depression.

"Magic" can work for another reason. Your depression can lift because of a strong belief in the curative powers of the ritual. For example, a belief that a feeling of misery and lethargy was demon-inspired could be the sort of explanation that would serve as a mental "pill" leading to a sense of hope. The shaman's explanation, that your strength would return in time, could explain why there was no immediate relief from the malaise but there was hope for eventual relief. A relief from worry or preoccupation about the dull feelings of depression could contribute to a positive change of mind that eventually leads to a positive shift in the biochemistry associated with depression to a biochemistry associated with well-being.

From primitive times up to the recent present, little was known about how depressive thinking melded with depression. Our modern knowledge about how thinking affects both our emotions and our biology moves us further from magical ways of knowing toward an evolving science where evidence weighs more than myths in how we meet such challenges as overcoming depression.

THE POWER OF BELIEFS

We are a believing species. It is impossible to remain conscious and not have beliefs. Our beliefs weave through our lives and give a certain sense of constancy and stability to what we do and to how we feel.

The power of belief was recognized and used by the eighteenth-century BC Babylonian king Hammurabi. When Hammurabi introduced his legal codes, he faced the problem of enforcement. He knew his agents could not be everywhere to apprehend people violating his laws. So he told his people that the laws came directly from the sun god Shamash. He said that if his agents did not discover those who violated the god's laws, the god would surely see the violation and would sooner or later punish the offender.

If anyone doubts the power of beliefs, consider the World War II kamikaze pilots who showed that beliefs can trump life. Some—perhaps the majority—of these suicidal pilots believed that by crashing their planes into U.S. ships, they would go directly to heaven. Some pilots may have understood that this proposition was a myth but still went on the suicide run because they believed that they would be socially censored if they didn't volunteer.

Depressive beliefs can sprinkle the path of melancholia with dispiriting ideas such as, you can never escape the grips of depression. If you believe this proposition as truth, it feels like reality. However, while the emotions that flow from this thought are real, the underlying ideas are seriously flawed. As in the ancient ritual described above, logic can grow from an unrealistic belief and become part of a logic-tight compartment that is, at first, impervious to contradictory facts. It is often through a slow process of accommodating to new information that the compartment collapses.

Even when depressive propositions of truth are both false and debatable, they are no less powerful. There is a big difference between knowing that a depressive belief can cause grief and developing a conviction that can override it.

It is a fact that we can hold on to false beliefs even when faced with strong contradictory evidence. That is a quirk of human nature. It is also a fact of human nature that science can erode our myths, but magical ways of knowing can remain appealing and dominating. It takes time to replace the old with the new by accommodating to systems of belief that are factually grounded.

False and Factual Beliefs

We all have false beliefs. Some fit snugly into what we see, making them resistive to change. At one time, people thought the world was flat because it looked that way. Eventually most people came to understand that the world is a sphere. Physical fact, then, replaced a visual illusion. However, in ancient times the belief about the world being flat caused no recognizable harm. Given the times, the belief was irrational but not notably harmful. In fact, it may have been helpful. At a time devoid of adequate navigational devices, sailing ships that stayed in known shipping lanes and those that stayed within sight of the shore were unlikely to be lost.

Some beliefs are false and harmful. A pessimistic belief that you will stay depressed forever can both deepen a depressed mood and support a self-fulfilling prophesy. Such beliefs, when recognized and understood, are contestable and changeable.

Depressive thinking represents a distortion of what most people recognize as reality. This biased, distorted, unrealistic, and overly generalized form of thinking can continue to exist even though it violates fact, logic, and reality. Depressive helplessness beliefs, for example, are inconsistent with many factual aspects of reality. If you label yourself helpless, and this view represents your general state of mind, you have probably excluded from your thoughts exceptions to a helplessness view. For example, if you can walk, blink, or stretch, you are not completely helpless. If you can question an idea, you are not completely helpless.

Despite glaring flaws in depressive thinking, when these beliefs are active, they can impact what you feel and do. They can decrease your tolerance for frustration, increase your level of distress, and keep the depressive sensations swirling.

Filtering Reality Through Depressive Beliefs

Imagine awakening one morning with nothing to believe in. You have no causes. You have no passions. You have no justification for living. Is the absence of such beliefs the same as depression? Possibly.

The positive things you believe in can fade when you listen to the roar of depressive beliefs. You can believe in your ability to solve problems, but when depressed, you shift to believing that you can do nothing right. Following a significant loss, your beliefs in a bright future can be overtaken by a belief that you'll never survive the loss and the future will remain forever bleak.

While bound by a significant depression, your everyday beliefs can fall into the background of your thoughts, replaced by thoughts that bulge with negativity. When active, these depressive beliefs can wash out your hopes, wishes, desires, and what you find pleasurable in life. What you once believed in can go into hibernation as the winter of depression lingers on. Yet, beliefs that counter depressive beliefs coexist within us all and await a resurrection.

Our beliefs, including depressive beliefs, are like filtering systems. When activated, the filter allows in information that supports the belief. It blocks contradictory information by ignoring the information, or explaining it away. This mental filtering helps sustain beliefs, even those that routinely lead to poor results. A compulsive gambler, who believes in beating the odds, is likely to squander much and gain little. It matters not that past experience tells a story of losses that overwhelm gains. In a fit of depression, a belief that depression will never end fuels itself and finds reason for itself.

Beliefs that contradict reality are changeable. Nevertheless, the process of negating entrenched depressive beliefs and experiencing the power of functional competitive beliefs normally proves challenging. This chapter examines how to meet this challenge.

THE ABC WAY TO DISABLE DEPRESSIVE THINKING

With any continuing depression, it is rare to find a straight line between events, thoughts, and reactions. When people feel depressed, they often have multiple distressing thoughts that go through their minds. This flow of thought symbolically consists of dots, gobs, fragments, jagged lines, and other interlinked and unconnected thoughts. Thus, you may think about events that you associate with your depression and ruminate about a specific event. Then your mind jumps to how miserable you feel and then on to more pessimistic ideas.

A flow of depressive thought is rarely linear. It's more like a cacophony of clashing sounds. These thoughts can go from pessimistic to feelings of worthlessness, to self-blame, to blaming others, and so on. You can profitably monitor and give these depressive thoughts a linear order, thus making them easier to examine and dispute. For example, you can organize your thoughts and address depressive thinking using psychologist Albert Ellis's (2003a) ABCDE method. The letters stand for activating events, beliefs, consequences, disputation, and new effects. Let's see how the system works.

Activating Events

A neighbor's cat enters through an open window and shreds the fabric of your expensive couch. You get a flat tire. A person in front of you in line gabs with a clerk while you're in a hurry. Your best friend comes for a visit. You get a pay raise and a letter of commendation for your work. What do these situations have in common? They are activating events that can evoke evaluations that can lead to emotional and behavioral reactions. For example, you might feel angered upon seeing the cat scratch your couch if you thought, "The owner of this damned cat should have kept it locked up. I can't stand this." You'd likely feel differently if you disliked the couch and now had an excuse to buy another—perhaps at your neighbor's expense.

Beliefs About Events

The B is the centerpiece of the system. Activating events are normally filtered through your beliefs. If you believe that you are helpless to exit from your depression, you are likely to filter your experiences to exclude exceptions to this core belief. You are likely to exaggerate the importance of conditions that fit with this belief. Then, thoughts and life experiences that can counteract depressive beliefs readily slip into the background. However, bringing rational thinking to the foreground of your thoughts and strengthening this thinking is a prescription for combating irrational depressive thoughts.

Ellis divides beliefs into rational and irrational. He couples rational beliefs to functional motivations and actions and connects irrational beliefs to dysfunctional emotions and behavior.

Rational Beliefs

Healthy rational beliefs are ordinarily objective patterns of thought that lead to constructive actions and benefits. Rational belief systems are propositions of truth that are functional and reality-based. They can support personal development and the pursuit of meaningful personal goals, including the reduction and prevention of depression. You can view these beliefs as sensible when they attach to healthy emotions and actions.

If one idea is rational, it doesn't mean that a contradictory belief is irrational. In the area of personal development, there can be many rational perspectives about the same situation. For example, when there are different strategies to accomplish the same result, it doesn't mean that one approach is rational and all others are not. Disabling depressive beliefs through reasoning is a rational approach. You can also teach yourself to change irrational depressive thinking through problem-related behavioral actions. This latter approach can be rational if you believe that activity trumps depression.

As a practical matter, attacking depressive thinking through reason can affect how you behave and feel, and attacking depression through purposeful activities can positively intertwine with your thinking and emoting. But if you think that questioning depressive thinking and engaging in purposeful actions builds a bridge you can cross from a state of depression to one of liberation from depression, that doesn't mean that taking antidepressants is irrational.

How can you tell if a belief is a healthy, rational belief? Such beliefs represent reasonable, objective, flexible, and constructive conclusions or inferences about reality that support survival, happiness, and healthy results. The questions that follow are an aid to determining if a self-development belief is healthy and rational. Does your belief

- promote productivity and creativity?

- support positive relationships?

- prompt accountability without unnecessary blame and condemnation?

- encourage acceptance and tolerance?

- strengthen persistence and self-discipline?

- serve as a platform for conditions that propel personal growth?

- correlate with healthy risk-taking initiatives?

- link to a sense of emotional well-being and positive mental health?

- lead to a realistic sense of perspective?

- improve your career performances and opportunities?

- stimulate an openness to experience and an experimental outlook?

- direct your efforts along ethical pathways?

If your belief fits with several of these positive criteria, it is likely to be functional and rational. For example, if you believe that it is important to meet your responsibilities, that belief normally promotes advantages. Suppose you believe the "do it now" view leads to greater personal efficiency, effectiveness, and less stress. If you truly believe this and act upon that belief, it is likely that you'll routinely do reasonable things in a reasonable time in a reasonable way in order to accomplish more with less strain and more satisfaction. Follow the "do it now" prescription and the chances are that you'll gain a growing sense of personal control.

Rational beliefs can be tested by their results. If you believe that you can help yourself overcome depression through reducing depressive thinking, and you act according to the belief, the chances are you'll eventually gain relief from depression.

Irrational Beliefs

We all have irrational flaws in our thinking, and some of these are hard to see. They are sometimes called "blind spots." By accepting that you will sometimes think irrationally, you are more likely to tolerate depressive thinking within yourself as you act to change it.

Irrational beliefs refer to any thoughts that are inconsistent with reality. You think grasshoppers can communicate with crickets because they both make sounds with their legs. That's irrational. As far as we know, there is no inter-species communication between grasshoppers and crickets. However, this belief is unlikely to have any meaningful effect on your mood, behavior, or life. It may be irrational, but it is probably not harmful.

Harmful irrational beliefs are arbitrary, subjective, unscientific, and illogical. When our irrational beliefs are rigidly fixed, we are likely to operate out of a logic-tight compartment where gross misrepresentations of reality continue unabashed because we feel married to them. By definition, harmful irrational beliefs are unhealthy. They cloud your consciousness with distortions, misconceptions, over-generalizations, and oversimplifications. They limit and narrow your outlook. You can normally find harmful core irrational beliefs present in destructive conditions such as impulsiveness, arrogance, defeatism, condemnation, depression, anxiety, hostility, insecurity, addictions, procrastination, prejudice, envy, compulsions, and obsessions.

In identifying harmful depressive beliefs, here are some classic questions. Does the belief

- link with a mood of depression and exaggerate that mood?

- promote a sense of pessimism, fatalism, or defeatism?

- match up with a sense of helplessness?

- generate feelings of worthlessness and self-blame?

- interfere with your relationships?

- impede your ability to manage basic activities of daily living?

- detract you from pursuing meaningful personal goals?

If your belief meets any of these seven criteria, it is likely to be irrational and is likely to prove depressive.

When irrational depressive beliefs actively dominate your consciousness, the rational ones tend to fade into the background. You can bring them out of hiding and strengthen them so that they become active, dominant thoughts. They can sound like a faint murmur, if they are heard at all. When rational thoughts are the active thoughts, the depressive thoughts tend to fade.

Consequences

Irrational beliefs have their own emotional and behavioral consequences. But some consequences are positive. You take a sugar pill that you believe is an antidepressant. You believe it will work. You feel better. This is the placebo effect. A placebo is an inert substance that can lead to actual chemical changes in the body. In that sense, an irrational thought can be positive. In a way, it is like the belief of the primitive tribespeople who believed that a ritual followed by migration would lead to an escape from the life-draining demon Kazzze.

Harmful irrational beliefs have both emotional and behavioral consequences, as well. When you believe that you are helpless to change and you have no hope, and then you blame yourself for what you claim you can't control, you engage in a pattern of irrational thought that has the power to evoke negative emotional consequences. An emotional consequence can be an anxious-based inhibition. When you believe you can't do anything to defeat depression, you are likely to languish with a downtrodden emotional sense of helplessness. This is an emotional consequence.

A behavioral consequence can be withdrawing from activities with significant others. Behavioral consequences include an increased rate of procrastination on following through on self-help measures to curb depression. The consequences can include a lower response rate to other people. Behavioral consequences can have a downward spiraling effect: you can feel worse as you retreat into yourself.

Connecting emotional and behavioral consequences to depressive beliefs opens opportunities to cut the connections. Judging depressive thoughts, rather than accepting them as self-judgments, can help reduce their impact. Increasing activity levels can lead to behavioral consequences that counteract depression.

Disputation

It's in human nature to be suggestible, to develop false beliefs, and to hang on to those beliefs as though they were absolute truths. But we also have the ability to think rationally and to resist buying into blanket depressive thinking statements.

A person who has never experienced a significant depression may at first puzzle over how people with depression can hold on to depressive thoughts. Can they not see that the thoughts are unreal and only serve to perpetuate an already miserable state? But this assertion of rationality may be irrational. Depressive thoughts are well connected to each other and connected to depressive sensations. It takes time to develop competitive networks of thought that substitute for and can uncouple the depressive variety of thought from their associated emotions and sensations.

Knowing the difference between depressive thoughts and their rational counterparts is no assurance that the rational perspective will prevail, for knowing about something is different from believing. It is through a process of information gathering, questioning the negative, plus seeking positive alternatives, that you can blueprint a new response pattern within your brain in the form of a powerful new set of antidepressive beliefs.

New information about depression can lead to new ways to view the process and a reduction in depressive thinking. Changes in perspective come from education.

A process of falsifying depressive thoughts, repeated many times, can lead to a conversion from "knowing about" to conviction. Through this active process of developing a competitive antidepressant belief system, you simultaneously build a coping frame of reference. But you have done much more for yourself. By recognizing and disputing depressive thinking, you have shown yourself that you are not helpless and you have hope.

Disputation is where you apply scientific ways of knowing and doing, along with common sense, to counteract your depressive thinking. Chapter 5 materials on critical thinking and Socratic reasoning apply to the disputation process. By disputing depressive thinking, you get a double positive: You deflate the effects of negative thinking, which can have a calming effect. You also free your thoughts and time for pursuing experiences that you are more likely to value. The following disputation methods illustrate one way to strengthen your rational connections while weakening harmful depressive beliefs.

Apply Reason

Here is a way to question (dispute) hopelessness thinking and helplessness thinking in order to reduce their impact and advance your clear-thinking skills:

Believing that your life will stay miserable is an example of a hopeless depressive thought. There are many ways to dispute this belief. You can start with these observations: Hopelessness is an overly generalized prediction that people who feel depressed often make. It is also a conjecture. Unless you can know the future (and we know that is a false belief), you can't predict the future with certainty. How can you use this information to challenge a hopelessness prediction?

Believing that you can do nothing to alleviate your suffering is an example of depressive helplessness thinking. Much of the material in this book focuses on challenging this helplessness thought. If you have tools to defeat depression, then how does it follow that you cannot put some to use to test the hypothesis that you are helpless to change?

Rationally speaking, when you articulate your observations and questions in a way that gives direction to solving personal problems associated with depression, you increase your chances of disengaging from irrational blind spots in your thinking. Such a disengagement can feel relieving.

Take Action

Challenging helplessness thinking can be accomplished in part through practical actions. You tidy your abode even though you'd rather withdraw into darkness. At a fixed time each day, you jog in place for five minutes, or you do some other form of exercise. You do something altruistic, such as anonymously sending toys to an orphanage.

You may find through taking practical actions that you don't feel quite so emotionally drawn into yourself. You can find that you dwell less on events that displease you, and that you have less negative thoughts about yourself. But you may also begin to experience a growing sense of confidence in yourself as a doer, rather than a stewer. Such a perspective shift can start a forward spiral, which leads to a disengagement from a downward spiral of depression.

By teaching yourself to think about your thinking, by separating sensible from depressive thought, and by engaging in problem-solving behaviors, you position yourself to disengage from automatic depressive thinking. The skills you develop to counter this thinking predictably grow in strength through practice.

New Effects

When you engage in "do it now" activities to counteract depression, you identify and challenge depressive thinking and engage in problem-solving activities. Through this process, you are acting to do and to get better. The acid test for this process lies in the effects that you produce for yourself. If you find that by acting against depressive thinking, feelings, and actions, you feel a growing sense of relief and control, you've produced a positive effect. As this effect increases in frequency, intensity, and duration, depression is likely to decrease.

As you apply cognitive skills to a process of ridding yourself of depression, an electroencephalograph can measure changes in your brain waves. As you develop your cognitive problem-solving skills, your brain waves change in positive ways (Deldin and Chiu 2005). This is a meaningful effect.

Neural imaging devices, such as functional magnetic resonating imagery, show that the functional changes you make in your thinking lead to structural changes in the brain (Goldapple et al. 2004). Reasoning and problem solving activate the prefrontal cortex, which is the part of the brain we associate with reason and logic (Keightley et al. 2003).

The brain includes interrelated neural networks. By strengthening and expanding those that relate to reason and problem solving, you can make some rather permanent changes that tend to strengthen over time.

The very promising research on neural imaging of cognitive interventions is, perhaps, one of the more exciting developments of the twenty-first century. Eventually we may be able to see specific "color" changes in the brain when, say, depressive thoughts are successfully challenged. A visual view of the brain that couples with positive changes in feelings can prove very reinforcing.

Through applying the ABCDE system, you've made yourself your own shaman with the power to vanish the demon of depression. But rather than rely on magic, your shaman is up to date. This shaman relies on science and on the recognition that making positive changes takes time. You can make real gains through a process that can be measured by both brain imaging methods and your own knowledge that you can exercise control over your negative thoughts. The process requires activating and strengthening your rational capabilities.

■ *Amy's Story*

Following a bitter divorce, Amy had been mildly to moderately depressed for approximately three years. This conscientious and sensitive person's depression was complicated by a highly self-critical attitude, brooding, self-doubts, and a decline in her ability to tolerate frustration and anxiety. She saw herself as a wet mop who was pushed around by others. Amy believed that she got no respect from members of her family and her employer. She felt trapped.

In her second session, Amy appeared weepy and upset over unkind comments about her appearance made by her older sister, Molly. She saw Molly as the "perfect person" who never admitted to any faults but who was quick to find fault with others. Amy saw herself as vulnerable and unable to defend herself against her sister. During this session, she felt depressed and anxious. She flitted from one thought to another, creating a kaleidoscopic picture of different colored distresses. She found it difficult to focus.

Following an upsetting event, Amy, like many who feel both anxious and depressed, had a difficult time organizing her thoughts. She found it especially challenging to separate her depressive and anxious thinking from her legitimate gripes. So she and her therapist took extra time that day on problem organizing so that she could move toward her goal of reducing her distress over her sister's comments, of standing up for herself, and of getting better control of her thoughts and life.

As Amy progressed with a problem-solving analysis, she used an ABCDE model to get a fix on her problem and figure out what to do.

The ABCDE model is linear in so far as each step logically leads to the next. As a practical matter, however, most people focus on activating events and their emotions about the event. So, in working with a cognitive behavioral therapist, you might talk about what happened and how you felt. You'd start with the activating event and emotional and behavioral consequences, then look at what you were perceiving and thinking at the time. You can also follow this process on your own using techniques described in this chapter. The following is Amy's ABCDE exercise.

Activating Event

First, Amy looked closely at what triggered the kaleidoscope of distressing thoughts. Molly had paid a visit and said, "You didn't answer my e-mail quickly enough" and then went on to say, "What's wrong with your hair? You need to get your act together. You need to lose weight."

Amy, at first, focused on what had happened and on how bad she felt. This is common. Thinking about your thinking is usually far down on the list of things to do when you feel distressed. Amy noted the conditions she associated with feeling upset and then described her emotional and behavioral experiences under the heading of "consequences." She then came back to describe what she recalled thinking at the time. If you, at first, find it natural to jump over the beliefs category and then come back, that is an acceptable practice.

Beliefs

We broke out Amy's beliefs into a dichotomy of irrational and rational thoughts about the event. As they were clearly the more dominant, we started with the irrational thoughts first. Then we worked on teasing out the rational thoughts. This proved somewhat challenging. Her rational ideas about the event were present, but they were obscured by her stressful and somewhat catastrophic depressive thinking. (Sometimes you will find yourself inferring the rational thoughts. That is a positive step on the path to teaching yourself to develop a rational perspective.) Here's a table outlining Amy's irrational and rational thoughts.

Irrational Thoughts	Rational Thoughts
"I'm not attractive enough."	"I don't like being put down."
"I'm not smart enough."	"Molly's negativity annoys me."
"I can't do anything right."	"I'd prefer not to deal with this situation."
"I'm overwhelmed."	"It's better to stand up for myself than quit."

By seeing her irrational-rational dichotomy of thought, Amy's first comment was "Wow. I sure did a number on myself. Molly was a pain, but I was a bigger one." Amy felt encouraged that her awareness of her depressing thoughts and their rational counterparts suggested that she was not locked into the negative. She had an alternative. She found this perspective emotionally freeing.

Consequences

Following Molly's comments, Amy's stomach dropped. She reported feeling a variety of negative emotions followed by discernable behaviors. Her emotional consequences included anxiety, anger, and depression. Her behavioral consequences were that she became sick to her stomach and vomited and that she withdrew.

Disputation

Both Amy and her therapist thought that the process of recognizing the irrational and rational elements in her thoughts was a useful exercise. Connecting the dots between event, thought, emotions, and behavior gave her a linear organization for this process. In the process of doing this exercise, Amy significantly calmed down. She reported that she could clearly see how her thinking grew to catastrophic proportions. This awareness, she believed, could help her to maintain her perspective in the future when she faced her sister's negativity. However, beyond recognizing the dichotomy of irrational and rational thoughts, Amy and her therapist expanded the analysis to include self-questioning and disputation. Here is an example of how Amy went about disputing her irrational thinking about her sister's comments.

Questions	Answers
"What if I'm not as attractive as my sister wants me to be?"	"My attractiveness is partially controllable, but I am more than my looks."
"Where is the law that says I need to be as thin as my sister insists?"	"Maintaining a reasonable weight is a reasonable goal. It's my choice, however, as to what I weigh."
"How is my worth contingent on my sister's opinion about my appearance and intelligence?"	"It's contingent only if I let it be."
"If I'm not the person my sister wants me to be, what's wrong with being the person I am?"	"I can always give myself unconditional self-acceptance."

"What do I mean when I think I'm out of control?"	"This is a reflection of the distress I cause myself when I convince myself I am helpless in my ability to defend my interests. I'll work to develop my assertiveness skills."
"What do I mean when I tell myself that I'm overwhelmed?"	"I'm accepting hogwash. I can reframe my situation by looking at what I can control and what I would best work toward improving."
"What do I mean by 'a nervous breakdown'?"	"This is emotional reasoning. Nerves don't break down. The breakdown is with my thinking. I take my feelings of distress and magnify them. I believe I can't cope now or ever. I can learn to recognize and challenge and change this thinking."

Effects

Here's a list of potential effects that Amy produced with this process:

■   "Stop vomiting."

■   "Have a sense of optimism that I can learn to recognize and question negative thinking."

■   "Stick up for my rights by telling my sister that her criticisms are both unhelpful and alienating. If she wants to get along with me in the future, she had better stop the negativity."

■   "Have positive sense of self-worth."

■   "Reduce helplessness and hopelessness depressive thinking."

■   "Gain personal control of thinking, emotions, and actions."

As Amy learned more about the ABC approach and practiced using it, she felt significantly better. Learning to organize her thinking made a difference. She felt hopeful. Over time, she also figured out how to express herself constructively with her sister.

Amy noted that her sister continued to harp about her weight and appearance, but that she was able to put her sister's statements into perspective. She also asserted herself more with her sister. With some trepidation, Amy told Molly that she appreciated her concerns, however, she liked her own hairstyle, her weight was on the low side of the average range, and she was satisfied with her choice of clothing. Molly defended her comments. Amy could see that she wasn't going to change Molly's views, but she did get Molly to agree to keep her comments to herself about Amy's appearance. For the first time in many years, Amy saw that she could stand up for her rights. She stopped describing herself as a "wet mop."

ABCDE EXERCISE

When you feel in a depressive rut, use the following ABCDE self-help form to address your depressive thinking. Follow Amy's example and fill in the blanks.

A (activating event): _____

B (beliefs about depressive sensations, events, or thoughts)

Functional beliefs (rational, factual, plausible, reasonable, predictable): _____

_____

Depressive beliefs (self-handicapping beliefs, misconceptions, distortions, and so forth): _____

_____

C (consequences)

Emotional consequences from functional beliefs: _____

Emotional consequences from depressive beliefs: _____

Behavioral consequences from functional beliefs: _____

Behavioral consequences from depressive beliefs: _____

D (disputing depressive belief systems)

Prime questions to ask and answer: _____

Prime actions to take: _____

E (new cognitive, emotive, behavioral effects)

Results of prime questions: _____

Results of prime actions: _____

THE STEPPING-STONE APPROACH

Depressive ideas and beliefs can be organized under themes such as worthlessness, helplessness, and hopelessness (Knaus 1982). The themes can be ordered according to the distress or discomfort they promote. This ordering is like using stepping-stones to cross the stream of depression and then moving on without depression on your trail. To get to the second step, you take the first. To get to the third, you take the second. But here's the rub. You start with the toughest step first. Luckily, you can break the toughest step down into simple parts. And when the most depressing theme is evaluated, challenged, and derailed, the weaker themes will sometimes collapse. Metaphorically, the stream dries up and you don't need the stepping-stones any longer. What follows is an illustration of how this stepping-stone approach works.

■ *Betty's Story*

Betty became depressed after her company went bankrupt and she lost her job. She had the symptoms of a moderately severe depression. She woke early and couldn't fall back asleep. She complained of a depressed mood, difficulty concentrating, and forgetfulness. She isolated herself in her apartment, often refusing to answer the telephone. She viewed herself as a worthless person with no future. She believed that she could do nothing to help herself.

When she didn't "snap out of it," her worried parents literally dragged her into therapy. Thereafter, Betty's first steps involved educating herself about depression. She quickly learned about the research on depression and the benefits of physical exercise. She complained that she didn't think she could exercise on her own. Her parents agreed to exercise with her. Each day, they would come to her apartment. After pressing her to try, they usually succeeded in getting her to walk with them. They kept the pace brisk and walked for about forty-five minutes each day. Following this approach, Betty began to show signs of improvement. When depressed, you can often use all the support you can get.

Her depressive thinking was especially burdensome. She agreed to take a closer look at what she was thinking and to try a stepping stone approach. Through this method, she would first separate her depressive thoughts according to themes and then order them according to her level of discomfort when the theme was on her mind. Since her themes tended to interlace, the process of parting them proved challenging, but she persisted and succeeded. She did this by matching the beliefs against the criteria for rational and irrational thought. Not surprisingly, her depressive thinking fit the irrational criteria. Next, Betty ordered the themes according to their degree of negativity.

Seven Steps to Defeat Depressive Thinking

1. Identify depressive themes.

2. Compare according to strength.

3. List ideas to support belief.

4. Evaluate the self-defeating ideas, not yourself.

5. Create a chart to organize the themes.

6. Create challenges for each emerging depressive idea.

7. Persist and practice in disputing self-defeating ideas using the tools provided here.

Here is the approach Betty followed:

1. She identified four major depressive themes: worthlessness, helplessness, hopelessness, and self-blame.

2. She compared each theme according to the level of stress she associated with it. She thought that her feelings of worthlessness were stronger than either her sense of helplessness and hopelessness. She thought her sense of hopelessness was more distressful than her sense of helplessness. Self-blame, though painful, was the fourth corner of a depressive box that entrapped her.

3. Betty's next step was to come up with examples of beliefs that she held to, within each theme. Then, she weighed the ideas according to their stress effect. For example, the worthlessness theme included this ordering of ideas: "I'm stupid. I'm not living up to my potential. I can't do anything right."

4. Betty made a chart for each theme. Within each chart, she listed the depressive ideas that supported the theme.

5. She wrote down challenges for each separate depressive thought, challenged this belief, and recorded the results. Each time she detected new emerging depressive messages, she added the theme to her chart, and came up with ways to challenge the associated ideas. This served as a coping tool.

6. Through persistence and practice, Betty began to build her skills in disputing negative depressive thought. Through this process, she built a coping frame of reference to use against her depressive thinking.

A closer look at Betty's stepping-stone approach follows:

The Worthlessness Theme

Betty's most troublesome theme was worthlessness. She believed that her self-worth depended on her performances and upon what others thought about what she did. For example, she took her company's bankruptcy personally. She thought that if she had done more, the bankruptcy would not have happened. Beyond falling into this demandingness trap, Betty worried about interviewing for a new job. She feared that she would not present herself well, and no one would hire her.

Self-blame and worry thinking had predated her depression by years. Indeed, she recalled thinking as a child that she could only be good if she did perfectly well. Her parents recalled that she was too hard on herself. They wanted her to do well, but they were also remarkably accepting and tolerant of her mistakes. They would have been happy for her if she was happy flipping hamburgers at a fast food restaurant.

Betty's three "worthlessness" examples were "I'm not smart enough," "My performances are inadequate, and that's awful," and "I am inadequate." The following chart describes Betty's disputations and results:

Worthlessness Theme		
Beliefs	**Questions**	**Results**
"I'm not smart enough."	"If I were more intelligent, how would my life be any different?"	"More intelligence can speed my ability to solve problems. Still, I can make good use of my current abilities rather than lament about not having more of what I already have."
"My performances are inadequate, and that's awful."	"What is wrong with doing reasonable things reasonably well instead of perfectly well?"	"The view that I can still do well without having to do perfectly well, and that's not awful!"
"I am inadequate."	"How does my global worth depend on each performance I make?"	"My 'self' can't be defined as totally one way or another. Much of what I do and think changes according to my mood and situation. Of the consistencies in my life, I act fairly toward others, meet my responsibilities, and routinely seek ways to improve. That observation dismantles my global inadequacy belief."

By recognizing, evaluating, and challenging demanding, perfectionist thinking, Betty gained ground in defeating an irrational process of negative beliefs that had promoted considerable anxiety, inhibition, and grief since her childhood.

Next, Betty looked at the circularity in this part of her depressive thinking. She thought that she was inadequate because she was not smart enough. Yet she thought she needed to be smart enough to feel worthy. Not being smart enough meant that she could never be worthy. She mapped this process according to primary and secondary premises and her conclusions: Her primary premise was that she was not smart enough. Her second premise was that she needed to be perfectly smart to be worthy. Her conclusion was that she was inadequate because she wasn't perfect. Now her job was to break the circle by questioning the premises and conclusion. She found all three points logically flawed.

As Betty evaluated her belief that she was not smart enough, her first question was: smart enough for what? To invent time travel? To rule the world? To live a fulfilling life? Betty figured she did not want to invent time travel, which was impossible. She did not want to rule the world; that was too big a responsibility. But she could do things to increase her odds for living a fulfilling life. She was clearly smart enough to do that.

Next, she looked at the idea that to be worthy she had to be perfect. She had already partially dealt with that part of the circle. The following question sapped more power from her perfectionist belief: "If I can't be what I can't be, what's wrong with enjoying and developing the self that I am?" She had only one reasonable answer. She had a right to enjoy her life. One problem was to find ways to improve her life experiences without judging her global self.

In an innovative way, Betty decided to apply a perfectionist standard to her perfectionist thinking. If her thinking was flawed, it was worthless, not she! With this new perspective gripping her thoughts, she had clarity on a direction she could take. Her inadequacy conclusion no longer held. The basic premises upon which her sense of inadequacy was based, she saw, were flawed beyond belief.

Once the layers of her perfection onion were peeled, she saw another distressing conditional-worth idea that distressed and depressed her. The idea was that something was wrong with her because she was not living up to her potential. She questioned that belief in the following way:

Belief	Question	Result
"I'm not living up to my potential, and that makes me worthless."	"Even if true, how does it follow that failing to achieve my full potential renders me totally worthless?"	"Reaching full potential is a vague and probably unrealistic ideal."

Betty hadn't originally connected the idea of living up to her potential with her sense of worthlessness. It is common for people to add to their thought log as they slow the flow of automatic depressive thinking. They often discover dysfunctional core beliefs. Once Betty recognized the negative implications of this core belief, she went to work to challenge and purge it.

Betty periodically had a revival of contingent-worth ideas (they are practiced and habitual). But now she had powerful tools to recognize and contradict them.

The Hopelessness Theme

You can be in a hopeless position when you have twenty minutes to get to the airport and you are stuck in bumper-to-bumper and stop-and-go rush hour traffic. Hopelessness in depression is another matter. Here you have options, yet you believe you can't change. In this mind-set, you have no possibility of succeeding, improving, getting help, or finding a solution. But this idea of hopelessness is a myth. Like the mythical Sirens who captivated the minds of sailors and lured them to shipwreck and disaster, you can transfix yourself with fatalistic thoughts. But is the hopelessness conjured in the mind as much of a myth as that of the blind poet Homer's description of the mythical Sirens?

The human mind is made for adaptability. We can generate different ideas, make predictions, and move toward positive future opportunities. We can avoid excessive risks and visible dangers. We can solve problems. Yet, we sometimes forget that these capabilities are within reach if we reach for them. Here is the adaptive approach Betty took to deal with her sense of hopelessness.

Hopelessness Theme		
Beliefs	**Questions**	**Results**
"I don't have what it takes to change."	"What do I want to work at changing that I consider both realistic and worthwhile?"	"I've begun to change negative beliefs. I started exercising to work against depressive sensations and mood. I've made progress. I can make more positive changes because I'm doing that now."

"I'm going to suffer forever."	"Where is the proof that my mood will remain constantly negative?"	"The answer is, there is no proof that my depressed mood will continue forever. Education about depression gives me a different prediction. The odds favor that I will free myself from symptoms of depression. Unrealistic ideas are subject to evaluation and revision. Physical exercise helps boost endorphins, or feel-good brain chemicals. In short, I have many ways to change that I have the power to initiate."

Hopelessness can be among the more painful of the depressive themes. But like the worthlessness theme, this belief is so general that it is unprovable.

The Helplessness Theme

Helplessness is ordinarily higher on a person's theme list. In Betty's case, helplessness was third on her list. Here is how she examined and dealt with her thoughts of helplessness.

Helplessness Theme		
Beliefs	**Questions**	**Results**
"I am helpless to change the discomfort I feel or the events around me."	"How does that view compare with what I actually do? What other perspective is likely to prove productive?"	"Complete control is a myth. Seeking to understand is a softer, more progressive approach toward meeting challenges and solving problems."
"I can't do anything right."	"Where is the proof that I can do nothing right?" "What is 'nothing'?" "What do I mean by 'right'?"	"I can challenge the idea that I can do nothing right by making a list of ten things I do okay every day. This can range from brushing my teeth to getting a refund for a greeting card to writing a poem. This action provides a set of contradictory data to compare to a blanket 'can't do anything right' statement. The statement is false when the facts contradict it." "'Nothing' is an overgeneralization. Such blanket statements don't take individual situations into account." "'Right' is a matter of definition. The effectiveness of actions occurs in degree. It's impossible that all my actions are not right."

Dealing with Blame

Blame was subtly woven through the worthlessness, hopelessness, and helplessness depressive thinking themes. Betty blamed herself for the way she thought. She told herself it was her fault for putting herself into a situation that she saw as hopeless. She also thought it was her fault that she felt so helpless.

Self-Blame Theme		
Belief	**Question**	**Result**
"Everything bad that happens is my fault."	"How can any human being legitimately take the credit for all that does or can go wrong?"	"Taking the credit for matters outside of my control makes no sense. Even in those instances where I am clearly to blame, fixing a problem is better than blamefully dwelling upon it."

The themes thinned as Betty moved from worthlessness to hopelessness to helplessness. By the time she got to self-blame beliefs, she was in a position to quickly brush off the idea as an illegitimate conclusion about her self.

Betty got a big boost up from depression by learning how to think about her thinking. By defusing her depressive thoughts, she gained relief from depressive thinking and the physical symptoms of depression that she experienced. She felt calmer.

RELAPSE PREVENTION

After she drafted her charts, Betty made revisions. As she learned more, she added questions and challenges to her four negative themes. For example, she had a strong interest in the history of the ancient world. Several weeks after drafting the helplessness chart, she copied down a quote from the Roman orator Cicero's *Six Mistakes of Man*: "the tendency to worry about things that cannot be changed or corrected." The things that could not be changed or corrected she saw as a legitimate form of helplessness. She also mused that her tendency to worry about possible disasters was something that she could change.

By forcing herself to follow through, even when she felt inhibited by depression, she gained an experiential understanding that she was not helpless. If she could act to change, her life was not hopeless. By meeting tough challenges, she could see that worthlessness was an illusion and self-blame was normally without merit.

Progressively, with some lapses, Betty came to believe that she could turn her knowledge about depression into a waterfall to douse its embers. As Betty learned more ways to negate negative thinking, she found a growing sense of tranquility. Here are some of the positions she adopted:

- Accept that negative depressive thoughts may be automatic, but you don't have to take them personally.

- Recognize that automatic depressive thinking will arise from time to time, especially following a twinge of mild depression, a negative mood swing, or having had an unpleasant experience.

- Disengage from believing the depressive thinking message. Thinking habits are habits because they attach to activating events, such as depressive sensations, down moods, and losses. Put them into perspective through matching them against the criteria for rational and irrational thought, separating the rational from the irrational parts, and challenging the erroneous emotive content, which is vulnerable to the question of proof and evidence.

- Refuse to engage in any form of global self-blame. This theme often distracts from problem solving. To help herself maintain perspective in reducing both perfectionist and self-blame thinking, Betty put on her refrigerator an observation from Plutarch, a Greek biographer and essayist who lived in the first century AD: "To make no mistakes is not in the power of man; but from their errors and mistakes, the wise and good learn wisdom for the future." She figured if Plutarch's thought had survived, it had merit.

Over time, Betty conquered depression while continuing to use her charts as reminders. Over twenty-one years, she had experienced no more than a few days of mild depression. She was genuinely pleased with what she had accomplished in her life to that point. She looked forward to the next decade.

Ellis's Approach to Prevent Relapse

If you have had a depression and want to prevent a recurrence, here are some things that Albert Ellis (pers. comm.) suggests:

- Assume that depression is partly caused by your damning yourself for your poor behavior and/or damning the world as an awful place.

- Use the principles of rational emotive behavior therapy (REBT) to give up this kind of damnation and to achieve unconditional self-acceptance (USA), unconditional other-acceptance (UOA), and unconditional life-acceptance (ULA).

- Strongly, powerfully, and emotionally work at achieving USA, UOA, and ULA.

- Persistently act against your self-downing and life-downing.

- Each day, fill out at least one REBT self-help form, such as the ABCDE exercise after Amy's story in this chapter.

- Persist at actively and forcefully disputing your three main irrational musts: "I absolutely must perform well!" "Other people have to treat me considerately!" "Conditions absolutely should be the way I want them to be!"

KEY IDEAS AND ACTION PLAN

What are the key ideas that you got from this chapter? What actions can you take?

Key Ideas

What are the key ideas that you found helpful?

1. _____

_____

2. _____

_____

3. _____

_____

Action Plan

What actions can you take to progress?

1. _____

_____

2. _____

_____

3. _____

_____

POSTSCRIPT

In this chapter, we looked at a rational emotive behavior therapy framework for counteracting depressive thinking and two examples of how people suffering from depression used cognitive behavioral methods to curb different depressive thoughts. The next few chapters will probe deeper into worthlessness, hopelessness, helplessness, and self-blame thinking. We'll look at tried-and-true as well as innovative ways to end their impact and unlink them from depression.

CHAPTER 8

Ending Worthlessness Thinking

A small egg rested on the top of a haystack beneath an oak tree. Upon seeing the egg, a farmer picked it up and put it into the henhouse. A chicken sat on the egg. It hatched. The baby bird grew into a chicken hawk. Growing up among the chickens, the hawk pecked kernels of corn from the ground. Believing it was like any other member of the flock, it lived its days thinking it was a chicken.

Anyone can behave like a chicken, even when they are more like a hawk. When we tether ourselves to false beliefs, such as thinking that pecking corn is our lot in life, this is similar to believing that depression is endless. In a depressed state of mind, the "who am I?" question is commonly answered by the label "worthless." This form of negative thinking automatically blurs the mind from other views. Accepting such beliefs as fact aggravates depression.

Fables like the hawk among the chickens suggest that we are what we believe ourselves to be. There is a certain validity to that view. Our beliefs are an integral part of our life philosophy. Some define our identity. What you generally think about yourself will normally influence how you feel about yourself. But what if your primary beliefs about yourself were negative and led to distressful results?

Your view of yourself structures many of the things that you do. See yourself as having integrity, and you are likely to act with integrity. View yourself as bold, and you are likely to do bold things. View yourself as worthless and you are likely to feel miserable and have many complaints about yourself.

Self-views can and do vary based upon mood, situation, and perceptions. But a pattern of self-doubt, second-guessing, and hesitation can lead to self-downing, avoidance of challenge, needless inhibitions, and an elevated risk for anxiety and depression. An amalgamation of self-doubt/downing tendencies, a biological proclivity toward depression, and sufficient stress can prime the pump of depression.

When depressed, it is especially important to avoid doubting yourself, deflating yourself, and giving up on yourself.

Sweeping generalizations such as thinking of yourself as worthless, inept, "bad," or useless stretch credulity. These thoughts are changeable. Extracting, contesting, and deflating worthlessness self-talk removes a particularly toxic ingredient from a depressive stew.

> **Worthlessness beliefs distress rather than define us.**

Let's take a brief excursion into the world of "self" where you may find that how you define your worth can reflect your sense of self. This excursion will begin with a theory of self. Then it will look at a theory of personal worth. Perhaps through this excursion you'll see how to take away discordant depressive thoughts about yourself and bring relief from that aspect of your depression.

A PLURALISTIC THEORY OF SELF

Socrates' prescription for wisdom is to "know thyself." He asserted that the wisest are those who know where their ignorance lies. Without recognizing ignorance, there would be no basis for developing knowledge.

When it comes to self-awareness and development, Socrates' prescription seems close to the mark:

- A process of self-inquiry can sharpen self-knowledge.

- Using questions and reason for discovering "truth" can yield a growing sense of inner control and ability to command events around you.

- Using reason to examine assumptions positions you to separate verifiable from speculative assumptions.

Through this process of inquiry you are better positioned to "know thyself" through recognizing and deflecting erroneous thoughts about yourself and identifying fruitful avenues for filling gaps in your self-knowledge. Such efforts form a platform for increasing your perspective on the richness that resides within yourself.

What is this entity called *self* that is wise to know? People commonly define the self as "what you think about yourself." A few might argue that the self is an illusion. Therefore, there is no self. Whether real or an illusion, most of us tend to think about ourselves a lot. But what is this self that we think about?

When depressed, you may be inclined to think categorically about yourself by defining yourself as worthless. But the self is too complex to be so easily classified. A broader perspective on the self can contradict narrow depressive thinking about the self and help alleviate that part of a depressive burden.

Getting to a broader perspective involves doing something else first, which is to give yourself valid reasons to expand upon your concept of self, to see that "self" in perspective, and to accept that self with all your personal attributes included. With a strong and stable self-concept, you are less likely to negatively pigeonhole yourself. Here are some arguments for accepting the self as pluralistic:

- Psychologists Gordon Allport and Henry Odbert (1936), in their search for what makes up the self, found 18,000 human qualities listed throughout a standard English dictionary.

These words included emotions, talents, and traits. They found about 4,500 trait words including warm, dominant, sanguine, inventive, friendly, quick-witted, motivated, bold, shy, and stubborn. The words describe part of the complexities that go into what is a gigantic composite picture of the self.

■ Human beings have about eight primary emotions and about five hundred cognitively toned variations on these basic themes. Basic emotions include delight, anger, and fear. Emotional variations include angst and lassitude. Emotions can be mixed, such as feelings of disgust and anger.

■ There may be over 120 factors that go into what we call "intelligence." Our intuitive abilities, insights, imagination, and creativity add to this intellectual complexity.

■ Values are an area of great diversity. In a simple sense, values are what we deem important. Higher level values include tolerance, integrity, responsibility, and freedom. Fundamental values include following the rules, reciprocity, politeness, and assertiveness. We are all touched, in one way or another, by cultural values, national values, and self-values.

■ Our facilities come into play practically every day. Some of us have artistic talents, leadership capabilities, and organizing strengths. We have faculties for doing such things as sensing whom we can rely upon, structuring plans of action, inventing, learning, teaching, protecting, and changing. We also have faculties for inertia through negative thinking.

■ Your complexity grows when you consider what goes into the many roles you play, such as parent, prophet, pal, or patriot.

■ You can add to your self-definition using externals such as the type of clothing you wear, the automobile you drive, your job status, or how much money you have invested.

How do the complexities of being human blend into your definition of self? Do you view these factors differently when you feel depressed? Do some of these qualities go into hibernation when you are depressed? Can you discover them again?

Doing a Personal Features Experiment

If you think worthlessness thoughts about yourself, you may find it useful to try to shift perspective and think pluralistically. The pluralistic self has many attributes and coexisting conditions of the mind. Thinking pluralistically about the self can promote flexible thinking about the self. Building a solid self-concept to override a depressive one won't happen overnight, of course. The effort takes time. But the reward can be great. Where can you begin? Start by pitting a label of worthlessness against a pluralistic view of the self. From a self-development point of view, it is implausible that you can be completely worthless and also multidimensional and complex. Getting to that point of awareness can prove challenging.

Most people follow the same patterns, beliefs, and interests. Once an idea is fixed in the mind, it tends to persist. That's one reason why self-change normally proves to be challenging. For example, as a habit of mind, worthlessness thinking entrenches itself in memory and beliefs, thus making this negative process resistant to change. However, if you find yourself locked into a self-limiting mind-set about yourself, practice thinking multidimensionally about yourself. This approach can eventually compete effectively with entrenched depressive thinking habits.

If you are not used to pluralistic thinking about the self, but want to explore this option, be forewarned. When you first try to think pluralistically, you can evoke a conflict of the mind against itself. When old habits of thought are confronted by fresh ways of thinking, you might filter the new information or contort it to fit established beliefs.

To counteract a worthlessness thinking habit you'll need ammunition—perhaps a lot of it. Old habits rarely retreat without a struggle. They can spontaneously recover when you are off guard or feeling vulnerable.

Doing a personal features experiment can provide ammunition for supporting an alternative way to contradict worthlessness thinking. To explore this self-concept development approach, you can write down all of your personal features within these categories: values, faculties, emotions, attributes, and roles:

Values include responsibility, honesty, or a good meal. What you value is what you normally view as important.

Faculties include reading, writing, calculating, cooking, negotiating, repairing. Your faculties will normally have related skills. For example, you might occasionally restore furniture. That process can break down into an expanded list of faculties such as acquiring, repairing, sanding, staining, varnishing, and so forth.

Emotions include happiness, sadness, frustration, and joy. In their simplest form, emotions break out into pleasant and unpleasant states. When depressed, emotions tend to be unpleasant and negative. When in a depressive state of mind and emotion, look beyond depression and think about the range of emotions that you once were capable of experiencing. What were these emotions? When did they occur?

Attributes include being outgoing, quiet, bold, friendly, quick-witted, passive, active, caring, compassionate, sensitive, or hard-nosed. These are the sort of distinctive features of a personality that can stand out to other people.

Roles involve the various parts you play throughout the day and throughout your life, such as student, teacher, protector, or organizer.

PERSONAL FEATURES EXPERIMENT

What are your personal features? Fill in the blanks under these categories.

Values	Faculties	Emotions	Attributes	Roles

Now, compare your list against the label "worthless." When depressed, if you think of yourself only as worthless, ask yourself: "How can I be only one thing, worthless, and at the same time operate in a world of roles and complexity that involves an expression of my values, faculties, emotions, and attributes?"

Human complexity is a reality. A pluralistic theory of the self takes this complexity into account. According to this theory, you are more than the sum of all your evolving values, faculties, emotions, attributes, and roles.

If you worked to adopt a pluralistic theory of self, would this view decrease your depression and improve the quality of your life? There is no guarantee for this, but there's a good probability. For example, seeing yourself as evolving and pluralistic can contradict a tendency to shrink yourself into a narrowing funnel of depressive thinking. Such a shift can feel emotionally freeing.

A pluralistic concept of the self potentially offers more advantages than a negative-but-global self-view. Anyone who dislikes feeling stunted in their emotional growth, due to a negative self-view, can act to change the view. You are capable of an infinite variety of thought. Therein, you have an opportunity to untwist depressive self-views and replace them with functional new thoughts about the self.

The Self on the Horizon

At one time or another, most people wonder who they are and what makes them tick. There is no single answer to the "what is a self?" question. The question tempts an answer of complexity and also variability.

In an allegorical sense, the self is like the horizon. When you stand in different places you can see the horizon in different ways. You can have different perspectives about the horizon, as you can have different perspectives on your "self." Yet, as scenes change, the horizon remains a constant. There is also a constancy about the self, just as there is variability and changeability.

In looking at the horizon, you may think you see the earth meet the sky. This perception is real, but it is also an illusion. Although you can see the horizon, you can never touch it. Could the same be true for the self? We experience the self and know we have recognizable qualities that distinguish us from others. You can experience a sense of self, but that sense of self can shift with changing circumstances and ideas about the self. We can't grasp the full essence of the self any more than we can see all possible horizons. But does that make the existence of a self less valid?

Like changes on the horizon, changes in our lives are inevitable. The horizon changes. It sometimes appears bright (optimism, successes). It sometimes darkens (sadness, gloom, depression). Coming storms appear foreboding (anxiety). Mirages appear (faulty self-image). Then the weather changes and the clouds vanish. Through the seasons in our lives, the horizon can look different. We sometimes assume that others see—or should see—the horizon in the same way that we do. Yet each of us can have different views about the same scene. We can also have related views. Although perspectives can differ, facts remain the same.

A THEORY OF WORTH

In a practical sense, people who display special skills gain advantages. High skill performers in the arts, business, sports, and the professions gain financial advantages. So does the mechanic who quickly diagnoses and fixes an automotive problem. He provides a service that is valued. There are big advantages for performing effectively and disadvantages for weak performances. But are either top or lower levels of performance a measure of human worth?

It is possible to define human performance and worth as the same. The seventeenth-century British philosopher Thomas Hobbes described human worth as measured by what people contribute to society. Personal contributions provide a way for people to feel esteemed by others and to esteem themselves. There are many ways to make contributions, so no person needs to be excluded from this formulation. But does it make sense to use "contributions" as a definition for self-worth?

The word "esteem" comes from the sixteenth-century French word *estimare* meaning to set a value on. Esteem basically means to value or judge someone or something as favorable. Self-esteem ordinarily is a prelude for judging self-worth. But seeking self-esteem can have a boomerang effect. What starts out to be positive can turn to something negative, such as when what you esteem yourself for ceases to be available or doesn't occur in the degree you desire.

From a self-approval standpoint, if there is a big fly in the self-worth and self-esteem ointment, it is the presence of contingency. A *contingent-worth* process boils down to labeling yourself based upon your ratings of what you do and what you think others think of you. So if you see yourself doing good things or getting praised, you can esteem yourself. But what happens if you get criticized for what you do, or if you believe that others think badly of you?

Throughout life, there are disappointments, reversals, losses, and frustrations. Does that mean your worth is diminished when such events occur? What does it mean when "fortune smiles" and you hit a home run on the stock market, or a rival leaves a field open to you? Do such conditions elevate your worth as a person? Only if you think they do.

People who ordinarily operate on a contingent-worth theory are likely to feel good about themselves when they do well and feel frustrated when their performances fall below their standards. Contingent-worth valuations reside in the background of thought, becoming activated when conditions elicit them. Like a swarm of bees buzzing around your head, it can be difficult to draw your attention away from them. Such a preoccupation with worth-based contingencies leads to yo-yo thinking. You are up when you meet the contingency and down when you don't. When these self-judgments are persistent and intense, they fertilize conditions for depression. But the contingent-worth theory is largely based upon a definition. Other views are possible.

Failure and Failings

One contingency affecting your self-worth may be depression. When depressed, you are more likely to view yourself as a failure compared to when you feel upbeat. If you fall into the *failure trap* and are looking for an exit, you can look at the failure issue from another angle.

Human beings have failings. One failing is succumbing to depressive thinking where you categorize yourself as a failure. You can work to change failings. Failure can characterize an action, but failure, as an overgeneralization, is too sweeping an expression to characterize a person.

Failings are part of a changeable human process that also includes nonfailings, accomplishments, and capabilities. You are normally better off working to rectify failings than to engage in the irrational act of branding yourself a failure.

While it is true that you can fail at some of the things that you undertake, failures do not make you a failure. A realistic perspective can help mute this thinking. For example, the inventor Thomas Edison made many thousands of attempts to find a filament for a lightbulb he tried to develop. When asked how he was able to tolerate such failures, he quipped that he did not see this as a series of failures. He saw the process as a way of discovering what didn't work.

Unlike Edison's approach to discovery, some failures can be hard to accept. You may have lost the love of your life to a rival. Such experiences are dramatic and memorable, and if you didn't feel rotten, something would be wrong. Nevertheless, such significant losses do not make a person a failure.

As with the hawk among chickens, you are what you think. But what you think you are when depressed may not fairly represent who you are.

PLURALISM-WORTH COMPARISONS

The act of pitting a pluralistic theory of self against a contingent theory of worth creates an opportunity to see self and worth paradoxically. If you are more than what you do, then how can what you do be all there is to you? If you are, for example, a person with multiple characteristics, multiple roles, multiple abilities, multiple dimensions of intelligence, and multiple experiences, then how could you be worthless, even if you made a colossal mistake, if an acquaintance despised you, and if you suffered from depression?

Contingency worth theories are different from pluralistic theories of self. From a self-development point of view, it is important to separate the two. If you have a choice—and as a pluralistic thinking person you absolutely do—why not rate your performance rather than yourself? You can grade performances, but defining your global worth based upon your changing performances is an arbitrary act.

You have a choice between thinking pluralistically about the self or accepting a simplified depressive label, such as "worthless." Arguably, adopting a pluralistic self-view helps negate a negative self-view. As Albert Adler implies, you would best work against negative habits of thought, as this process has entanglements and traps that need to be discovered and defeated.

A pluralistic outlook represents a choice, but it also represents a truth. Moving toward this more enlightened state involves a lifetime effort. It is an effort, however, that becomes easier with practice.

> You have more control over worthlessness thinking than you do over the color of your eyes or the size of your feet.

Accepting yourself does not mean that whatever you do or whatever you lack in your life is okay. Rather, it means to take reality for what it appears to be, change what you can, and work around what you can't. Acceptance involves giving in to reality, without fighting it. With this philosophy in mind, you are likely to concentrate your attention on what you can accomplish and what you can do to enjoy your life.

When you unconditionally accept yourself, you continue to be responsible to do the best you can, within the time and resources that you have available. Within this ethical system, if you act badly, you risk self-censure and external consequences. However, when you work at promoting self-acceptance, you are likely to feel open to your experiences and to stretch for self-improvement.

ABC METHOD FOR DEFUSING WORTHLESSNESS THINKING

Depression typically includes worthlessness thinking such as, "I'm no good. I'm worthless. I'm a failure." When active, such depressive thought labels can influence how you feel and what you do. But, these labels reflect thinking not *being*.

Global negative self-attributions can be challenged through a Socratic five-step process of defining key terms, gathering examples, gathering exceptions, questioning the definition, and contrasting the examples. Through this five-phase process, you can show yourself that you cannot possibly be only one way. It becomes tougher for overgeneralizations to fertilize the weeds of unreason. You can further defuse worthlessness thinking with the ABC method (see chapter 7).

The following chart shows how to apply the ABC method to defuse worthlessness thinking and to develop a strong, positive, realistic self-concept.

Activating event (experience): "A series of errors due to difficulties attending and concentrating."
Rational beliefs about the event: "Lapses in attention and concentration happen when depressed. This is unfortunate but the way things temporarily are. I'll likely operate less efficiently than I would prefer."
Emotional and behavioral consequences for the rational beliefs: "A sense of regret for lapses in concentration. Acceptance of a temporary disability."
Irrational worthlessness beliefs: "I make too many careless mistakes. I'm a failure. I've always been a failure. I'm worthless."
Emotional and behavioral consequences for the irrational worthlessness beliefs: "Shame. Disparagement. Anxiety. Depression. Withdrawal. Avoidance of challenging activities."
Disputes for irrational worthlessness beliefs: "(1) Although errors are unfortunate, how do errors, connected to a symptom of a depression disability, make me a total failure? Sample answer: Lapses in attention and concentration are expected when depressed. There is no reason to expect anything different. Errors are likely. (2) How does a temporary lapse in concentration result in a permanent sense of failure? Sample answer: It doesn't. An extreme generalization about the self does not prove itself. This is as illogical as saying that I am a completely noble person for throwing a piece of trash into a wastebasket. (3) How does a lack of concentration mean I am worthless? Sample answer: This conclusion is the result of a faulty major premise, that there should be no lapses in concentration when depressed. The premise is irrational. Lapses in attention and concentration are part of the depressive process. The secondary premise is that I am a failure because of errors resulting from lapses in concentration. The premise reflects an overgeneralization and is disputable. The worthlessness conclusion that follows is assumptive. It is based upon primary and secondary premises that lack validity. When matched against a pluralistic theory of self, this conditional-worth theory collapses under the weight of its own absurdity."
Effects of the disputes: "Despite depression and disappointment about operating less efficiently than normal, a calmer outlook."

When worthlessness thinking links to your depression, use the ABC method to map and counteract this thinking. You can use the following chart as a guide.

Activating event (experience):

Rational beliefs about the event:

Emotional and behavioral consequences for the rational beliefs:

Irrational worthlessness beliefs:

Emotional and behavioral consequences for the irrational worthlessness beliefs:

Disputes for irrational worthlessness beliefs:

Effects of the disputes:

KEY IDEAS AND ACTION PLAN

What are the key ideas that you got from this chapter? What actions can you take?

Key Ideas

What are the key ideas that you found helpful?

1. _____

_____

2. _____

_____

3. _____

_____

Action Plan

What actions can you take to progress?

1. _____

_____

2. _____

_____

3. _____

_____

POSTSCRIPT

A positive sense of self and worth can be pivotal to evoking feelings of well-being, resiliency, and optimism. By bringing a theory of worth closer to a pluralistic theory of self, you can operate with a broader perspective and use that perspective to counteract circular worthlessness thinking. Building a broader sense of self into a self-worth equation can help mute the mood of depression.

CHAPTER 9

Defeating Helplessness Thinking

When depressed, do you feel overwhelmed, besieged, incompetent, inept, and unable to manage? Do you believe that you can do nothing to exit from the misery that you experience? If you believe that you can do nothing to stop feeling stuck in depression, chances are you will generally view yourself as powerless and defenseless.

When helplessness thinking takes over, it reflects the message that you are unable to constructively act, and you are therefore going to remain stuck in a depressive quagmire. When helplessness thinking dominates, you are stuck. But such thinking is changeable!

You have the power to think about your thinking. You can learn to develop competing systems of thought and actions to counteract depressive helplessness thinking and free yourself from this form of defeatism. Start with a why question: "Why do I think I'm helpless?"

AN INABILITY TO ACT OR SUCCEED

What is helplessness? A standard dictionary defines it as an inability to act or succeed. A second definition includes the idea of feeling depleted of strength. Does an attitude of helplessness in depression fit these two definitions? Sometimes.

When depressed, if you believe that you are generally helpless to act, that is a mental myth. You have the power to act against depression. True, you may experience difficulty attending and concentrating. Your mood is down. You can experience yourself trudging through the day. You feel fatigued and

> Helplessness is like a bird that thinks it has a wounded wing. But what if the wing is strong enough to bring the bird back to flight?

disinterested in acting. Every bone in your body can resist action. Nevertheless, most of the capabilities you had before depression descended did not vaporize. They may be available in lesser degree, but they remain accessible.

The second definition of helplessness involves feeling depleted of strength. When you feel depressed, you probably do experience a depletion of strength. A persistently depressed mood, lower energy levels, and higher levels of fatigue are to be expected.

There are different ways to decide what this means. If you view depletion as a temporary symptom of depression, this is radically different from defining this state as permanent. When you interpret the thoughts and sensations of depression as temporary, but of longer than desired duration, you are less likely to get depressed over feeling depressed.

Helplessness and Successes

When it comes to overcoming depression, what does success mean? Success can be defined as an achievement. Actions against depression are achievements. Reading this book signals that you are willing to explore the possibility that you can overcome depressive thinking to rid yourself of depression. That action represents an achievement, and, thus, a success.

To boost your opportunities for accomplishment, set your sights on progressively mastering depression. It ordinarily takes time and a knowledgeable approach to chip away at the depressive process, gain relief, and prevent relapse. If a specific effort does not alleviate depression, you may have discovered what won't work. That's a success. You may also need to allow yourself more time with the technique. That knowledge represents a success.

WHEN HELPLESSNESS IS REAL

Helplessness thinking in depression is like a voice of desperation and defeat that can tightly weave through a depressed mood. Helplessness can involve the belief that both depression and life's events are outside of your ability to assert control. This form of thought may or may not be a prime cause of depression. It is, nevertheless, a frequent symptom of a depressed mood.

Helplessness is not the reason people get depressed. It's usually a seriously distressing experience that thunders into depression. There are many things in life that we can't control that don't evoke depression. You probably can't prevent earthquakes. Unexpected events can disrupt your interests and goals. You trained for months for a marathon race. You accidently broke your leg on the morning of the race. Most can unhappily accept these out-of-control occurrences without faulting themselves or thinking helplessness thoughts. On the other hand, if you were to blame and defame yourself for events you can't control, yet view yourself as helpless to control these same events, you have a paradoxical perspective.

Most reasonable people would recognize that there are insurmountable barriers that they cannot effectively act against. Atlanta psychotherapist Edward Garcia (pers. comm.) has an interesting helplessness exercise that puts this idea into perspective. Garcia suggests that you go over to a solid wall. Put the palms of your hands on the wall. Push against the wall. See if you can topple it. As hard as you try, the wall will stand. You're helpless to bring it down. You probably could not care less if you don't have the strength to push down a wall. This act may not be that important at all. On the other hand, ridding yourself of depression is often meaningful, and unlike the wall, depressive ideas can fall.

BOOSTING YOUR PROBLEM-SOLVING EFFECTIVENESS

In Aesop's story of the crow and the pitcher, a thirsty crow stood before a pitcher half-filled with water. Because the water was out of reach, the thirsty bird couldn't reach down to drink. The clever crow dropped pebbles into the pitcher until the water rose to where it could drink. This type of problem solving has an obvious value. But can problem solving be employed in the service of defeating depression? Yes!

An obvious question is, what is a problem? A problem exists when we have a gap between what we want and what we have, and the process of finding a solution is still to be found or applied. The crow was thirsty and wanted water. A pitcher held water. To get the water to the top of the pitcher, the crow had to find a way to cause it to rise.

Whether a problem exists or not is dependent upon need. If you are not depressed, learning ways to counter depression may be a low priority. When you suffer with depression, you want to free yourself from depression. Now the desire for a solution can rise to where you have a problem to solve. By focusing your efforts on solving problems, you can help yourself defeat depression (Nezu 1985).

You can get started in solving relevant personal problems through the use of the *bits-and-pieces* procrastination technology technique. Instead of facing a large problem, which can seem overwhelming, you break it down into chewable bits and start with the first logical step. Upon starting and completing step one, you proceed to step two. That's the bits-and-pieces way. This process illustrates that you can take corrective steps. Applying bits-and-pieces technology shows that you are not helpless.

HELPLESSNESS QUESTIONING

Helplessness beliefs morph into hopelessness, and vice versa, to form a vicious spiraling downward circle of depressive thought. A radically different view is possible, however. The fact that you think helplessness thoughts carries an optimistic meaning. Your mind is active. With an active mind, many things are possible. This includes using an active mind to reverse depressive helplessness thinking.

The following three-phase helplessness questioning exercise describes how to pit the mind against itself for personal gain. Following the idea that depressive helplessness thoughts reflect the reality of depression, but not necessarily reality, the phases are: identifying the helplessness message, questioning the message, and coming to a nonhelplessness resolution. The following example describes the process.

Helplessness Message	Self-Questioning	Resolution
"I'm helpless to change."	"Is helplessness a depressive thinking example? Is it a fact-based belief that predicts for all time that you are utterly unable to take any step whatsoever to break from a depressive rut?"	"Helplessness thinking represents an example of depressive thinking. Since people cannot guess the future with certainty, helplessness is a hypothesis. There is practically always something to do to step up from a depressive rut."
"I feel overwhelmed with too many responsibilities and without the energy to act."	"The key words and phrases that depict attributions are 'overwhelmed,' 'too many,' and 'without the energy.' What does 'overwhelmed' mean? What constitutes 'too many?' What does 'without the energy' mean?"	"Key words and phrases in helplessness thinking can point to exaggerations. Instead of accepting the key words in a helplessness thinking monologue, clarify the meaning. This exposes the myths in the words. An erroneous myth soon loses credibility."
"I am to blame for being weak and unable to control depression."	"How am I blameworthy for a persistent depression?"	"Contesting depression without burdensome blame."

HELPLESSNESS QUESTIONING EXERCISE

List your helplessness messages, question them, and see what results.

Helplessness Message	Self-Questioning	Resolution

By acting to falsify negative helplessness beliefs, you've shown yourself that you are not helpless.

THE HELP-FULL/LESS PARADOX

New York City psychologist Diana Richman (pers. comm.) points out the paradox that people create for themselves when they purchase self-help books and yet describe themselves as helpless. People can still believe they are helpless, even while they take steps to achieve their desired outcomes. Since individuals so often negate actions that reflect the reality that they can, and do, help themselves, Richman suggests a "helpFULL-helpLESS" exercise to resolve this paradox and break from a cycle of depression.

Helpful thinking is more conducive to combating depression and attaining your goals than maintaining a helpless style of thinking. Helpful thinking involves three prime beliefs:

1.   "I can organize and direct my efforts toward achieving my goals."

2.   "I can explore areas of uncertainty and unknown outcomes."

3.   "I can withstand the discomfort of hard work."

Helplessness thinking involves three prime beliefs:

1.   "I am not able to take actions toward achieving my goals because of external life conditions."

2.   "I could not stand not knowing if I will attain my desired outcome."

3.   "I cannot bear the discomfort of hard work."

Richman's exercise challenges the perception that you have been helpless to achieve your goals throughout your life.

HELP-FULL/HELP-LESS EXERCISE

First list goals in the helpful thinking column that you achieved when believing that you could and would take actions toward achieving those goals. Next, list goals that you failed to achieve and/or outcomes that might have resulted in avoiding the discomfort of taking action. Examples are listed below. You fill in the rest.

Help-FULL Thinking Goals	Help-LESS Thinking Goals
"Obtained job in desired field."	"Avoided rejection from job interviews; no job."
"Negotiated price on motor vehicle."	"Avoided salesperson thinking I'm a cheap person."

Compare the lists and review the choices that you have made throughout your life. Revisit how you perceived and experienced the process of executing short- and long-term goals that included a healthy help-FULL thinking outcome. Then, revisit what you perceived and experienced during the process when thinking in a help-LESS style. Through this comparison of listed items, you may discover that in those situations in which you thought helpfully, your actions did create the desired difference. You truly do have a choice in how you shape your perspective.

Now list your current goals and the help-FULL thoughts that you will maintain during the process:

Current Goals	Help-FULL Thoughts

The choice between thinking in a helpful or a helpless manner can exist in a phase of mind that is independent from the sensations of depression. In short, you can feel depressed and still think helpful thoughts and take helpful actions. Apply this approach, and you might soon discover that helpful thoughts can result in self-help actions that will lead you out of the depression abyss.

ABC METHOD FOR DEFUSING HELPLESSNESS THINKING

Helplessness thinking can be so much a part of daily life that it is taken for granted. In a helplessness mind-set, when presented with tools for change, you are likely to put them aside without testing them. The common hidden message is this: "The techniques may work for others, but I can't do them." This perspective illustrates how helplessness thinking is a lodestone weighing against positive initiatives. The following chart describes a sample approach to defuse helplessness thinking and to advance competency thinking.

Activating event (experience): "A strong sense of inertia that seems like a wall preventing acting against depressive helplessness thinking."

Rational beliefs about the event: "This dull resistive feeling is a natural impediment to positive relief from depression. It is a problem process that will take a simultaneous act of will and effort to disrupt. However sluggish I may feel, I will take the step of applying the ABC template to this thinking, and see what results."

Emotional and behavioral consequences for the rational beliefs: "A feeling of sluggish resistance is likely to continue, for a while, even following focused actions. Eventually, acting on the rational belief can divert me from depressive helplessness thinking and promote a valid reason to experience a sense of control over the helplessness thinking process."

Irrational helplessness beliefs: "I can do nothing to change. I'm trapped. I'm doomed. The feeling of depression is too heavy, too weighty."

Emotional and behavioral consequences for the irrational helplessness beliefs: "Helplessness thoughts continue to amplify the feeling of inertia that gives credibility to the thinking."

Disputes for irrational helplessness beliefs: "(1) Where is the proof that there is 'nothing' that I can do to change? Sample answer: This judgment makes no sense. Making an effort may not guarantee a desired result, but making an effort can represent a change. (2) What does 'trapped' mean? Sample answer: Literally, 'trapped' means an unpleasant situation which is tough to escape. Trapped, as a form of depressive thinking, can convey a different meaning, such as an inescapable misery. Action taken to address depression-related problems can help unravel this trapped view. (3) What does 'doomed' mean? Sample answer: Doom refers to certain destruction. The use of the word 'doom' in reference to depression sticking is an uncertain prediction. (4) In what way is depression *too* weighty? Sample answer: The key words are 'too' and 'weighty.' It is a reality that depression can feel weighty. Adding the word 'too' suggests being overwhelmed with depression. Sticking with 'weighty' to describe the experience of depression sounds valid. 'Too' sounds like an exaggeration. (5) What examples support the trapped, doomed, too weighty connection to depression? What exceptions contradict the beliefs? In what ways are these thoughts exaggerations? Sample answer: By questioning such depressive helplessness propositions in this way, I have already shown myself that I am not helpless."

Effects of the disputes: "An acceptance that depression may continue, but a growing sense of mastery over depressive thinking demonstrates an ability to organize and regulate my efforts to deactivate this form of thinking."

When helplessness thinking is linked to your depression, you can use the following chart as a guide to map, question, and counteract specific helplessness thoughts that mingle with your depressed mood.

Activating event (experience):
Rational beliefs about the event:
Emotional and behavioral consequences for the rational beliefs:
Irrational helplessness beliefs:
Emotional and behavioral consequences for the irrational helplessness beliefs:
Disputes for irrational helplessness beliefs:
Effects of the disputes:

KEY IDEAS AND ACTION PLAN

What are the key ideas that you got from this chapter? What actions can you take?

Key Ideas

What are the key ideas that you found helpful?

1. _____

   _____

2. _____

   _____

3. _____

   _____

Action Plan

What actions can you take to progress?

1. _____

   _____

2. _____

   _____

3. _____

   _____

POSTSCRIPT

Believing you can't manage or cope can create inner feelings of anxiety that can lead to resignation and hopelessness. This state of mind and a depressed mood can feel like a prison with walls of desperation bound by bars of depressive thoughts. Counteracting these thoughts has several bonuses. You can gain a sense of pleasure from a calmer state of mind and body. You can think more flexibly. You can feel legitimately optimistic.

Conditions pass, perceptions change, and the unmanageable becomes tolerable or doable. So, when you feel a sense of helplessness over understanding or controlling what is happening around you, consider Helen Keller, who was born both deaf and blind. She found a way to gain meaning in a dark and silent world and to make meaningful contact with others. This didn't happen overnight, but it did happen.

CHAPTER 10

Hopelessness and Optimism

"Clickety clack" went a wheel as it slowly rolled in a fixed circle digging a groove into the soft soil. A small mouse ran in front of the wheel. The rut caused by the rolling wheel was too high for the mouse to get by. The poor creature ran to survive. Then, a storm drenched and shorted the motor that drove the wheel. It stopped. Rainwater filled the rut. The mouse swam out.

Preoccupied with survival, the mouse had little time for hopeful thoughts. Nevertheless, there was "hope." An unanticipated change made the difference. Whether the mouse had faith, trust, and confidence in a positive outcome or not, chance intervened.

When depressed, you can think pessimistically about your future. Still, thoughts do not control chance and probability. So, there may be much reason for hope, even when you can't see it. For example, hopelessness thoughts can get short-circuited by reason.

CHANCE AND THE MIND

In the bleakest of times, chance can play an unexpected role. If you are parachuting from an airplane, and your parachute doesn't open, the outcome doesn't look good. Although rare, some parachutists whose chutes failed to open survived due to an odd twist of chance.

The story of Kate Adamson (2002) sheds some additional light on how chance and probability can link to positive outcomes. After suffering a stroke, Kate looked like she was in a coma. She survived on life support. Her physicians thought she was in a vegetative state. At a point in time, Kate's life support was ended.

> When you believe you are trapped and have a very remote chance of prevailing, take the path that gives you a chance.

Kate was aware of what was happening around her. She recognized people and heard what they said. Although she was aware, she could not move and respond other than to occasionally blink her eye, which her husband noted.

When Kate was eight days off her feeding tube, her husband threatened to sue the hospital and insurance company that had denied treatment. The tube was put back. Today, Kate is back to living a full life. Her journey back to a normal life started with an eyeblink. She recorded this experience in her book, *Kate's Journey: Triumph Over Adversity*.

There truly are very desperate situations. Suppose you had a few days to live because you had an incurable cancer. Is that not a hopeless situation? The answer boils down to chance and probability. The odds are strongly against you, but the outcome is not guaranteed.

Here is an example of how hope temporarily triumphed over cancer. A patient within days of death from an advanced case of lymphosarcoma, a malignancy involving the lymph nodes, survived beyond what his physician expected. In his final days of life, the man pleaded with his physician to administer an experimental cancer drug. The man didn't qualify for its use. The physician, Bruno Klopfer (1957), administered a shot of the drug in the hope that his patient would die peacefully over the weekend. Klopfer reasoned that his patient would know that all that could be done was done, and this knowledge could make his last hours peaceful.

The following Monday, Klopfer returned to see his patient sitting up and laughing with the nurses. He actively tried to convince other cancer patients to take this miracle cure. Was the recovery Klopfer observed a dramatic example of a placebo effect? Did the man's jubilant state of mind evoke a powerful immune system response to fight the cancer? (It appeared to Klopfer that the man's cancerous tumors had noticeably shrunk.) Would the man have spontaneously recovered without his strong belief in the ability of the drug to cure?

We cannot be sure about the cause of the spontaneous recovery and relapse. However, the man took action and succeeded in acquiring the "miracle" drug. Thereafter, he improved.

The patient recovered to the point where he returned home to resume a normal life. Thereafter, he read a news report that said the drug was ineffective. After he read the story, the disease returned. What happened? Had he lost hope?

The mind can sometimes influence the course of a disease. There is a growing body of evidence showing that hope and optimism are physically healthier states of mind than hopelessness and pessimism (Peterson, Seligman, and Vaillant 1988). Optimism—even when unrealistic—correlates with a sense of control. This state of mind can promote physical health advantages (Alloy and Clements 1992).

Perspectives on Suffering

Viktor Frankl (1963), an Austrian psychiatrist and founder of logotherapy, was a death camp survivor. Following his death camp experiences, he asserted that social conditions can never fully set the boundaries for the human spirit and cannot deprive people of a freedom of will. Free will remains possible under even dangerous and oppressive circumstances.

> Choose hope over hopelessness whenever you can.

During World War II, Frankl was incarcerated in four different Nazi death camps. Rather than dwell on his dismal situation, he looked for meaning in what he saw. Thus, he would find meaning in the smallest events, such as watching an ant move a crumb.

His insight, that people can find meaning despite very limited freedom of choice, led to his emotional survival under the most dangerous and potentially disturbing of circumstances. He lived through his reason and not through fear.

Frankl saw that people can live life through their higher mental processes. This provides freedom from unreasonable fears as well as pessimistic expectations. He thought it best to live in the present moment and to prepare for the future. He accepts that life can be hard and that positive change involves work.

Radical Change in Perspective

Clifford Beers (1908), who spearheaded the mental health movement of the early twentieth century, made a remarkable recovery from a severe bipolar condition. It began when he determined that he need not imprison himself with his past follies, indiscretions, and failures.

In his book, *A Mind That Found Itself*, Beers described his exit from depression. Beers turned his world around from a terrifying pessimism to a determination to oppose stigmatism toward people with mental illnesses. He started to operate with an optimism that his efforts would prove fruitful. Thereafter, Beers made great strides.

Optimism is a belief in future opportunities and successes. This state of mind represents a confidence that such events will be a part of the future. Although optimism can include the idea that things will turn out all right, optimism can be a passive act of waiting. A realistic optimism includes constructive actions toward positive results.

Changing from needlessly pessimistic depressive thinking to a realistic optimistic view can be accelerated. Pessimistic thinking involves a static view about the future, where nothing good will happen and miseries will remain the same. Shifting from this static thinking to a more optimistic view involves recognizing the fluidity in situations, adapting to this reality, and acting to shape parts of the future through what you do in the present. An initial step in this process involves helping yourself build mental flexibility by

- exploring novelty, change, and improvisation

- a willingness to withstand a lack of structure, control, certainty, and predictability

- tolerance for ambiguity, complexity, and feeling different

- making independent judgments

- knowing when to suspend judgments

- accommodating to changing information

- inching forward when bold steps cannot be taken

The actions you take to shift from pessimism to intellectual flexibility, counteract hopelessness thinking.

Acceptance of uncertainty, tension, and suffering	**Converts**	Fear of depressive thinking

into

Acceptance of risk and opportunities to devise and achieve performance and mastery goals.

The key word here is "converts." This word links to a process of maintaining an open perspective, recognizing and rejecting needlessly negative thinking, taking steps to advance toward meaningful goals, and accepting limitations. In this process, you may not be able to choose situations, but you can decide how to view them and the beliefs you apply to them.

HOPE AND HOPELESSNESS

"Hopeless" can legitimately refer to specific situations. If you are four-foot-two, your chances of playing center for a National Basketball Association (NBA) team is practically nil. But, if you are four-foot-two, you probably don't aspire to play center for the NBA. Instead, you direct your efforts toward what is reasonable that you can accomplish. As the old saying goes, "Different strokes for different folks."

Some situations provide no hope for change. Aging, for example, is inevitable. But do you have to feel miserable about this reality? Even when one situation is hopeless, what opportunities are available in others?

When you compare a hopeless situation with hopelessness thinking, the difference can be dramatic. When a situation is hopeless, such as aging, acceptance of this state may not change this reality. But you can feel remarkably free to go about making the most of life despite the aging process. Hopelessness thinking is a state of despondent resignation that adds misery to the unpleasant aspects of an unfortunate situation. This form of thought can significantly restrict your will to move forward.

Hopelessness depressive thinking goes beyond the boundaries of facing a hopeless situation. Hopelessness thinking can include abstract beliefs such as these:

■   "My future looks dismal."

■   "Nothing will ever work out."

■   "Whatever I do will be futile."

■   "I will never get better."

■   "This is the way I am (miserable)."

Hopelessness thinking can be specific where an unfortunate event links to a fatalistic resignation:

- "I lost my job (and will be out of work forever)."

- "I botched this sale (and may as well quit because I can't do any better)."

- "My pet Puffy died (and I can't go on)."

Hopelessness thinking ordinarily includes one or more of the following related themes:

- an expectation that the future holds unescapable misery

- a conclusion based on a prophesy that the present is not only bleak, but the future will stay the same or get worse

- a helplessness idea that you are powerless to change your state of being

- a fatalistic dramatization of a state or situation

- the elimination of chance, hope, and change from the mental equation

Is there a role for pessimism? Sure! Defensive pessimism is sometimes a reasonable response. Imagine going to a used car lot with the optimism that you will get the best price on a great automobile by trusting everything the salesperson says. You might not like the outcome. Defensive pessimism might cause you to do your homework before making a decision.

The Power of Illusion

What is hope other than a belief and expectation that matters will turn out well? But hope is an illusion. Chance and probability can interfere with this mental invention.

> Hopelessness forecloses on opportunity.

Psychological illusions are something you believe to be true but are not that way at all. They are reality distortions about someone, something, or some condition. People who think they drive better after a few drinks are afflicted by an illusion of false competence. People who believe that their intuition is inevitably accurate may sometimes be right. But human intuition is often far from perfect. People who think they can do nothing to defeat their depressive thinking can fuel a self-fulfilling prophesy. You believe you will fail in any attempt to overcome depression. You fail to try. You continue to feel depressed.

If psychological illusions are partially or wholly false, they can be shed. But this process can be challenging. The power of a psychological illusion is that after you see it, the illusion may continue to influence your perceptions, emotions, and actions. When some of my clients first identify their own depressive thinking, the thoughts often continue automatically. That is because psychological helplessness illusions stealthily flow along the channels of the mind. When you take the stealth out of the equation, you still have the habit to contend with. Yet, first watching yourself go through a negative thought habit is often a preamble to changing the pattern.

Alternatively, when you first see through the hopelessness illusion, you may feel relief. Often this relief is temporary. It is useful to think of relief as a preview experience. This preview provides a peek into future positive possibilities. You are likely to have a hopelessness thinking habit to contend with. Habits that are made can be broken.

In a process of curbing hopelessness thinking, preview experiences show the possibilities. Your future efforts show the actuality of what you can do when you put your mind to the task of defeating hopelessness thinking.

Countering Hopelessness Illusions

Seeing an illusion is a first step in exiting that part of a depression trap. But, how do you see what appears veiled from view, especially when you have no feedback except that which comes from you? The answer is simple: You can tell an illusion by its results. If a predictable flow of pessimistic thought connects with a dismal mood, suspect a hopelessness illusion.

Here are some examples of hopelessness illusions: "It's no use going on." "I have no life." "It's all over for me." What can be said about such hopelessness thoughts? They reflect a point of view where you have no way to succeed, can't cope, can't change, or are incapable of improvement.

Dead-end hopelessness thoughts convey futility. But is this futility an illusion? Probe a little deeper to see. What does it mean when you tell yourself, "It's no use going on"? Does this mean that nothing over the next three years could possibly happen to change your thoughts or life situation? The illusion is that your destiny has already been determined. Can you prove this to be true before you experience the future? If you can predict the future, you could have unbridled power.

Is there a quick way to identify hopelessness thinking and label it so as to more efficiently recognize and deal with these thoughts? Challenging hopelessness thinking takes time. But you can improve with practice.

Hopelessness thinking involves fatalistic prognostications that are based upon conjecture, jumping to conclusions, and overgeneralizations. Instead of accepting them, view them as assumptions or hypotheses. Then, challenge them.

Asking and answering coping questions is a way to debunk hopelessness depressive thinking. For example, can you prove that the future is fixed and unchanging? Can you say that a fluid future depends upon your mood?

Through raising and examining these questions, you can discover that core hopelessness assumptions are hard to support. There are alternative views that can undue a hopeless view. The unexpected happens. This makes the future open to alternative possibilities. What does it mean when a change in perspective liberates the mind from depressive torment? Does that suggest an alternative view has taken hold?

The "Prove It" Technique

The "prove it" technique is a three-phase exercise for challenging hopelessness thinking. The first phase is to list hopelessness thoughts, such as "my future is dismal." The second is to cite examples to support the thoughts. The third is to list and explore alternative views and possibilities.

Start by seeking examples that you use to support hopelessness thoughts. For example, if you think your future looks dismal, expand upon the issue with examples of how your future looks dismal. List them. Then look for contradictory facts, evidence, or reasonable alternative ways of viewing a situation. Then compare a hopelessness proposition of truth with an alternative proposition of truth. Can you prove that either view is absolutely true?

By punching holes in hopelessness thinking, you can diminish the emotional impact of this form of thought. This exercise can help boost your perspective, and such a boost can lead to relief from distressful speculations.

"PROVE IT" EXERCISE

List your hopelessness thoughts, examples to support the thoughts, and alternative ways of thinking.

Hopelessness Thought	Examples	Alternatives
1.	1.	1.
2.	2.	2.

Disputing a Hopelessness Theory

Does hopelessness thinking represent a fact or a theory? It is a fact that people think hopelessness thoughts. But what happens when you treat hopelessness as a theory? A theory reduces complex data to a short, simple formula. It involves a set of ideas, facts, and propositions. Theories can be tested. This approach is radically different from accepting hopelessness as a fact.

Hopelessness in depression boils down to a short, simple theory such as, "Life is bad and won't get better." When actively believed, this pessimistic theory bleaches out hope. Because of the enormous impact that hopelessness thinking has on mood and actions, this belief bears scientific scrutiny.

You can challenge a hopelessness theory by using the power of the scientific method. Following this approach, you raise legitimate questions about hopelessness thinking. To apply scientific thinking to a hopelessness theory, ask these questions: Where is the irrefutable evidence to support the hopelessness belief? What are the facts that disconfirm the theory? For example, if you think that "life sucks," look for the evidence that supports this type of hopelessness theory. Look for exceptions. Through this process, you might discover why hopelessness in depression is a theory with holes in it.

In choosing between a fixed hopelessness theory and the scientific method of discovery, you are normally better off choosing a scientific approach. Granted, applying the scientific method to hopelessness thinking takes an extra effort. That effort involves putting attention and concentration onto the process, asking coping questions, and insisting on factual answers that you can independently confirm. In the short run, this is a more arduous method than automatically relying on a hopelessness theory as a way to explain a depressive sense of reality. The effort can be worth it, however. Through practicing the scientific method, you can build the sort of mental muscles that can contest hopelessness beliefs.

ABC METHOD FOR DEFUSING HOPELESSNESS THINKING

You can help yourself defeat hopelessness thinking by doing something else first. One preliminary action is to raise questions about hopelessness thoughts and seek fact-based answers. This process can lead to a by-product of relief from this form of thinking.

The following chart shows how to engage the ABC method to counteract hopelessness thinking and boost your chances for developing a realistic sense of optimism:

Activating event (experience): "A dark grim mood that lingers."
Rational beliefs about the event: "A depressed mood is unpleasant, distracting, and inhibiting. I'd strongly prefer to feel differently. But the mood is what it is, and will continue until it passes."
Emotional and behavioral consequences for the rational beliefs: "A sense of philosophical acceptance and emotional tranquility about a painfully unpleasant ongoing experience. A realistic optimism that depression will pass when it passes."
Irrational hopelessness beliefs: "I can't stand this feeling. It has gone on forever. Things will never change. I will never get better. I'm doomed."
Emotional and behavioral consequences for the irrational hopelessness beliefs: "The mood remains. The conditions associated with it remain. The dire predictions can lead to a sense of desperation without hope. There is a deepening of the depression and immobilized agitation."
Disputes for irrational hopelessness beliefs: "(1) Although a lingering feeling of depression can feel oppressive, why can I not stand what I don't like? Sample answer: I can, but I still don't like the state I'm in. (2) What is the gain for telling myself that depression will go on forever? Sample answer: There is no meaningful benefit for making a fatalistic proclamation. This state has gone on longer than I'd prefer. I'm not in a position to predict all chance and opportunities to defeat a lingering depression. (3) What are the 'things' that will never change? Sample answer: Forever is a long time. Many things can happen between now and then. Is it possible that my perspective can change with new information and the passage of time? (4) Where is the proof and evidence that I am a fortune-teller with certain knowledge that I can neither do nor get better? Sample answer: Mythologies of the mind fictionalize reality. Their presence may be real, but what they represent can be no more than a figment of reality. (5) What do I mean by 'doomed'? In what way am I doomed? Can I prove this doom theory beyond a reasonable doubt? Can I show the world that there can be no exceptions to this theory? Sample answer: Doom is a form of extremist depressive thinking. Like ink can color water, it can blur clarity. Although doom thinking can color clarity, this pessimistic prophesy is vulnerable to clarity."
Effects of the disputes: "Abandon hopelessness thinking."

The process of developing rational thinking skills will not diminish the significance of a loss, but it can diminish the depressed mood and various unpleasant physical symptoms of depression that are associated with that thinking. You gain skill in the use of this method when you act to remove the surplus misery associated with hopelessness thinking.

When hopelessness thinking is linked with your depression, you can use the following chart as a guide to map and counteract this thinking:

Activating event (experience):
Rational beliefs about the event:
Emotional and behavioral consequences for the rational beliefs:
Irrational hopelessness beliefs:
Emotional and behavioral consequences for the irrational hopelessness beliefs:
Disputes for irrational hopelessness beliefs:
Effects of the disputes:

KEY IDEAS AND ACTION PLAN

What are the key ideas that you got from this chapter? What actions can you take?

Key Ideas

What are the key ideas that you found helpful?

1. _____

_____

2. _____

_____

3. _____

_____

Action Plan

What actions can you take to progress?

1. _____

_____

2. _____

_____

3. _____

_____

POSTSCRIPT

Chance and probabilities are part of life. So, if you wait for hopelessness thinking to lift, you may be rewarded for your patience. Chance can intervene. But waiting and doing are not at odds in this instance. By acting to recognize and question hopelessness thinking, you need not give up the possibility that an accidental happening can deal a blow to an unrelenting pessimism. Moreover, learning to effectively deal with hopelessness thinking can lead to new discoveries about your clear-thinking resources and your ability to apply them.

CHAPTER 11

Restraining Blame

Like the air, blame is found everywhere. When something negative happens, you'll hear people asking "who's at fault?" When a nation's economy falters, the leadership is typically targeted for blame. The grass on your lawn starts to brown and you blame the hot sun. In a depressive state of mind, you might blame yourself for feeling the way that you do. Blame can be needless in other ways, such as in psychological seesaw games where people elevate themselves through devaluing others (Potter 1952).

At the sharp edges of blame, some live their days finding fault and riding themselves over infractions that most might not notice or would automatically ignore. When excessive blaming continues unopposed, it becomes a reflexive response without reflection. This blame-trap thinking contributes in multiple ways to depression and to other of life's needless miseries (Knaus 2000).

Can you avoid blame? Perhaps if you are in a coma. But someone might blame you for that too! Even if you acted with great diligence in your responsibilities, oversights, errors, and lapses can evoke blame. The clothing you wear could offend someone who prefers a different color, and you could be accused of having bad taste. In short, there is no escaping blame. The question is, what blame is relevant, what is not, and how do you deal with blame when it is needless or excessive?

As practically everyone knows, blame is often spread for no good reason at all. What is not so widely known is that blame is a significant threat to positive mental health and a factor in depression.

Most people don't intentionally bring the misfortunes of needless blame upon themselves. Nevertheless, when blame blends with depressive thinking, this negativity is normally out of sync with the situation.

This chapter will look into the world of blame. It will examine why you are not to blame for your depression and what you can do to curb needless blame that coexists with depression.

BLAME AND THE BRAIN

Depression is not the fault of the person who suffers from this darkened mood. No one wakes up one morning and says, "I believe I will think depressing thoughts today and cause myself to feel miserable."

Depression is not a character flaw. Depression is not a choice. It's a psychological, biological, social, and environmentally related condition. Choice comes into play in what you decide to do to free yourself from depression.

When people have the flu, they feel ill. They show symptoms. The public doesn't see the infecting virus, yet the symptoms are understood. If you felt sick with the flu, many of your normal abilities would temporarily fade. You would likely experience difficulty attending and concentrating, have a diminished interest in life, find eating unpleasant, and your ability to engage in normal activities of daily living would be impaired. In this state, you are unlikely to blame yourself for the flu. Blaming yourself for depression makes as much sense as blaming yourself for the flu.

The public can't directly see automatic thoughts of depression masquerading as self-blame or directly see the neurotransmitters and cerebral blood flow changes to certain areas of the brain that relate to this negative thinking. (Neurotransmitters are chemical messengers released from a nerve fiber that help pass messages from one neuron to another.) The public ordinarily doesn't see the computerized pictures of the brain when it's altered by depression.

There is an observable difference in the way the brain looks when you are depressed compared to when you are not. You can see this difference in the results of computerized neuroimaging methods such as a PET scan (positron-emission tomography) or fMRI (functional magnetic resonance imaging). When you are depressed, parts of your brain will look cooler. Thus, the depressed brain looks different from a nondepressed brain.

Depression is what it is. It is no more of a choice than is a vulnerability for the flu. Unfortunately, when depressed, many blame themselves, others, or circumstances for their depression. Nothing worthwhile is gained through such blame. By refusing to blame yourself for depression, you act kindly toward yourself. You are then in a better position to get tough on curbing depression.

PATTERNS OF BLAME

Functionally, blame is a process of objectively finding fault before assigning consequences. This social blame idea has a specific purpose, which is to establish accountability. You are speeding in a school zone and get ticketed. A colleague ducked his share of a group project, leaving you with the responsibility. You don't like the position in which the person put you. You take corrective action. This is a rational approach. In these two senses, affixing blame is part of an accountability process.

Blame comes in many forms, such as generalized blame, self-blame, blaming others, blaming the past, and blaming situations. Generalized blame is characterized by such statements as "people are not to be trusted" or "I can't do anything right."

Self-Blame

Without a sense of ethics or social responsibility, self-blame is not likely to exist. The ability to make ourselves accountable for our actions separates ordinary people from psychopaths who could not care less about anyone or anything other than themselves. However, self-blame can go to irrational extremes, such as blaming yourself for acting helpless against depression, declaring yourself worthless, or chastising yourself for phony reasons. Here your ethical compass is skewed in the wrong direction.

One insidious form of self-blame can come from viewing yourself as deficient. When self-blame links to such thinking, you can view yourself as not attractive, smart, or athletic enough. Imagine if your contingency for happiness was a need for something that you thought was impossible to obtain, such as thirty more IQ points? When this deficiency/blame mode of thought is active, happiness, success, and worth are out of reach. However, consider this view: "I am the only me I will ever be, so I might as well act to do the best I can with the resources I have available."

Blaming Others

At any time, you can typically find external conditions upon which to project blame. The reason you feel depressed is because of government corruption, a sneaky rival, parents who gave you a rotten childhood, discrimination, a lousy education, a narcissistic mate, an unfair boss—the list goes on. By blaming others for your depression, you narrow your choices. Following this logic, to get better you have to change other people and the circumstances they create. Good luck!

Blaming others can also have a self-righteous feel. Self-righteous blame thinking can sometimes, in the short term, feel rewarding. Because self-righteousness can cloud judgment, sour relationships, and set the stage for more distortions, it has few long-term benefits. The short-term gains are rarely worth the long-term pains.

Blaming the Past

In the twilight zone between self-blame and blaming others, we can find victim thinking. You can view yourself as the consummate victim. Here is an example: "I suffered a series of losses, including a pet parakeet who flew out of an open door, automobile repair problems, a flooded basement, and a reduction of my hours at work leading to financial strains. That's why I feel depressed." While multiple aversive conditions can contribute to depression, how you think about such situations can mediate surplus distresses that can accompany depression. Blame is not a solution for depression.

True, you and others can bear fault for some disturbing and harmful results that occurred in your recent or distant past. But what can you do to change the past? The past is kaput. Your ability to defeat depression lies in what you can do now.

Whatever the causes for a current depression, your present and future depends on your efforts to do and get better. You have a great ally—yourself and your ability to conjure different views, hold them constant, and look for the evidence or plausibility for each. So it is possible to see yourself take charge of your present and future, even when it was not possible to control aspects of your past.

Blaming Situations

You walk down a street, stumble, and look at the ground. You see nothing unusual. Yet you think there must have been an obstacle. This is known as blaming an imaginary condition.

A limb falls from a tree and damages the hood of your automobile. You can take a philosophical view that such random events enter the lives of all. You can also blame the tree, blame your community authorities for not ordering the limb cut, or blame yourself for where you parked your car. Whatever and whomever you blame, the problem remains. The solution involves notifying your insurance company, getting a repair estimate, scheduling the repair work, obtaining a rental vehicle, and so forth. These solutions don't change, independent of who or what is to blame.

Another form of stress can accompany an unanswerable "why me?" question. Depressive thinking that stems from blame thinking can involve "why me?" questions. But this is rarely a question of inquiry as it is a form of implied blame that can reflect and feed into a sense of total helplessness.

There is no universal answer to the "why me?" question. Things are as they are. The more interesting question remains, "How do I make the most of what I have?

EXTENSIONS OF BLAME

Blame often involves extensions. These extensions include intolerance, condemnation, and punishment. Thus, when feeling depressed for an unacceptably lengthy period, you might internalize blame and become intolerant toward yourself. When depressive extensions of blame include punishment ("I must have done something wrong and deserve to suffer"), depression can blister with added stress.

Extensions of blame can be externalized. You're driving in traffic, and another motorist cuts in front of you, causing you to hit your brakes. If you act as though the person violated your territory and now deserves to have his or her automobile crash into a tree, welcome to the world of extension-of-blame thinking. In an extension-of-blame mental state, it wouldn't matter if that person acts charitably, has a close-knit family, and is known for his or her integrity. What matters is this person did something bad to you by violating a rule of the road and now deserves punishment. (See chapter 15 for more information on the blame-anger connection and resolutions.)

Another view could lead to a quite different reaction, thus suggesting the potential value in working to think flexibly without compromising your values. Consider this perspective: If the person driving slowly were your best friend, would you think the friend deserved to lose control of the vehicle and crash into a tree? You might still disapprove of your friend's driving, but your thoughts and actions are likely to be more rational and tolerant.

Blame extensions involve demands that you or others be a certain kind of person, hold the "right" beliefs, or act according to unmovable expectations; intolerance for deviations; condemnations for deviations; and punishment. When persistent, blame extensions can translate into domestic violence, and domestically violent men are likely to be significantly depressed (Maiuro et al. 1998).

Indirect Extensions

Blame extensions can be indirect and still unmistakable. Blame phrases such as, "What's wrong with you?" "Can't you get anything right?" or "Were you brought up in a barn?" are the tip of this iceberg.

Indirect extensions of blame bristle with negative implications. "What's wrong with you?" is a way of blaming you for being you. Most people who are subjected to these shame-through-blame questions respond defensively by making their own accusations in response. Yet some sensitive individuals become emotional casualties of blame extensions, and this carries over to depression.

Uncovering and Defeating Blame Label Illusions

A psychological illusion is something you believe to be true but isn't that way. For example, you may think that depressive thinking reflects your identity, but it doesn't. You may label yourself by telling yourself that you are worthless, but the label "worthless" represents a generalization, and such a generalization is a form of illusion. At another place and time, your self-view may change.

A cue to illusory depressive thinking resides in the verb "to be." I am helpless, for example, is a generalization because of the verb. Can you be only one way? Is every other person on the planet only one way? Such questioning helps to strip the veneer from an illusion of helplessness.

What if you were to relabel yourself "wonderful"? When depressed, the word would have little credibility. While labeling yourself "wonderful" is far better than labeling yourself "helpless," or "worthless," both extremes reflect an illusion. Who can be only one way?

There is a quick technique for addressing generalized "to be" thinking in depression. Substitute the word "act" for the verb. By saying that you "act helpless," you can examine whether you can act in only one way or you can act in other ways or change your actions.

By radically shifting from making global statements about yourself to addressing actions that you can change, you reduce the risk of giving yourself a dose of double troubles where you blame yourself for being helpless or being worthless.

BLAME EXONERATIONS

To avoid the extensions of blame, most will find ways to excuse their blameworthy behavior. This exoneration tactic is seen at all levels of society.

When a national policy fails, who is to blame? Whoever holds the power determines who or what is to blame. In 1958, Chinese communist leader Mao Tse-tung initiated the Great Leap Forward agricultural reforms. This forced peasants onto massive collective farms. The Great Leap left millions dead of starvation due to empty grain silos. How is this to be explained? Enter one of the more creative exoneration ploys of history.

The disaster, Mao asserted, was not due to his policy. The empty grain silos were caused by greedy sparrows. He blamed the birds for stealing the grain. Then, declaring war on the sparrow, Mao recruited millions to hunt them out of existence. Mao exonerated himself at the expense of the sparrow.

It is the rare person who seeks and then squarely faces truth. Why is this ordinarily so hard? If blame were not unpleasant, "tell the truth," "be open," and "level with others" would be the rule. But the golden rules of honesty are more the exception when something important is at stake, such as personal image.

Because blame is recognizably unpleasant and can lead to unwanted consequences, most prefer to maintain positive public images and to avoid blame. Yet, in most instances, apologies can go far to repair rips in relationships.

In conditions of blame, exoneration ploys frequently come into play. Exoneration ploys are ways to maintain a good public image while cloaking real or imagined faults and actions. These ploys take many forms, including excuses, finger-pointing, white lies, identifying loopholes, shifting blame, omitting relevant information, denial, rationalizing, and convoluted admissions, such as "nobody told me not to do that." Often this exoneration process is part of a vicious circle looping back to more blame excesses and extensions.

Sometimes exonerations take the form of blaming: "Other people are the problem." "The world is corrupt." "There is too much unfairness." When you believe that you have saved face, these ploys can result in a specious reward in the form of relief. However, face-saving successes can lack credibility in the eyes of the beholder, and your lack of transparency and truthfulness can lead to distrust.

It is often easier to blame parents, education, an indifferent universe, the devil, an unhappy marriage, unfairness, bad breaks, strangers, or genetics for worries and troubles. While externalizing blame is an expedient way to blow off responsibility, the solution can contribute to a bigger problem, depressive helplessness. At the same time, there is no need to correct faults or make amends when someone else is at fault.

BLAME AND PROCRASTINATION

Self-blame is ineffective when it comes to ending depression. Nor will self-flagellation save the day when it comes to uprooting procrastination. It's been tried before, with poor results.

If self-blame isn't productive, then how about social censure and blame? Attempts to use blame to evoke social emotions (shame, guilt, embarrassment, humiliation) to curb procrastination typically flop. For example, nineteenth-century procrastination books for children describe tragic tales about people whose procrastination led to death (Barr 1857), who brought failure and disgrace upon themselves (American Sunday School Union 1848), or who caused agonizing grief to self and others (Margaret 1852). On the lighter side, a more contemporary children's story series describes procrastination as a way that people can get themselves into a pickle (Reinach 1977).

Persistent procrastination is rarely assuaged by ridicule, threat, guilt, or humor. That is because procrastination is a complex, automatic habit process made more complex when coexisting with depression. If you feel depressed and simultaneously blame yourself for procrastinating, refuse to blame yourself for having an automatic procrastination habit. Then take a first step to follow through on what is presently useful for you to do. Practice this approach many times, and you can progressively reduce combinations of procrastination, blame, and depressive thinking.

REDUCING BLAME EXCESSES THROUGH PERSPECTIVE

Given a choice, most reasonable people would prefer to think clearly. Moreover, few would go out of their way intentionally to learn and practice blame-excess techniques and stretch out this form of negative thinking. It's hard to imagine that a self-help book titled *The Joys of Self-Blame and Self-Deception* would make the best-seller list.

A realistic perspective can counter blame excesses. Perspective involves weighing what is going on in your life according to its relevance. A fact-based perspective is an insulation against needless pessimism. In this apportionment process, it's clear that even when some aspects of your life go poorly, other parts are likely to be going better.

When blameworthy conditions and negative thinking initially dominate your attention, a broader perspective can be a relief. This broader view can involve accepting the right of others to hold views you don't like. It can involve putting up with irritations but also rectifying and correcting problems.

REDUCING BLAME EXERCISE

Perspective is an important component in reducing blame excesses. When blame excesses affect your sense of emotional well-being, the following seven steps can help you develop a realistic perspective. Start by listing the blame situation, then apply the steps.

Blame situation:
1. Specify the causes, effects, and actual damages.
2. Describe your reasoned thinking about the situation.
3. List blame-thinking excesses.
4. Devise an alternative for blame-thinking excesses.
5. Among your action choices, decide a direction.
6. Implement the action.
7. Revise as appropriate.

ABC METHOD FOR DEFUSING BLAME THINKING

The following chart shows how to apply the ABC method to blame thinking:

Activating event (experience): "A lingering depressed mood."
Rational beliefs about the event: "Down moods are unpleasant."
Emotional and behavioral consequences for the rational beliefs: "The down mood continues but is not exacerbated by added negativity. Activities continue, but at a pace that reflects the level of depression I experience."
Irrational blame beliefs: "I brought depression upon myself, and therefore I am to blame."
Emotional and behavioral consequences for the irrational blame beliefs: "A worsened sense of depression. Withdrawal."
Disputes for irrational blame beliefs: "How am I totally blameworthy for feeling depressed? Sample answer: The various causes for depression suggest that this disability occurs because of a vulnerability for depression, and conditions that evoke it. Unless I can convince myself that I should be singled out for blame, I had better accept the vulnerability and learn to apply my abilities to mute depression's effects."
Effects of the disputes: "Relief from the ravages of blame."

When blame thinking is linked with depression, you can use the following chart as a guide to map and counteract this thinking.

Activating event (experience):

Rational beliefs about the event:

Emotional and behavioral consequences for the rational beliefs:

Irrational blame beliefs:

Emotional and behavioral consequences for the irrational blame beliefs:

Disputes for irrational blame beliefs:

Effects of the disputes:

KEY IDEAS AND ACTION PLAN

What are the key ideas that you got from this chapter? What actions can you take?

Key Ideas

What are the key ideas that you found helpful?

1. _____

   _____

2. _____

   _____

3. _____

   _____

Action Plan

What actions can you take to progress?

1. _____

   _____

2. _____

   _____

3. _____

   _____

POSTSCRIPT

We live in a blame culture. Blame is a norm. Blame recognition and management is rarely taught in the schools. Yet blame excesses, extensions, and exonerations are a significant part of our social interactions and are implicated in depression. A great deal could be gained by shrinking the frequency of blame excesses by helping kids develop critical thinking skills to substitute for automatic blame-trap reactions.

CHAPTER 12

Avoiding the Perils of Perfectionism

Perfectionist thinking represents an attitude that says "I must be perfect, or I'm worthless," or "you must be perfect, or you are condemnable." Perfectionism sometimes includes the idea that "it has to be exactly the way I want it to be, or it is no good." When this black versus white philosophy is active, you will practically always find gaps between where you are and expect to be and a reason to feel frustrated and distressed.

When it's active, perfectionist thinking can take many forms, such as demanding that you should make no errors, that you must be in control, and that you have to be totally competent. Within this mind-set you can think, "I goofed up," "This shows I can't do anything right," "It's my fault things go wrong," or "I should have done something different." This self-critical attitude can contribute to, or reflect, a sense of helplessness that can add to your vulnerability for depression. A combination of demanding self-talk ("should," "must") and alarmist self-talk ("awful," "terrible," "can't stand") elevates the risk for depression (Cox and Enns 2003).

Black-white perfectionist thinking has a punishing aspect. If you believe that your worth depends upon perfect performances, a perfect appearance, or perfect judgments, you are likely to painfully demean yourself when you focus your attention on your imperfections. This blame game distracts from self-development. A perfectionist mind-set also can apply to how you view other people and situations in which you find flaws. When this defect detection process is ongoing, it invariably leads to frustrations that can couple with a miserable depression.

No one is perfect. You can find variability with everyone in terms of their disposition, intelligence, characteristics, and behavior. Some have quirks. People's thoughts get muddled under stress. We all make mistakes. We have gaps in our knowledge. Memory is imperfect. Yet when perfectionist thoughts storm through the mind, the normality of human fallibility often gets shelved. However, you can teach yourself to quell this mental storm. If you find yourself in the perfect person trap, you can learn from this chapter how to spring free and drop the risk of depression associated with this mind-set.

A TRAGIC PLAY

In the world of perfection, some act like they believe the answer to overcoming their miseries is to be perfect, and so they play out their script in this tragic play. But a perfectionist attitude is often the very state of mind that promotes needless stress, such as when you anticipate failure and rejection or when you can't forget something that did not go right. If you count yourself among those who expect too much of yourself, others, or events, learning to overcome perfectionist expectations drops your risk for depression and increases your opportunities for happiness.

Those who enter the world of perfectionism play out a script that allows no room for error or for improvising. In many ways, the script is like a Greek tragedy. In ancient Greek plays, we see many forms of human frailty, including making wrong assumptions, arrogance, and magical thinking. These tragic plays often end with lament.

Unlike classic Greek tragedies, where a lamentable outcome is foretold, you can shape your present so that in the future you need not depress yourself over unreasonable expectations. You can improvise to reach that point.

The following is a perfectionist script in a tragic play that is commonly acted out in the theater of the mind. Here is the background to the scene. The main character is called Perfect. Perfect is a creature of the mind that hangs on to the expectation that perfection is the law of life.

As the play begins, Perfect is surveying a world where nothing is right. Perfect insists on no mistakes. Thus absorbed, Perfect does not see beyond the stage it plays on.

On one particularly dark and dreary day, Perfect calls forth its cohorts. They come in swarms. Insecurity arises, then ducks, hides, and pulls the strings that ring a bell for Despair. The Judge scans the horizon for fault. The Critic blames all. Picky comes to nitpick. Then the keeper of Perfection's scrolls rolls out ten commandments of perfection:

1. Make no mistakes.

2. Be perfectly knowledgeable.

3. Be all that you think others want you to be.

4. Always be strong.

5. Never show vulnerabilities.

6. Utter only unassailable statements.

7. Show more intelligence than anyone else.

8. Exhibit no flaws.

9. Anticipate all things in advance of their occurrence.

10. Make others see and do things your way.

This play is an ongoing tragedy. But you can rewrite the scrollkeeper's commandments. Most of the important things you accomplish result from a gradual process of learning through doing, not from inflexible perfectionist thinking.

DIMENSIONS OF PERFECTION

Perfectionism can serve multiple purposes. It can represent a personal theory for how to establish control and how to experience success and happiness. It can serve to combat insecurity. It can serve as both an explanation for and solution for depression. For example, if you were perfect, you wouldn't feel depressed. But this is superstitious thinking.

> **Few things in life are all black or all white.**

Being a perfectionist is like avoiding the path of a black cat to avoid bad luck. By meeting perfectionist conditions for gaining worth and security, you try to avoid bad luck, disappointment, feelings of worthlessness, discomfort, and despair. But this is an impossible dream. You can do nothing to stop actions already in process or that are inevitable, such as the spinning of the earth or the rising of the sun. Moreover, perfectionism normally detours you from discovering what you can do.

You can divide perfectionism into absolute and relative levels and along personal and social dimensions. In *absolute perfectionism*, the standard is total perfection. Anything less is unacceptable. In *relative perfectionism*, falling beneath a preset standard is unacceptable. You receive a B– on a paper. You emotionally pound on yourself for not getting the B that you set as your minimal standard. Basing your worth on either absolute or relative perfectionist standards is an invitation to feel insecure.

Personal perfectionism involves your expectations for yourself. Here, you fail yourself when you fall short of your expectations or standards. To avoid failure, you may avoid situations that you think can lead to this result. In this way, you can preserve the belief that if you tried, you could have succeeded perfectly well. But it is unrealistic to tell yourself you could have succeeded perfectly well when you have yet to try.

You've entered the world of *social perfectionism* when you think that others should unwaveringly exhibit the morality, fairness, courtesy, and consideration that you expect from them. Under the mandate of social perfectionism, you see people as unredeemable unless they follow your rules.

Psychiatrist Eric Berne (1964) describes how a process of pressuring others into narrow slots of conformity fits with a critical parenting style of thinking. This style includes badgering others to be perfect, strong, or pleasing. Berne asserts that by recognizing these inner voices in ourselves and others, we can better prepare ourselves to extract some positive aspects from them, rather than be driven by them.

Perfectionism has more twists and turns than a ball of twine. For example, the "should have" twist can cause consternation and misery. Imagine living a life of Monday morning quarterbacking where you second-guess prior decisions and fault yourself because you didn't do what you should have done. When this line of thought is active, you risk condemning yourself for what you didn't think to do or for what you thought to do but didn't. This state of mind raises your risk for depression, providing you are vulnerable to this disability.

The "should have" perfectionist message includes blame for not doing what might have been. If you fall into this trap, try substituting "could have" for "should have" and see if this takes the edge off of the demand; balance the picture by what you did that you think was okay; consider that no one is infallible and no one does everything perfectly, then consider why; remind yourself of the scrollkeeper's first commandment, "Make no mistakes," and query yourself as to how that could be; ask yourself how a fallible person can be infallible, and then answer the question.

If you define your worth based on what you can't directly control, you're on a slippery slope. But in the area of self-development, there is a way off the slope. This is the no-failure plan. You start to look at challenges you face as experiments, where you try to find out what works and what doesn't. Whatever the results, you've succeeded. In this way, you've philosophically eliminated failure in self-development matters.

DEPRESSION AND PERFECTION

Psychologist Albert Ellis (1994) found a pattern of thought in depression that includes perfectionism and a negative self-concept. He saw that perfectionist demands coupled with self-downing contribute to a downward depressive spiral. Even Sigmund Freud, who got hung up on an oral-fixation theory as a cause of depression, saw this relationship. Freud (2005) suggests that self-criticism is partially responsible for melancholia (depression).

Psychiatrist Karen Horney (1950) was among the first to make the connection between demands, irrational claims, and neurotic misery. Her description of neurotic misery refers to a pattern of demands, anxiety, and depression.

Perfectionism can reflect an ideal. But the process has a thorny tail that lashes back upon itself with a vengeance. For example, some people suffer from the "I am not" pattern. Here, the formula for happiness and success rests with being something you are not. To achieve success, you have to be more beautiful, talented, powerful, or charming in a way that you can never be. For example, your IQ needs to be fifty points higher, or else you won't find the right mate. So you don't try or end up settling rather than selecting. This "I am not" pattern is a prelude for depression. It can seem pretty depressing if your solution for a better life involves meeting standards where you routinely fall short.

> No one is perfect. No human is a god.

A LANGUAGE OF PERFECTION

You tell yourself that you should make a bank deposit before the bank closes at 4:00. Here you demand nothing. The use of should is conditional. On the other hand, "should" can be a demand referring to how things should be, such as "I should never look foolish."

"Should," "must," "ought," "require," and "expect" are part of a vocabulary of perfectionism that can activate stress. When part of a perfectionist outlook, these words can be the source of much misery. For example, "should," when used as a judgment word, can have a strong emotional impact. If you fail to do what you tell yourself you should do, you may condemn yourself for not living according to this demand. But we live in a fluid world where change is ongoing. It is impossible to anticipate everything and to respond perfectly to what you anticipate.

When you believe that you must have what you think you need, what happens when you don't get it? What does it mean when you make a mistake and then tell yourself that you should not have erred, or that you should have done something different from what you did? The eighteenth century English poet Alexander Pope has an answer: "And, spite of Pride, in erring Reason's spite, One truth is clear, whatever *is*, is *right*."

PREFERRING VS. DEMANDING

Demands and requirements are part of our social communications. They are common in the military, the schools, in religions, in corporations, and in governmental agencies. There are many times where requirements are reasonable and realistic. You insist that a long overdue report get submitted. You require a two-year-old child to stay in your fenced yard to avoid the risk of running into a busy street. You may hold to certain values, such as responsibility and integrity, and these values operate as imperatives for how you choose to live your life. However, some requirements are objectively meaningless. You blame someone for falling short of perfection. Your favorite team loses an important game, and you blame the coach for not acting according to your script. But how does that rearview thinking change anything?

The spirit of this requiring philosophy is that "I should have acted differently." "I must not make mistakes." "People ought to act fairly." "I must have others think well of me." While such outcomes are often desirable, translating them into requirements is like hitting a barrier and telling yourself that it should not exist.

Some perfectionist ideals seem desirable, even when they cannot be permanently attainable. What reasonable person wouldn't want to achieve the ideals of happiness, success, approval, control, comfort, and certainty? Make them into requirements, however, and you can undermine these desirable states. Irrational demands normally promote stress, and stress is both uncomfortable and misery making.

A preferential view is radically different from irrational requirements or demands. A preferential philosophy involves desires, wishes, and wants. These conditions of mind serve as positive motivators. Going after what you want, experiencing happiness, or gaining approval is a big part of this preferential philosophy.

Preferring a result has a different "feel" than demanding that you must get what you think you need now. From a self-development perspective, a preferential philosophy has these advantages:

- You are likely to feel less self-inflicted stress.

- Perfectionist extension-of-blame thinking will decline.

- You are likely to appear friendlier and more open, agreeable, and approachable.

- You'll have fewer perfectionist fear-of-failure expectations; you'll experiment and learn more.

- You are likely to focus more on problem solving than on helplessness thoughts.

- You are likely to think more clearly and creatively.

- You are more likely to follow up on responsibilities and so will procrastinate less.

- You'll experience a broader range of positive emotions.

The following table shows the differences between the language of requiring and the language of preferring.

Requiring Outlook	Preferential Outlook
expect	prefer
demand	wish
require	desire
insist	want
need	favor
got to	care for
should	hope
ought	like
must	aspire

CHARTING YOUR EMOTIONAL RESPONSE

Emotions that are activated by irrational demands include negative affects such as anger and anxiety. Preferential thoughts normally activate determination and other forms of positive motivation.

Use the following chart to predict the emotions resulting from a demanding versus a preferential perspective:

Demand Thinking	Emotion	Preference Thinking	Emotion
1. expect	1.	1. prefer	1.
2. demand	2.	2. wish	2.
3. require	3.	3. desire	3.
4. insist	4.	4. want	4.
5. need	5.	5. favor	5.
6. got to	6.	6. care for	6.
7. should	7.	7. hope	7.
8. ought	8.	8. like	8.
9. must	9.	9. aspire	9.

Building preferential resources takes more than substituting a desire word for a demand word, however. Saying "desire" when you mean "demand" is rarely helpful.

What about eliminating such words as "should," "ought," "must," "require," "expect," or "demand" from your thoughts? That's not likely. Try to eliminate your Social Security number from your memory. It's only through years of disuse that this can happen, if at all! The memories of words don't evaporate by decree. Accept that, and you have unraveled another string on the perfectionist ball of twine.

You can make yourself aware of how irrational demands can influence how you feel and what you do. You can train yourself to accept a preferential view of yourself and the world, if that seems desirable. Making such a shift from a demanding to a preferential philosophy often starts with an awareness of the connection between demands and stress and questioning the premises behind the demands. For example, if you demand your own way all the time, here is a question to ask yourself: "Why must things be only as I expect them to be?" If you think that others—even strangers—have stringent expectations for you, and you shy away from people because of this, here is another question: "What makes me think I have ESP and know what others expect me to do or to be?" Through such self-questioning steps, you can move in the direction of reducing depressing strains from perfectionist claims.

You can deactivate perfectionism by

■   Thinking in degrees. Instead of saying "I failed," you might say, "I got forty percent of what I wanted."

■   Qualifying your thoughts and responses: "I generally approve of the position of X, but differ in this respect."

■   Considering perfectionist thinking as an assumption or opinion. This makes the thought less of an absolute and makes it more accessible to review and reason.

QUESTIONING IF-THEN LOGIC

All-or-nothing perfectionist thinking commonly links to "if-then" conditional worth messages: "If I'm not what I think I should be [perfect], then I'm worthless." "If you violate my expectations, then you are condemnable." "The world should be fair, and if it is not as it should be, then it should be destroyed."

If-then perfectionist logic has other twists. "If I don't do what I think you think I ought to do, then I'm unworthy." Charles Horton Cooley (1902) called this reflection about what others might think a "looking glass self."

The problem with perfectionist if-then logic lies in getting yourself boxed into a demoralizing system. In this box, perfectionist thinking twists like a viper, then bites with a devastating venom. "Then" represents a belief ("worthiness is based on perfection") and the "if" provides the reason ("infallible actions, thoughts, and consistency make for perfection"). So if you are perfect, then you are worthy, and if you are imperfect, then you are not. This type of reasoning is known as a non sequitur. One point doesn't realistically follow the other. In short, it doesn't add up.

Okay, so step outside of this box. If you are not perfect, how does it follow that you are worthless? Where is the evidence, proof, or facts to support your argument?

Albert Ellis (1988) asserts that worthiness is a definition. He notes that you can decide to give yourself unconditional self-acceptance (USA). This is where you accept your global self, even if you don't like some of the things that you do. Although this is more easily said than done, compare the perfectionist philosophy with USA using the following acceptance exercise. Which choice do you prefer?

ACCEPTANCE EXERCISE

Fill in the blanks with your own examples of perfectionist thinking and actions that can extend from this thinking. Then come up with alternative USA thinking and actions that can extend from it.

1.   Personal examples of perfectionist thinking that relate to feelings about yourself:

2. Actions that can extend from perfectionist thinking:

3. Alternative USA thinking that relates to feelings about yourself:

4. Actions that can extend from USA thinking:

Unconditional self-acceptance doesn't absolve people of responsibility for their actions. Rather it is a means of maintaining perspective and avoiding needless intolerance.

BREAKING THE BONDS OF SELF-IMPRISONMENT

Perfectionist thoughts bond with negative emotions such as anxiety and anger and states such as depression. You can set the stage to switch from a demanding to a preferential view by first contrasting a static state of perfectionist self-imprisonment with a process of self-development.

State of Self-Imprisonment

A state of perfectionism is one of self-imprisonment with these characteristics:

- Attainment of certain "needs" is seen as a solution for perceived inadequacy, incompetence, lack of internal order, or emptiness.

- Failure to attain these needs leads to distress, which is usually perceived as an inability to attain what you want.

- Inner demands and expectations fuel strain and tension.

- Lacks must be filled by someone else because of a perceived personal incapacity for attaining desires.

- External effort directed toward pressuring, coercing, mandating, or manipulating to get your way.

A Process of Self-Development

A self-development process has these positive characteristics:

■ Person believes goals are attained through individual initiative and innovation. This can occur in collaboration with others or alone.

■ Joy and accomplishment are seen as by-products of working to develop skills and competencies.

■ Effort is directed toward creating positive results.

■ As a by-product, meeting productive (sometimes creative) objectives can lead to happiness, accomplishment, or friendship.

■ Concrete goal attainment opens opportunities for meeting new challenges and goals.

APPLYING THE ANALYSIS

Expand your counter-perfection analysis by applying it to your own experience. Use a pencil with an eraser. You might want to erase or add ideas.

What actions can you take to get beyond perfectionist demands that bond with negative emotions? (What ideas can you doubt? What actions can you start to take that oppose perfectionist thinking?) _____

_____

_____

What actions can you take to strengthen a goal-directed problem-solving approach? (What hopes, aspirations, and wishes do you have that you can work to achieve? How can you make yourself accountable for keeping promises that you make to yourself?) _____

_____

_____

If your goal is perfection, there are some ways to achieve it. "Whoa," you say. "After this discussion on the perils of perfectionism, it seems more important to curb than encourage these tendencies. Why give a mixed message?"

In some respects, you are already perfect. You know the alphabet from A to Z. Is that not perfect? You know your multiplication tables. Is that not perfect? It's what you do with this knowledge that makes the difference.

In another respect, you are the perfect embodiment of yourself. No one can be a more perfect you than you. You can build on that resource you call your "self" to gain advantages, avoid penalties, and enjoy your life.

ABC METHOD FOR DEFUSING PERFECTIONIST THINKING

The following chart shows how to apply the ABC method to perfectionist thinking:

Activating event (experience): "Imperfect performance."
Rational beliefs about the event: "I'd prefer to do better next time."
Emotional and behavioral consequences for the rational beliefs: "Disappointment. Work to improve performance."
Irrational perfectionist beliefs: "I should have done better. I'm stupid."
Emotional and behavioral consequences for the irrational perfectionist beliefs: "Distress. Withdrawal."
Disputes for irrational perfectionist beliefs: "(1) Where is the law in the universe that says I must behave flawlessly? Sample answer: There is no such law. (2) Can I accept myself even when I don't like my performance? Sample answer: Acceptance is a choice. However, acting with tolerance and self-acceptance frees my mind for problem solving, and the opportunity to do better."
Effects of the disputes: "Still disappointed over performance. Renewed efforts to do better. Sense of self-acceptance."

When perfectionist thinking is linked with your depression, you can use the following chart as a guide to map and counteract this thinking.

Activating event (experience):

Rational beliefs about the event:

Emotional and behavioral consequences for the rational beliefs:

Irrational perfectionist beliefs:

Emotional and behavioral consequences for the irrational perfectionist beliefs:

Disputes for irrational perfectionist beliefs:

Effects of the disputes:

KEY IDEAS AND ACTION PLAN

What are the key ideas that you got from this chapter? What actions can you take?

Key Ideas

What are the key ideas that you found helpful?

1. _____

_____

2. _____

_____

3. _____

_____

Action Plan

What actions can you take to progress?

1. _____

_____

2. _____

_____

3. _____

_____

POSTSCRIPT

The nineteenth-century English writer Samuel Johnson early recognized the perils of perfection and presented them in an 1820 essay in *The Rambler*. Johnson (1962) saw perfectionism as a habit of mind of magnifying details against perfectionist standards, which leads to decreased understanding and increased unhappiness.

Johnson had it right about perfectionism as a habit of mind. By modern standards, perfectionism is more than being a stickler for details and getting upset when anything falls short of a perfectionist standard. It's an attitude of mind that you can take for granted until you learn that when perfectionist thinking is active, it can promote stress and strains. By raising serious questions about the validity of the "shoulds" and "oughts" of perfectionism, you can do yourself considerable good.

CHAPTER 13

Low Frustration Tolerance and Depression

Frustration occurs when you have a goal blocked, when you face a barrier you can't immediately overcome, or where there is a gap between what you want and what you get. Frustrations are an inevitable part of life. You get caught in traffic and miss an important meeting. Your insurance company refuses to pay a legitimate claim. A mathematical equation stumps you. You apply for a job and don't get it. You lose your keys and can't get into your house. You don't see eye-to-eye with someone. You feel depressed and don't function as you'd normally prefer.

As long as you have wishes and desires and face unwanted barriers, frustration is inevitable and normal. Expect it.

Frustration is motivational. Without frustration, you probably wouldn't have an emotional incentive to solve frustration-provoking problems. However, frustration can be viewed as intolerable, and at that point, it can prove disabling.

Frustration can motivate avoidance. Managing and tolerating frustration may be the single most important thing to do when facing challenging personal conditions such as depression and anxiety. If the mental health field put as much time into finding ways to help people boost their tolerance for frustration as it has done for "self-esteem," I predict people would be far more productive in their efforts, report greater satisfaction with life, and have fewer stress-related health problems.

Your tolerance for frustration has a bearing on how you go about facing the ordinary and extraordinary frustrations of life. Unfortunately, while you are depressed, frustrating circumstances don't go on vacation. Depression brings fatigue. Fatigue normally frustrates wishes to feel more energized. Your tolerance for frustration is likely to grow worse.

> If you fear discomfort and frustration, Atlanta psychotherapist Ed Garcia (pers. comm.) suggests that you consider this question: Has there been anything in your life that you accomplished that did not derive from discomfort? If discomfort is part of making a significant change, what is there to fear?

When depressed and fatigued, you are likely to experience a decreased tolerance for frustration. Managing the ordinary and extraordinary events of the day can seem arduous. A diminished ability to cope with frustrations can contribute to a downward spiral where an already darkened mood deepens.

Frustration involves unpleasant sensations. When these sensations come into focus, they tend to persist. Frustration sensitivity, along with a depressed mood, can extend and support helplessness and hopelessness thinking. By acting to develop high frustration tolerance, you are less likely to descend further into the pot of pessimism called depression.

This chapter will look at inappropriately low frustration tolerance and depression, probe the connection between low frustration tolerance, depression, and substance abuse, examine the relationship between procrastination and depression, and dig into how a high-frustration-tolerance perspective can boost your chances for ending depression.

LOW AND HIGH FRUSTRATION TOLERANCE

Low frustration tolerance (LFT) refers to when you impulsively overreact to situations that impede what you expect or want. Millions who are primed to avoid discomfort, who demand quick fixes and instant gratification, fall into the LFT trap. A substance abuser wants to consume a favorite substance *now*. An anxious person wants a magical pill to promote confidence. A new counseling client wants quick relief.

Frustration tolerance exists on a continuum. At the high-frustration-tolerance end of the continuum, you understand what you want to accomplish and are willing to sacrifice and persist even when the going gets tough. Your mind feels freer. You experience more spontaneity and exhilaration of spirit. You view yourself as in charge of your life and accountable for the decisions you make and actions that you take. With high frustration tolerance, you are likely to experience a positive self-concept, accomplish more, and experience greater satisfactions with less stress and strain. In an LFT mode, you are primed to overreact to inconvenience and hassle. You are likely to believe that you have more than your share of distresses and crises. Most of us live our lives fluctuating between these extremes. However, the emotional advantage goes to those whose tolerance for frustration is normally high.

Here are some examples of LFT reactions:

- You have a "short fuse" when things don't go your way.

- You gobble handfuls of potato chips even when on a diet.

- When delayed, you tend to tap your fingers or pace.

- You ask questions, then don't pay attention to the answers.

- When things do not happen quickly enough, you put your hands on your waist, sigh, or express other body movements to signify impatience.

- You buy on impulse.

- You act cranky and irritable when you don't immediately get what you want.

- You tend to dramatize your complaints.

- You harbor grudges and recycle them in your mind.

Frustration tolerance is not a constant thing. It can depend upon perception and situation. When ill, hungry, or after losing sleep, your tolerance for frustration can drop. When you feel in a good mood, you are likely to feel more tolerant. When depressed, your tolerance for frustration is likely to decline.

False Rewards

Psychologist George Ainslie (Ainslie and Monterosso 2003) points out that diversion from purposeful activities can result in a specious reward. You duck a problem. You feel an immediate sense of relief. But your relief comes from avoidance. That's why the reward is specious. It's useful to be aware of this connection, refuse the reward, and instead follow through with a constructive action.

Frustration Distresses

Stress is a pressure or tension that evokes mental, emotional, and physical strain. Some stresses are short term, such as the fright you feel following a near accident. Others can be more durable, such as the undesired loss of a job. Self-induced stress can come about from beliefs of being a failure or a projected sense of hopelessness. When internal stresses are present with depression, a dysphoric mood can seem unbearable.

Stress of any sort can feel unpleasant, but not all stress is bad. Some forms of stress result from the positive efforts you make. I call this "p-stress" or progressive stress. Effort is directed toward solving problems, such as coping with a tense relationship, testing a promising new idea, probing an area of uncertainty, sticking with an unpleasant but important work project, or developing personal clear-thinking skill resources.

Distress (d-stress) comes about when you magnify your troubles, think life is too tough, view yourself as helpless to cope, and feel easily hurt by slights that are often more imaginary than real. The process includes lamenting, worrying, or fretting. The d-stress factor tends to feed upon itself. With d-stress in operation, you have more to feel frustrated about, and this can contribute to a declining sense of frustration tolerance.

The longer you spend in d-stress pursuits, the greater the risk of depression. And even if you don't develop a significant depression, d-stress distracts from the ordinary joys of living.

If you believe that you can no longer go on, you are likely to have an explanation, such as you are incapable of change or that a loss you experienced is unendurable. Such explanations reflect hopelessness. This d-stress attribution has the power to deepen depression. Helplessness and hopelessness thinking detract from your ability to deal with frustrations. When d-stress mingles with LFT, this combination of conditions can captivate your attention in a most unpleasant way. The process goes like this:

You encounter a frustrating condition.

⇩

You experience frustration.

⇩

You experience an impulse to discharge tension.

⇩

You dramatize the significance of the situation and your frustration.

⇩

You feel stressed and overwhelmed.

⇩

You view yourself as unable to control events.

⇩

You feel helpless.

When looking through a prism of depression, daily frustrations can seem overwhelming. Faced with an unwelcome frustration, you might d-stress yourself by saying to yourself, "Oh my god. This is awful. I'll never be able to manage. I can't take this." Helplessness self-talk blended with LFT impulses can feel like a maelstrom of misery. But d-stress is contestable and divestible.

In many states of depression, some people give up. The world seems too tough, and they feel too unable to move. They could not care less about doing anything. But for others, the gaps between where they are and would like to be take on a special negative meaning. Members of this subgroup tend to think they have suffered too long and that they need to get immediate relief from depression. In this urgent desperation, doing better is not enough. Immediate relief is a must. This form of perfectionist thinking couples with a low tolerance for frustration to add distress to depression.

Perfectionism combined with low frustration tolerance and depression is like a one-two punch. Here's an example: You suffer a loss. You tell yourself, "It shouldn't have happened. It must not be. It's awful and terrible. I can't stand the loss." This *awfulizing* takes a bad situation and escalates the misery.

The bad news is that LFT d-stress patterns can intensify depression. The good news is that the mental components of the LFT d-stress process are addressable. Training yourself in managing and tolerating frustration provides a way to build resilience against a wide range of unpleasant states that can range from alcohol abuse to xenophobia. Although high frustration tolerance links to self-confidence and less d-stress, this may be one of the more challenging human capabilities to develop and to routinely maintain.

DECREASING STRESS EXERCISE

The three glasses of stress in the illustration describe levels of vulnerability to stressful situations. Imagine that the content of each glass represents "stress." The glass on the far right would represent high stress tolerance because it can absorb more stress than the others.

You can use the concept of the stress glass to gauge your susceptibility to stress. Draw a glass on a piece of paper. List what stresses you face within the glass. Then, mark your stress level on the glass. Next, identify something that you can do to resolve (cope with) a stress. The idea is to lower the stress level by decreasing stressful mental, social, biological, and environmental conditions.

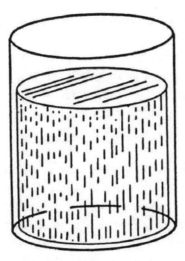
Low stress tolerance or
high stress vulnerability

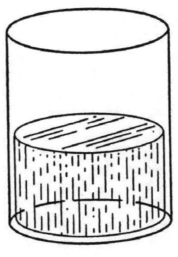
Moderate stress
tolerance or moderate
stress vulnerability

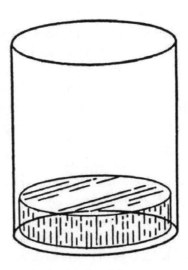
High stress tolerance or
low stress vulnerability

Bridgeport University Professor Emeritus Dom DiMattia (pers. comm.) suggests an *inventory approach* to put things into perspective to reduce the sort of distress that comes from awfulizing. For example, when you've had a bad week and you think, "Nothing went right, and that's awful," take stock. Identify what happened during the week that links to the emotional commotion you experience. Next, inventory what went well during the week. Then, inventory the ordinary occurrences of daily living that went as you would anticipate. Compare your "nothing went right" self-statement with the positive and neutral experiences that occurred during the same period. Does that change the picture?

Although this inventory approach can lead to a more balanced perspective, it does not take away the significance of recent negative events. Rather, you can use this technique to combat a stressful preoccupation with a few negative events by broadening your perspective. By using this reflective method, you can decrease the impact of awfulizing thoughts. Simultaneously, you position yourself to boost your tolerance for discomfort and to feel more in control of your thoughts and emotions.

LOW FRUSTRATION TOLERANCE AND SUBSTANCE ABUSE

About 25 percent of people with addictions suffer from depression. Thinking that life is too painful, some try to numb their sensations and fog their distressful thinking by escaping through mind-altering substances, such as alcohol, marijuana, or Valium. Over the long run, such self-medication efforts typically backfire. Alcohol, for example, often serves to drag a depression out.

When alcohol or drug abuse couples with depression, this can promote a vicious cycle of depression and abuse. It is challenging to kick a substance abuse habit even when you are not feeling depressed.

Nevertheless, breaking an addictive cycle is often a prerequisite to breaking a coexisting depressive cycle, for it clears the mind of addictive preoccupations.

If ever there were an area where LFT reigns, it is that of substance abuse. Once you're hooked, it takes a concerted effort to stop abusing addictive substances. The process of kicking such problem habits involves building up a tolerance for urges and cravings and learning not to capitulate to them. The higher you build your tolerance for frustration, the more likely you are to kick the habit.

Kicking a problem habit can give you a sense of control over your life. With this sense of control, you are less likely to have depressed feelings that link to the habit. You are also in a better position to deal with depression. However, people who go from alcohol dependency to sobriety may go through a period where their depression seems worse. The masking effects of the substance are gone. The issues that connect with depression may remain. New challenges can surface, such as how to handle sobriety, how to find purpose and meaning, how to address the residuals stemming from the habit (substance-related behaviors that cause personal harm and possibly harm to others), and how to come to peace with yourself and build from there. It is how you manage such new challenges that can make the difference. When building frustration tolerance is a prime objective that weaves through this process, you boost your chances for taking charge of your life and time.

■ John's Story

The following story illustrates how LFT and self-doubts weave through both depression and an alcohol abuse habit. To a casual observer, John was a success. He had a loving wife and great kids. It looked like he had it all. Yet John viewed himself as a loser. He saw himself as destined for failure. His tolerance for discomfort was low.

In public, John masked his depression well. He dressed sharply. He had a mellow, soothing tone of voice. He forced a smile. But that is not how he felt. He kept himself going through the day thinking that he'd drink at night and relax. He then drank to dampen his tension. The more frequently he drank, the worse his life became.

John made a major breakthrough when he made the connection between his depressive sensations, drinking thinking, and low frustration tolerance. That awareness gave him an important insight: his intolerance for tension and discomfort invited only greater intolerance.

When John kept a record of his thinking, he found that his mind switched from thinking about how rotten he felt to thinking about drinking. To remind himself of how this combination of depressive sensations, thought process, and alcohol consumption worked, he made up a card for his wallet where he wrote these four lines:

Depressive sensation
⇩
Depressive thinking
⇩
Drinking
⇩
Depressive sensation

John used the card as a reminder to pause and think through what was happening when he felt the urge to drink. He continued this reflective process until he tolerated his depressive sensations, refused to give in to LFT urges to drink, and stopped using alcohol as a solution for medicating his depression. This change took place over a nine month period. (In this area, quick cures are unusual.)

If you are using drugs or alcohol to quell depression, act to stop drinking or drugging. If addicted and you feel driven to consume, address the addiction. A compulsion to consume drugs and alcohol can trigger depression. At the same time, alcohol and drug use may temporarily cloak depression and contribute to a vicious cycle of substance abuse, depression, and masking depression through the consumption of an addictive substance.

Imbibing drugs and alcohol to dull the pains of depression is an unhealthy activity. Using substances to self-medicate against depression creates an entanglement with depression that is typically difficult to unravel. Although addiction and depression are a tough combination, they can be dealt with simultaneously.

Nicotine and Depression

You feel depressed. You light up. You distract and relax yourself. But this is no magic medicine. Take a look at these facts:

- Nicotine is an addictive substance.

- Smoking and depression can occur together and derive from common as well as separate mechanisms (Stage, Glassman, and Covey 1996).

- The risk for depression increases as the number of nicotine dependence symptoms increase (John et al. 2004).

- Approximately 60 percent of smokers who had significant difficulty quitting smoking had previous episodes of a major depression (Glassman 1997).

- Current and former female smokers are more likely to experience depression and more likely to go on antidepressant medication for depression than nonsmokers (Pomerleau, Zucker, and Stewart 2003).

- There is a correlation between increased smoking and depression among the elderly. Smoking can be associated with an increased depression or vice versa. Also, the incidence of depression increases with other unhealthy lifestyle changes, such as a reduced activity level (van Gool et al. 2003).

- Smoking elevates the risk for chronic diseases, such as coronary heart disease and emphysema. Chronic diseases increase the risk for depression.

When people smoke to dull depressive sensations, nicotine has some antidepressant effects (Balfour 1991). Nicotine affects brain regions that influence mood and feelings of well-being (Gilbert and Spielberger 1987). Nevertheless, depression will not normally lift using nicotine as an antidepressant. Once you're addicted, smoking creates repeated cravings for nicotine and does not appear to effectively address depression.

A significant number of depressed smokers are inclined to believe that quitting is risky when they are depressed. Quitting a smoking habit involves withdrawal, and withdrawal is mood depressing. Putting off quitting until depression is under control has some advantage. Unlike alcohol abuse, you can still think clearly when smoking, and dealing with smoking can be addressed after overcoming depression. On the other hand, you might consider that if you experience depressed sensations and withdrawal sensations at the same time, you can avoid having to face the withdrawal for nicotine later.

If you smoke and find yourself mindlessly reaching for a cigarette, listen for a stealth attack in the form of an addictive voice commanding you to consume. The addictive voice reflects low frustration tolerance. The voice has different themes. There is the "let the good times roll" voice, where you associate smoking with companionship and pleasant experiences. You may hear a defiant voice saying, "You smoke for pleasure. No one can stop you from doing that." You may hear a weepy voice that says, "You need something to calm down. Light up now. You can quit later." Recognition of this form of addictive thinking is a start. Acting to disrupt this stealth process can lead to progress in overcoming your addiction.

If you smoke and decide to quit, here are a few cognitive and behavioral tips:

- *Do a dollar cost analysis.* Put your expenses into perspective. Quitting smoking is clearly going to save you significant dollars. If you have a $5 a day habit, you can save $1,825 over a year. Can you think of a more productive use for those dollars? (Some people put what they save into a jar and deposit the dollars every week. Watching the dollars grow can feel rewarding.)

- *Withdrawal symptoms are temporary.* They typically pass in about two weeks. Knowing this is a time-limited event can help make the process tolerable.

- *Consider using a nicotine patch.* This approach will tend to ease withdrawal pangs.

- *Exercise regularly.* This will boost your endorphin level (a feel-good brain chemical). Increases in endorphin production can substitute for the effects of nicotine. You can also reduce a feeling of being winded due to a lack of exercise and smoking.

- *Make a plan.* The psychological reactions to smoking tend to last longer than the approximately two weeks of physical withdrawal. Later, you'll continue to associate smoking with certain times of day or with having a cup of coffee, studying for a test, moods, and sensory experiences such as taste, touch, sight, smell. Plan corrective actions for each of the main parts of the smoking habit. Execute the plan.

A key to an effective habit-breaking plan is that of making up your mind that you are going to quit. Pick a date to quit. Make a plan to do it. Execute the plan starting on the designated date. Chapter 14 includes techniques for dealing with unpleasant sensations. These techniques can be adapted to help you tolerate addictive cravings, urges, and sensations.

Acting constructively to promote good health helps to disrupt depression. And although any one action at any one time may not tip the balance, multiple activities spread over time can weigh on the side of freedom from depression.

PERSPECTIVES ON FRUSTRATION TOLERANCE DEVELOPMENT

The early cognitive behavioral psychologist Edward Chance Tolman (1922) observed that our expectancies, perceptions, and representations influence what we do. He taught that learning is goal-directed, purposeful, and involves a means-ends analysis, and people will select the easiest path to achieve a goal. The shortest path, however, may be the one that first requires accepting and facing frustration. Acting on this perspective can help alleviate many forms of needless stress.

Perspective helps you to accurately assign weight to events according to their importance and according to your ability to deal with those requiring attention. However, when depressed, perspective is ordinarily clouded by negativity.

When you focus on negative thoughts, you've lost perspective. This is like putting your hands before your eyes when looking at a full moon. The moon remains the same, but it is obscured from view.

Using PURRRRS to Boost Tolerance

In recognition of people's tendencies to overreact to frustration, the culture passes on warnings such as "haste makes waste." You'll also hear practical suggestions: "Look before you leap." "Count to ten." "Take a walk." "Think." These suggestions have a unifying thread: slow down! Cultural sayings also include "he who hesitates is lost." But how do you know when to slow down and reflect before acting and when to act without delay? The matter is that of context, perception, perspective, and common sense.

Boosting frustration tolerance involves hard-headed decisions on what you want to accomplish. It involves changing a habit of impulse or inhibition to one of reflection and purposeful action. You can adapt the PURRRRS approach from chapter 6 to address LFT depression reactions and boost your perspective. If you count yourself among those who try to self-medicate themselves through alcohol and other addictive substances, you can apply PURRRRS to the challenge of slowing down, reasoning, and abstaining. To use this approach, start by listing the LFT condition and respond using PURRRRS.

PURRRRS EXERCISE FOR LFT

Use the following chart to map your PURRRRS plan for boosting your tolerance for frustration. Start by describing what frustrates you.

Low-frustration-tolerance condition: _____

PURRRRS PLAN						
Pause	Use	Reflect	Reason	Respond	Revise	Stabilize
Stop.	Resist.	Think about what's happening.	Think it through.	Put yourself through the paces.	Make adjustments.	Persist and repeat.

Using the "Because" Technique

You can use the "because" technique to broaden your perspective on LFT self-talk. To use this technique, add the word "because" after negative self-statements such as "I can't take feeling frustrated," and then fill in the blank. Here is an example: "I can't stand feeling frustrated because . . ." This helps you to expand upon the issue and gain clarity, which provides a way to separate the important from the trivial.

You may answer the implied question after "because" with "I'm not competent enough to cope." With this clarification, you can follow up with other questions: In what ways do you cope less well than you would prefer? What is a minimal way to cope? If you don't cope effectively with a specific situation, is it possible for you to adapt ways you've used to cope in related situations? How might this be done?

LOW FRUSTRATION TOLERANCE AND ALTERNATIVE THINKING

People with a low threshold for frustration, who suffer from d-stress, tend to use language that worsens the misery: "This is awful." "I can't stand how I feel." "I'll never stop feeling depressed." "I won't get my life back." This frustration distress self-talk adds stress to stress and depressive ideas to depressive ideas. Let's look at a sampling of LFT distress talk and alternative views:

Alarmist phrases: "I am falling apart." "I can't stand it." Such catastrophic thoughts often extend to false conclusions, such as "I'm worthless." "I'm a loser." *Alternative view:* An alarmist phrase is not the same as a fact. Rather, it can reflect the mood you experience at the time of the thought. The question "Does what I think represent mood, reason, or reality?" can help put your thoughts into perspective.

Self-pity phrases: "I always ruin things for myself." "Nothing turns out right for me." "No one appreciates what I do for them." *Alternative view:* Self-pity phrases reflect an overly generalized projection of helplessness and hopelessness. As an alternative, use specifics to describe a situation, such as, "I got fifty percent of what I wanted." It is normally wise to avoid inflammatory language such as "always ruin" and "nothing turns out right."

Ineptitude phrases: "I will never be able to manage." "I can't control anything." *Alternative view:* These depressive thoughts blend helplessness with hopelessness. Terms like "never" bear special scrutiny. Look for exceptions to the never rule.

Self-referent phrases: "I'm a jerk." "I'm stupid." *Alternative view:* These thoughts are magnifications and overgeneralizations that represent a self-downing view. You can learn more about these extreme thoughts by reducing them to examples and then looking for exceptions. If there are exceptions, and there probably are plenty, then it is impossible that the self-downing statement is completely true. By uncoupling these thoughts from your self, you can gain considerable relief from depression.

In challenging frustration distress talk, step out of the box. Look for exceptions. Look for loopholes. Separate fact from fiction. Separate reason from emotion. In short, refuse to accept the negativity of frustration distress thinking without first examining and analyzing the thoughts. Letting them go unchecked is like sitting on top of an active beehive.

BREAKING THE INERTIA OF PROCRASTINATION

Is there a change you want to make, but don't? Does your frustration tolerance decline when you think about following through with timely and beneficial actions? Do you then delay action? This procrastination complication can be expressed through such thoughts as "I don't want to. I can't do it. I am too tired. It's too hard. I don't feel like it. It's too scary." This thinking can blunt efforts toward positive change.

A procrastination process is an inertial process where you follow the same path because you've followed it before. It doesn't matter if it's like wading through mud. This inertial pattern continues until you break from it.

Low frustration tolerance and procrastination commonly coexist to create the mud. In fact, LFT is probably the prime mechanism behind a procrastination habit. But there are other triggers. Procrastination may be triggered by perfectionism and fear of failure (see chapter 12 for techniques on challenging perfectionist tendencies).

Frustration Avoidance Habits

Frustration avoidance is a common response to frustration. Sometimes frustration avoidance makes sense. You avoid the frustration of assembling a child's toy by hiring someone else to do it. But in the area of self-development, frustration avoidance can be the wrong way to go. This avoidance process is like drifting with the flow of a stream. It's easier. But what if upstream is where an important goal lies? Suppose you want to overcome a handicapping fear or make a critical lifestyle change. By drifting with the current, you are obviously heading in the wrong direction. If you want to get upstream, you'll have to paddle harder in that direction.

Getting where you want involves breaking the inertia that comes with following a familiar, albeit destructive, habit such as frustration avoidance. This shift can be partially accomplished through teaching yourself to think differently. It includes recognizing that frustration is a normal part of any change that requires effort or where there is an element of uncertainty. The process involves accepting that in the long run, avoiding or escaping meaningful frustrations contributes to making life tougher. In the short term, it may be easier, for example, to give in to fatigue when depressed. Engaging in purposeful activity when fatigued can feel like paddling upstream. But that effort holds greater promise of freedom from depression than going in the opposite direction.

This upstream principle applies to practically every meaningful change that is in your interest to make. For example, people who are overweight, but keep gaining despite cycling through many diets, face an upstream challenge. A lifetime of moderate eating through portion control is a logical approach to stop the cycle and achieve and maintain a weight-loss goal. But we are psychological creatures whose old patterns can easily get in the way of our new interests, whether it is defeating depression, losing weight, or starting a business.

The Siamese Twin Challenge

How do you cut through the inertia of procrastination and depression to get upstream? You paddle to break the inertia built into both processes.

Atlanta psychotherapist Ed Garcia (pers. comm.) tells us that depression and inertia are like Siamese twins that stand like a boulder before a ten-ton truck. It takes a lot of power to push the boulder aside. This effort first strains a cold engine. All cylinders are not firing. But once you get the truck moving, even just a little bit, it builds momentum. The more it moves, the warmer the engine gets. As the momentum builds, it gets easier to push the boulder aside. Now you've started a new inertial pathway. This is the pathway where you point the truck where you want it to go. But you've got to get the truck in gear if you intend to expand your dormant potential to replace the dull chants of depressive thinking.

Garcia goes on to say that as you challenge your depression, you push yourself past the threshold of inertia. You can reclaim a sense of power that was there all along to discover.

The Five-Minute Plan to Overcome Inertia

Exposure is probably the most effective method for overcoming a strong but irrational fear. The idea behind exposure is simple. You put yourself into a position where you live through your fear feelings until the intensity drops. You can do this in a gradual, or graduated, way or by fully facing the fear. In either event, it's very important that you allow yourself to experience the fear until it becomes less intense. Otherwise, you reinforce self-defeating escapist behavior.

You're afraid of the dark, so you expose yourself to darkness. You can do this in a graduated way by using a dimmer switch to control the intensity of the light, thus putting this process under your control. You also can go into a dark room and sweat it out.

The principle of exposure applies to overcoming the inertia found in procrastination. Here is a practical five-minute technique for cutting through the procrastination barriers rooted in inertia.

Pick a practical activity that you resist doing that is in your interest to do. It can be anything from vacuuming your bedroom to filling out a college application. To break the inertia for the activity, commit yourself to working on it for five minutes. Agree with yourself that you'll start the activity and continue for five minutes (sort of like starting the truck). At the end of the five minutes, you can commit to another five minutes or quit. Repeat the five-minute plan until you're finished or decide to quit.

Once you start an activity, you often will feel an inertial pressure to continue. You can then view overcoming inertia as manageable because you've managed it.

The five-minute plan is a valuable tool for getting your engine started and keeping your truck moving. The plan is based on the dimmer switch idea. You decide the activity. You decide the rate of activity. You control what you do and the pace. Invoke the five-minute plan when you feel bogged down. Practice the plan until it becomes a habit.

What happens when you come to the point in this process where you pause or quit? You might have completed the project, and that is a good reason to quit. You might have more to do. In the latter case, take a few minutes to prepare for the next time you engage in the project. If you've decided to write the great American novel, record a few notes that describe what you plan to do next. By recording what you'll do next, you've given yourself a jump start, and you may find it easier to start again later at a designated time.

Of course, there is nothing magical about five minutes. Some do better working in ten-minute segments, others in half-hour segments, and others by committing effort to the first minute. Generally, small time frames are easier to commit to than longer ones.

For a subgroup of people who use the five-minute method, a quick and brief progress report, done at five-minute intervals, can provide a visual reward for progress and give a rhythm to the activity. For others, the interruption involving such recordings can feel frustrating. If you count yourself among the group where five-minute interval reports are motivational, here is a simple technique.

FIVE-MINUTE REPORT EXERCISE

The following chart maps a five-minute plan in progress. In each box, record what you did during that period. This will give you a visual running tally of your progress. It shows that the task consists of different phases that require time to do, progress is made in bits and pieces, and you can break an inertia that interferes with acting on a task.

Activity: _____

1st five minutes:	2nd five minutes:	3rd five minutes:	4th five minutes:	5th five minutes:
6th five minutes:	7th five minutes:	8th five minutes:	9th five minutes:	10th five minutes:

Although depression is a condition, not a choice, what you do about depression is a choice. The five-minute inertia-breaking plan is a choice to apply procrastination technology to get you going on what's important for you to do.

ABC METHOD FOR DEFUSING LFT DEPRESSIVE THINKING

You feel frustrated because you missed your plane. You tell yourself that you can't stand it. What is the "it" that you can't stand? Is it missing the plane, believing that you can't stand what you don't like, or the inconvenience and frustration? If you tell yourself that you can no longer stand feeling depressed, what is there about depression that is intolerable? The following ABC problem-solving sequence describes how to act against "I can't stand it" LFT distress talk.

Activating event (experience): "A depressed mood."
Rational beliefs about the event: "The mood is unpleasant. I'd prefer to live without it. But it is what it is and will pass when it does."
Emotional and behavioral consequences for the rational beliefs: "Acceptance of the unpleasant mood. An absence of double troubles over the mood."
Irrational LFT beliefs: "I can't stand it. It's too much."
Emotional and behavioral consequences for the irrational LFT beliefs: "Preoccupation with the mood. D-stress over the mood. Diminished tolerance for frustration."
Disputes for irrational LFT beliefs: "(1) Why can I not stand what I don't like (the mood)? Sample answer: I can stand it because I have stood it. But I still don't like experiencing a depressed mood. (2) What is the 'it' that is too much? Sample answer: My belief that I have suffered too long. However, suffering is often extended by dwelling upon the unpleasant. I'll work to grimly accept depression as time limited, debilitating, and unpleasant. I'll do what I can to go about my life with the temporary handicaps that accompany depression."
Effects of the disputes: "Acceptance of depressive mood and frustration about such tensions. Relief from a secondary mental misery imposed over the basic misery of depression. A clearer mind. A lesser preoccupation with the mood of depression. An optimism that depressive negativity can be overridden by rational reason. A corresponding increase in frustration tolerance."

When LFT thinking is linked to your depression, you can use the following chart as a guide to map and counteract this thinking.

Activating event (experience):

Rational beliefs about the event:

Emotional and behavioral consequences for the rational beliefs:

Irrational LFT beliefs:

Emotional and behavioral consequences for the irrational LFT beliefs:

Disputes for irrational LFT beliefs:

Effects of the disputes:

KEY IDEAS AND ACTION PLAN

What are the key ideas that you got from this chapter? What actions can you take?

Key Ideas

What are the key ideas that you found helpful?

1. _____

_____

2. _____

_____

3. _____

_____

Action Plan

What actions can you take to progress?

1. _____

_____

2. _____

_____

3. _____

_____

POSTSCRIPT

In primitive parts of the brain, frustration reactions can exist without formal thought and reason. Witness the reaction of a two-month-old who feels uncomfortable or hungry. Basic emotions such as frustration can trump reason until reason regains a foothold.

LFT self-talk is a cognitive distortion that leads to false predictions. Making these thoughts transparent, then thinking like a skeptic, can help expose false inferences and conclusions. There are some things in life that it pays to distrust. LFT self-talk is one of those things. Distrusting and disputing these thoughts is a prescription for gaining freedom from the stresses associated with them.

CHAPTER 14

Coping with Depressive Sensations

Hippocrates noted that *soma* (the body) can influence our thoughts and behavior. In that sense, our biology can be the activating event for irrational and dysfunctional thinking, as well as for positive and optimistic thinking. Aristotle taught that reason was immortal and independent of all ills and disturbances. Thus, reason could not be attacked by psychological distress or physical illnesses. Who was right, Hippocrates or Aristotle?

There is evidence to support Hippocrates' view. Prior to feeling the physical symptoms of a cold, you might feel cranky, irritable, and snappy. The change in your physical sensations can be a catalyst for the sort of thinking that associates with your irritability. We've all had days when we just felt good and in command, and typical daily annoyances had no influence over a positive mood. When you feel depressed, you may feel too tired and weak to care much about anything. That sense of giving up can reflect how you feel more than it does the other aspects of your life.

Aristotle has a point, though. It is possible to suspend judgment and refuse to capitulate to erroneous thinking when ill or depressed. However, when depressed and thinking depressively, without training, most people don't monitor their thinking sufficiently well to recognize when subjective depressive themes weave through their thoughts. Rather, they experience the thoughts as a reflection of reality. Refusing to capitulate to erroneous depressive thinking helps make reason independent of ills.

Physical sensations can influence your perceptions and color your thoughts. They don't have to, but they typically do. Depressive sensations are not only burdensome, but they can interact with a negative attitude of mind, such as viewing your situation as hopeless. However, logic can override depressive thinking. It takes a special effort to bring your thoughts to where they are not influenced by depressive sensations. That effort can make a positive difference.

RECOGNIZING DEPRESSIVE ATTRIBUTIONS ABOUT SENSATIONS

The unpleasant physical sensations that go with depression dramatically capture your attention (lethargy, numbness, fatigue, weakness, retarded movements, sleep disturbances, backache, headache, appetite, general body tension). These sensations can evoke depressive thinking about these conditions that can promote more unpleasant and stressful bodily sensations. How is this to be explained?

Most of us like to know how things work and why. When experiencing a change in mood, you may look for a reason. This is what is known as attributing causes to explain events. Attributions refer to how we explain things to ourselves. Social psychologist Fritz Heider (1958) is credited with creating attribution theory.

Psychologists Stanley Schacter and Jerome Singer (1962) have shown that we explain our sensations to ourselves. Wake up on the wrong side of the bed one morning and you might look for a reason to explain your mood. Suppose you decide that the reason you feel irritable lies in the poor way that your neighbor relates to you. Now the neighbor's faults swirl through your thoughts. The neighbor becomes the reason for your irritation. When your sense of irritability passes, you stop thinking about the neighbor.

Schacter and Singer propose that emotion is based both on a physical arousal and one's interpretation of that arousal. There are, of course, other catalysts for emotion, such as our perceptions and perspectives about ourselves, others, and life events. Nevertheless, how we label the sensations of depression gives a psychological dimension to this experience. For example, when you interpret a depressed mood to mean you are doomed, you are likely to stay stuck in that view until you recognize the flaws in this thinking and act to change it.

If you label depressive bodily sensations as unpleasant but understandable, this acceptance can shorten their duration and help prevent their recurrence. You may not immediately get over the sensations of depression, but without depressive thinking about these sensations, you can feel emotionally free. Acceptance and tolerance can, in the short term, take away some of the intensity of the depressive experience.

Acceptance and tolerance for unpleasant depressive sensations has a value-added benefit. People recovering from depression are more likely to reactivate negative depressive thinking when their mood changes or when they face setbacks (Ari et al. 1998). If you dramatize the significance of depressive sensations, you are more likely to experience a recurrence of depression (Parker and Parker 2003). Learning to think factually about unpleasant sensations demystifies them and serves as a buffer against them. Learning to reduce your sensitivity to the unpleasant sensations of depression can have a similar effect.

SENSATION SENSITIVITY

Coming like an onrushing tide, the physical sensations of depression are hard to ignore. It is understandable that you can fix on these unpleasant states. Such sensitivity to the sensations of depression is common.

Sensation sensitivity involves focusing attention on unpleasant sensations. Inadvertently putting depression-related bodily sensations under a psychological microscope can intensify them. I know nobody who does this intentionally. Nevertheless, as a species with the ability to categorize, explain, associate, and predict, we are subject to misreading the significance of what we feel—and sometimes to our detriment. Fortunately, we also have the capabilities to self-correct based upon valid new information.

When focused on unpleasant sensations, some may not recognize that they suffer from depression. Instead, they complain about stress, fatigue, appetite, headaches, gastrointestinal problems, a tightness in the chest, constipation, diarrhea, nausea, indigestion, sleep problems, pain in the joints—the list goes on. Multiple physical conditions are common among those with major depression (Simon et al. 1999).

Physical complaints during times of intense depression are common. But such complaints can and do exist independently of depression. It makes sense to determine their significance, and many will get medical examinations for this purpose. However, people with depression who believe they are sick rather than depressed rarely respond to medical treatment for the specific symptom(s). If they do, their response is short lived (Smith 2001).

When your focus is upon negative sensations and physical complaints, separating the physical from the psychological aspects of depression can yield an advantage. You are less likely to "bark up the wrong tree." Here are two questions to aid that separation: To what extent does your depression primarily involve physical sensations? To what extent do your thoughts about the way you're feeling contribute to the magnification of those feelings? Once these two issues are separated and clarified, you may be in a better position to address negative thinking about unpleasant depressive sensations.

A Depressive Sensation and Thinking Cycle

When depressive situations and thinking are connected, the linkage can lead to vicious cycles (Knaus 1982). A negative event can trigger depressive thinking, which activates a depressive mood. An unpleasant arousal can trigger depressive thinking, which, in turn, activates depressive sensations. And so on. The following diagrams describe how these vicious cycles can evolve:

Negative Events ⇒	Depressive Thinking ⇒	Depressive Sensations ⇒
1. goal blocked	"Shouldn't have happened."	anger and despair
2. personal loss	"I'll never recover."	general tension
Depressive Sensations ⇒	Depressive Thinking ⇒	Depressive Sensations ⇒
1. fatigue	"This will never end."	dullness, sluggishness
2. depressed mood	"I can't stand feeling this way."	frustration, agitation
Depressive Appraisal ⇒	Depressive Sensations ⇒	Depressive Thinking ⇒
1. "This will go on forever."	agitation	"I can't do anything to change."
2. "I can't control how I feel."	strain	"I'll never get over this."
Depressive Sensations ⇒	Depressive Thinking ⇒	Depressive Sensations ⇒
1. weakness	helplessness	tension
2. sluggishness	hopelessness	upset stomach

The above examples started with a negative event. But the activating event can be internal, such as a depressed mood. Thus, your mood can evoke negative thinking. You can also get into a spiral where negative events, negative thinking, and negative sensations play off of each other, which can add up to a maelstrom of misery.

Separating Thoughts from Sensations

You can explain sensations in different ways. It can be a biological change within the body. You smell a foul odor. The day is too hot. You have a toothache. Following a vague feeling of tension, you might give yourself a psychological explanation such as "life sucks," you have an unforgiving mate, or you have a dead-end job. But how factual are these psychological attributions when it comes to explaining a vague tension?

Separating sensations from appraisals is a starting point for unraveling this circle of misery if you want to reduce the intensity and durability of depressive sensations that are associated with such thinking. This reconstruction process takes time and practice.

Atlanta psychotherapist Ed Garcia (pers. comm.) says that when depressed, you might wonder, "Why is this happening to me?" This type of question can lead to a "poor me" attitude that takes a negative situation and makes it worse. To separate interpretation from sensation, Garcia suggests that it is often better to ask "*why* is this happening?"

By asking why, you have a greater range of possibilities to choose from. You are now in a position to go from what Garcia calls "soft" to "hard" thinking.

Soft thinking is like a floodlight that covers a broad area. The "why is this happening?" question is a form of soft thinking because you now have a broad range of possibilities to identify and choose among. By starting with soft thinking, you can avoid jumping to conclusions, such as the reason you are depressed is because something is wrong with you.

By first taking a soft-thinking approach, you might put your spotlight on a distressful depressive thought.

> Learning to tolerate and accept depressive sensations serves as both an intervention against depression as well as a means of prevention.

Selecting among the whys is a form of *hard thinking*. This is like focusing a spotlight on a narrower area. By moving from soft to hard thinking, you can examine the most likely explanation for depression and address those conditions you can verify that intensify and extend depression.

Although some physical conditions of depression can be outside of your control, you have a choice as to what you do about the depressive thinking connected to these sensations. By uncoupling depressive thinking from this process, you are in a better position to deactivate it.

RELAXATION INTERVENTIONS

The negative bodily sensations of depression can include stress sensations generating from anxious thoughts, depression about depression, and a variety of false attributions. By substituting relaxation sensations for stress sensations, can you set conditions for more positive thinking?

As depression deepens, and periods where you feel energized decline, ordinary stress can be challenging to manage. As distress over stress extends, the ancient remedy of putting yourself into a less stressful environment where you can "relax" can serve as a proactive step.

Relaxation sensations can mute depressive sensations such as tension. By reducing tension, you reduce the likelihood for depressive thinking. There are many ways to accomplish that result. The following imagery, breathing, meditation, and muscular relaxation techniques can be used to balance depressive bodily sensations with relaxation. This is not a one-shot deal, however. The secret in making these methods useful is in persisting with their use, usually in planned and spaced intervals. The idea is to use them to help yourself recalibrate your body from tense to relaxed.

Breathing for Relaxation

A simple, popular method to promote relaxation involves deep breathing. Here's how: Using your diaphragm, you slowly breathe in, hold your breath for a moment, slowly breath out, wait a few seconds, then breathe in again. Repeat the cycle for two minutes. Follow this approach at least twice a day. If this method helps you to feel relaxed, you are likely to continue with it.

Imagery Relaxation Methods

Those who can see their depression in images ("mud covering my face," "a dark hole I cannot crawl out from") may find relaxation imagery to be a counteracting force. This technique involves imagining relaxing scenes. In theory, as your body feels relaxed, your thoughts are likely to shift from depressive to peaceful.

Perhaps the best scene to imagine is a sensory image that you associate with relaxation. It could be a warm bubble bath or lying in the grass while counting the stars. To use your own sensory image, find a comfortable spot. Conjure and focus on the image. Hold it for about two minutes. If other thoughts intrude, return to the image.

If you find that relaxing imagery balances depressive sensations, you can try the following sensory images by focusing on each for what is a reasonable amount of time for you:

- Can you imagine a soft cloud moving slowly through the blue sky?

- Can you imagine a yellow rose swaying gently in the breeze?

- Can you imagine colorful tropical fish swimming in an aquarium?

- Can you imagine mist lifting slowly from a meadow as the sun breaks the horizon?

- Can you imagine a warm ray of sunlight on your forehead spreading throughout your body?

If this exercise helps you to relax, you might then structure relaxation imagery into your daily activities. Doing this exercise a few times a day for a few minutes can be the start of a process of recalibrating your body by substituting relaxation for tension.

Meditation Relaxation Methods

Meditation is associated with relaxation. To use this method, find a comfortable spot. Sit comfortably and repeat silently to yourself a single-syllable word such as "one" for about five minutes. As you think the word, breathe in and out in cadence. Here's how:

- As you breathe in, think "one" in a humming tone (approximately five seconds).

- As you breathe out, think "one" in a humming tone (approximately five seconds).

- If your mind drifts, go back to this cadenced inner chant as soon as you think to do so.

- Try this exercise for two weeks, twice a day, at a regular time.

The purpose of this meditation relaxation exercise is to answer the question "Is it possible for me to experience a sense of relaxation while meditating?" If the answer is yes, meditation may be worth pursuing.

Muscular Relaxation Methods

Edmund Jacobson's (1929) muscular relaxation method is based upon systematically tensing and relaxing the major muscle groups. To use this method, you seat yourself in a comfortable chair, or you can lie down. You squeeze a muscle group for five seconds, hold the tension for five seconds, then release the tension over the next five seconds until the muscle goes limp. This rhythmic squeezing and relaxing of different muscle groups can progressively lead to a sense of relaxation. Here are the steps:

- Make your hands into fists (slowly tighten, hold, and loosen).

- Close both hands into loose fists. Turn your wrists down until the muscles feel tense.

- Hold your hands out with palms down and stretch out your fingers vertically and horizontally.

- Grip your hands into loose fists and bend your fists down to put tension on your forearms.

- Shake your wrists. Let your fingers flop to loosen them. Then rotate your wrists slowly while tensing them.

- Straighten your arms to tense your triceps.

- Tighten your biceps by turning your elbows up as though you were picking up a heavy weight.

- Tilt your head back, putting gentle pressure on your neck muscles.

- Bend your head forward until your chin touches your chest.

- Gently rotate your head in a circular motion, then slowly bring this motion to a stop.

- Wrinkle your forehead.

- Frown and feel your brow crease.

- Close your eyes and tense your eyelids, keeping the rest of your face relaxed.

- Clench your jaw enough to create a sense of tension.

- Press your tongue against the roof of your mouth.

- Make a "Cheshire cat" type smile to tighten your cheek muscles.

- Shrug your shoulders back until you feel tension in your upper back.

- Shrug your shoulders forward.

- Tense your chest muscles.

- Tighten your abdominal muscles inward.

- Push your belly out so as to make a potbelly.

- Slowly arch your back muscles to produce a sense of tension.

- Tighten your buttocks.

- Flex your thighs.

- Tense your calf muscles by stretching your feet downward.

- Point your toes upward to feel the tension in your shins.

- When you complete this tension and relaxation cycle, imagine your body going limp like a rag doll.

If doing this muscular exercise helps you to relax, then doing muscular relaxation on a regular basis can prove useful to balance tension sensations of depression. By substituting relaxation for tension, this process can help recalibrate your body in a way that fertilizes conditions for clear and positive thinking.

Successful application of relaxation techniques does not take away an overwhelming loss, settle a major conflict, or eliminate an abusive situation. The idea behind using the techniques is to buffer the stress sensations of depression with relaxation as part of a process of helping the mind right itself.

Mobilizing for Action

Relaxation can set the stage for focused actions. When you are faced with a challenge, start with your favorite relaxation method. Follow this with a set of mobilization phrases. Then get into action.

To create a sequence of mobilization phrases, imagine a time when you operated at your peak or did the best you were able to do. This experience could include a sports performance, speaking up for yourself, or solving a challenging problem. Make up pithy phrases that build to a crescendo when you launch into action. Here is an example:

1. "I am feeling relaxed."

2.   "My confidence is growing."

3.   "My thoughts and emotions are focused."

4.   "I express myself decisively."

Once you have created your relaxation and action sequence, test it to see if this combination helps launch constructive actions.

■ *Barbara's Story*

Barbara was married with three children ages six, eight, and ten. She suffered from a mild ongoing depression that worsened at different points in her menstrual cycle. She reported that this irritability started after her first pregnancy. It worsened over the years. She found no medically effective remedy. She reported that her physician had run "every imaginable test and came up empty." She had been in therapy for three years to address her depression. She and her counselor worked to link her depression to early life experiences. She remained depressed.

Barbara experienced depression at two levels. Her ongoing mild depression erupted into a moderately severe depression that occurred every month or two and lasted for a week or more. During this time, she experienced considerable agitation, feelings of being overwhelmed, helplessness, and a sense of being out of control.

She withdrew at times, and her family had to "fend for themselves." At other times she felt agitated and erupted into angry outbursts. During these times, her husband reported that nobody in her family was safe from her "blame attacks."

To establish control over her responses to her ongoing mild depression and blame attacks, Barbara first recorded information to see if the agitated phase of her depression followed a predictable pattern. She marked days on the calendar when she had an anger attack. If she could predict when her depression intensified, she could devise a plan to manage herself during these periods.

Barbara's intensified depression sometimes started five days before her period, but this was inconsistent. However, she practically always recognized some of the early warning signals. She reported, "It was like a wave coming over me. I loved my husband the day before, and suddenly he became a devil. My kids became monsters. I now understand that my feelings have more to do with me than with them."

Once Barbara developed an awareness for the significance of her "wave," she wondered what she could do to disengage from it. A practical tactic involved first, to refuse to find fault and blame, and second, to use a button system.

The button system involved red, yellow, and green pin-on buttons. When she wore the red button, Barbara recognized a wave of tension condition. Her husband and children knew to back away. When Barbara wore a yellow button, this was a caution. On green button days, Barbara felt quite resilient and approachable.

The button exercise served several purposes. Her family stopped blaming themselves for Barbara's depression. It reminded her to stop blaming them. She saw herself as having control through deciding on what button to wear. The red and yellow buttons reminded her to think about her thinking. This process increased her sense of control.

Following successful use of the button system, Barbara obtained a part-time job. She had not worked for ten years. Now that all of her children attended preschool or school, she thought she could handle a part-time job. She joined an aerobics dance class. She previously enjoyed dancing. She soon came to look forward to that routine. Within a few months, her depression diminished. Simultaneously, the frequency and length of red button times significantly declined.

ABC METHOD FOR DERAILING IRRATIONAL THINKING ABOUT UNPLEASANT SENSATIONS

Acceptance is a typical first step in a process to lessen the intensity, frequency, and duration of depression—but it will not eliminate it. Acceptance of depressive sensations makes the experience more tolerable, and you can find added energy to advance your campaign against depression.

Positive change in this area is often measured by a diminishing strength of the sensations, their frequency, and how long they last. Acceptance suggests that you have developed a realistic perspective about the time it takes to change.

The following chart shows how to apply the ABC method to negative thinking about unpleasant depressive sensations.

Activating event (experience): "A sensation of general tension."
Rational beliefs about the event: "I don't like how I feel."
Emotional and behavioral consequences for the rational beliefs: "Acceptance of unpleasant depressive sensations."
Irrational beliefs about depressive sensations: "I can't control these feelings. They will go on forever. It's hopeless."
Emotional and behavioral consequences for the irrational beliefs: "Dullness. Sluggishness. Frustration. Agitation."
Disputes for irrational beliefs: "(1) Why is it necessary to control depressive sensations? Sample answer: This would be preferable, but not necessary. Accepting the sensations for what they are eliminates the sort of helplessness thinking that magnifies them. (2) Where is the proof that the negative sensations of depression will go on forever? Sample answer: Forever is a long time. Many things can happen between now and then, including a breakthrough plan for permanently lifting the mood and stress sensations of depression. There is no proof that depression will persist without abatement. (3) What is the 'it' that is hopeless? Sample answer: Does 'it' refer to your ability to think clearly? There is sound reason to believe that people can develop clear-thinking skills. Does the 'it' mean that tension is terminal? If so, where is the proof? In short, clarify what 'it' is first. Next, look at what you mean by 'hopeless,' and look for alternative opportunities. Chances are you'll find loopholes in hopelessness thinking."
Effects of the disputes: "Reduced frustration. Improved tolerance for tension. Decreased negative thinking about unpleasant depressive sensations. A lessening of depression."

When negative thinking about depressive sensations is linked with your depression, use the following chart as a guide to map and counteract this thinking.

Activating event (experience):
Rational beliefs about the event:
Emotional and behavioral consequences for the rational beliefs:
Irrational beliefs about depressive sensations:
Emotional and behavioral consequences for the irrational beliefs:
Disputes for irrational beliefs:
Effects of the disputes:

KEY IDEAS AND ACTION PLAN

What are the key ideas that you got from this chapter? What actions can you take?

Key Ideas

What are the key ideas that you found helpful?

1. _____

   _____

2. _____

   _____

3. _____

   _____

Action Plan

What actions can you take to progress?

1. _____

   _____

2. _____

   _____

3. _____

   _____

POSTSCRIPT

Occam's razor is a philosophical and scientific rule that holds the simplest of two or more competing causes is always the preferable explanation. For example, explanations for depressive sensations can include helplessness as the cause. This simple explanation may reduce uncertainty about what is happening, but it is like falling into a swamp. A more balanced explanation is that depression is unpleasant, and helplessness thinking is correctable. The sensations of depression are a sign of depression, nothing more.

You have the ability to think and learn in multiple ways. But exercising that capability means that you have to make choices. One choice is to accept and tolerate unpleasant depressive sensations without judging yourself for experiencing them.

CHAPTER 15

Dealing with
Emotional Stresses

Under ordinary circumstances, people lead complex lives, so an uncomplicated depression is exceptional. Just like you can have a headache and upset stomach at the same time, you can have a depression mingling with other troublesome states, such as perfectionism, low frustration tolerance, sensation sensitivity, anxiety, panic, trauma, anger, guilt, and shame. That's the bad news.

There is good news. You can address and defuse mixed emotional states that can coexist with depression through boosting your awareness of these processes and acting to defuse their impact.

The cognitive and behavioral methods in this workbook apply to a broad range of cognitively based stresses, such as anxiety. It is a good probability that you will experience one or more of these coexisting conditions either before or during the time you feel depressed. Although they add to the complexities of depression, you can parcel them out and address them separately. Such actions can improve your chances for defusing stresses related to depression, decrease unpleasant sensations that can aggravate depression, reduce the risk of relapse, and help prepare you to lead a happier, stress-free life. As anxiety appears to be the most common emotional accompaniment of depression, it's a good place to start.

ANXIETY AND DEPRESSION

Depression is often complicated by distressful emotional conditions such as anxiety (Stein, McQuaid, and Laffaye 1999).

- About 60 percent of those with a major depression have an earlier history of anxiety (Judd et al. 1998).

- Mixed depression and anxiety contributes to higher levels of work and social handicap, slower recovery, and a higher relapse rate (Sartorius et al. 1996).

- Addressing common cognitive features in anxiety and depression opens opportunities for an economy of effort that can reverse both conditions.

Anxiety is an apprehensive state of mind and body that includes vigilance and physical sensations such as heart palpitations, a sinking stomach, and sweating. It can range from butterflies in the stomach to terror. This vigilant state signals you to avoid a potential danger. You might tense at the thought of walking home alone after midnight. That is a rational form of anxiety, and your avoidance would be both appropriate and helpful. However, if you tense at the thought of giving a talk in front of a friendly group and start sweating and dodge the opportunity, you are responding to a misguided signal. Your avoidance is inappropriate and probably counterproductive in the long run. Although debilitating, this anxiety is correctable.

When anxiety revolves around imaginary fears, this irrational form of anxiety (i-anxiety) can have an emotionally handicapping effect. Like the other stress emotions described within this chapter, i-anxiety is an emotive cognition because this experience is strongly associated with irrational thoughts. By changing these cognitions, you can gain considerable relief from the tensions associated with them.

Anticipating a real danger relates to safety and survival. I-anxiety relates to imagined catastrophes involving social situations that have little to do with physical safety. In this tense state of mind, you may worry too much about your status, image, performance, and so forth. For example, Mike worries that he will lose his job. He's been worried about this possibility for several years now. Despite good performance reviews, he continues to fear the worst. One day when his supervisor walked past him without appearing to notice him, he jumped to the conclusion that he was going to be fired. His stomach became tied in knots. He had trouble sleeping that night as the thought of the possible job loss kept buzzing through his mind. The next day, his supervisor appeared in good spirits. He wasn't fired. He felt relief. This type of anxious worry prompted Mark Twain to quip, "I've had many troubles in my life, most of which didn't happen."

If you've experienced i-anxiety, the chances are that you've experienced many of the following:

- feelings of tension and difficulty in relaxing

- moodiness, irritability, and grouchiness

- difficulties falling or staying asleep

- expecting to make mistakes and being harshly judged (evaluation anxiety)

- diminished spontaneity

- procrastination

- fear of disapproval

- sense of inability to cope effectively

- difficulty in paying attention and concentrating

- worrisome fears that the worst can happen

- feeling "uptight"

- self-consciousness

- experiencing one crisis after another

- believing you are at the center of attention when you want to fade into the background

Depression, Anxiety, and Powerlessness

Depression and anxiety have related *cognitive signatures*, or predictable, telltale patterns of thought (Knaus 2002). Both states commonly include irrational thoughts of powerlessnesss, self-doubts, and self-downing.

A combination of anxiety and depression involves threats (anxiety) and loss (depression) that intertwine and reflect a sense of powerlessness, help-lessness, and worthlessness. With anxious tensions on the rise and depressive voices crying out, a sense of worthlessness emerges. Often this process starts with a catastrophic conclusion.

John saw the stock market tank one morning and alarmed himself with the thought that he would lose his retirement money. This catastrophic pro-nouncement extended into another. He saw himself as ill and handicapped with no one to help him. Because he was going to be poor, he caterwauled to

> Depression brings inertia and lethargy. Anxiety begets tension, fear, and inhibition. When combined, each state represents a different projection of avoidance, inertia, and discontent.

himself about how he was destined to suffer in silence without hope. Since he could do nothing about the market, he viewed himself as powerless to change his destiny. He felt worthless, thinking that since he was not smart enough to predict the market he would not have the intelligence to survive the crash. Then the market rebounded and his sense of depression decreased.

In i-anxiety, there is an imagined future danger and sense of helplessness about coping. In a depressed state of mind, your future thoughts are normally pessimistic. However, if you thought you could ably cope, you would be unlikely to experience either i-anxiety or depressive pessimism.

If you experience both anxiety and depression, here is some good news. Cognitive and behavioral methods for dealing with depressive thinking apply to dealing with anxious thinking. Many of the techniques available for dealing with depression also apply to i-anxiety.

Countering Anxiety

When you feel both anxious and depressed, listen for catastrophizing, self-downing, and help-lessness self-talk. Observe if these thoughts and anxiety sensations play off of each other. If you catch these thoughts in motion, you are in a position to question the logic behind the beliefs, examine realistic alternative views, and break the circle.

Most people prefer that others think well of them. This is a normal social desire. However, if you must have others' approval to feel worthy, this belief sets the stage for i-anxiety. If you fall into this need-for-approval trap, here are some questions: How does it follow that other people's approval or disapproval defines you? How does disapproval change the essence of you?

Look for loopholes in anxious logic. For example, what is your basic premise? If you think you are unworthy, then expand upon the issue. What does "unworthy" mean? What is your secondary premise? Do you believe you can be harmed because of your unworthiness? Expand upon the issue by asking and answering questions such as "harmed in what way?" If your conclusion is that you can't cope, look for exceptions.

Suppose you believe that you are generally powerless to protect yourself and thus vulnerable to harm. Here are some thoughts and suggestions:

- Although you may not control your destiny as fully as you wish, you still have choices. These choices involve decisions. You decide whether or not to brush your teeth. You decide to pull five weeds from a garden, open a book, or buy a loaf of bread. When you have choices, you make decisions. When you make decisions, you are not powerless.

- Put out birdseed for your feathered friends. Give a few dollars to a favored charity. Doing so illustrates that there are things in life that you can control.

- Ratchet it up. If you think you are too passive, read materials on assertion. Pick a basic exercise. Test the exercise.

- Redefine your i-anxiety as "speculation."

- Eliminate "failure" from your vocabulary. Look at your self-development actions as experiments. In an experiment, there is no failure. You learn what works and what doesn't.

- Write a poem about the power of worry. Here is an example: "Speculate, speculate, think about the worst that can eventuate." Here the idea is to poke fun at the anxious idea, not at yourself.

Through doing the above exercises, you position yourself to make a radical shift in your thinking from powerlessness to empowerment. The following exercise provides a structured way to address irrational powerlessness thinking.

CHALLENGING ANXIOUS THOUGHTS

List some examples of your i-anxious thoughts. Then challenge this thinking with techniques you've learned in this book, and record some rational thoughts that you believe give perspective on your situation.

Personal examples of i-anxious powerlessness thinking:

Challenges for i-anxious thinking:

Rational thoughts that lead to a broader perspective:

PANIC AND DEPRESSION

Have you ever suffered a sudden and intense fear associated with a pounding heart and a choking sensation where you have difficulty breathing? As the wave crests, you might grasp your chest fearing that the chest tightness you experience is the start of a heart attack. You feel shortness of breath, shaky, dizzy, or light-headed. You feel nauseated and think you are going to vomit. Your stomach might cramp, and your legs can tighten. You break into a sweat, experience hot flashes, or have chills. If you've experienced a similar dramatic combination of sensations, you've experienced a panic reaction.

Some people with panic have visited emergency wards over fifty times with the fear of having a heart attack. The physical evidence wasn't there, but the panic over that possibility was. As a precaution, you may already have had a medical examination to rule out coronary heart disease or another medical condition.

People in panic often fear a loss of control, feel detached from reality, think they are going crazy, and believe they face imminent death. You might think you are never going to get better and that your condition is unescapable. You might feel so frightened that you cry. And while you may not experience all of these unpleasant sensations, if you experience four or more of them, the chances are that you've experienced panic.

Because people are psychologically, biologically, and socially different, what goes into one person's panic may differ in form and degree from another's. However, palpitations and gasping for breath are common panic sensations that are normally experienced as threatening.

More than 50 percent of those who suffer from panic reactions eventually experience a major depressive episode (Tsao, Lewin, and Craske 1998). If you count yourself among the panic and depression group, the good news is that you have an excellent chance to overcome panic by using cognitive and behavioral methods (Ruhmland 2001). This is the gold standard for relieving panic. Using cognitive behavioral approaches with panic can yield relatively quick results (Penava et al. 1998).

Cued and Uncued Panic

Panic can be cued or uncued. In *cued panic*, certain situations such as smells, sights, or sounds can trigger panic. If you have had a near death experience, an associated sound can later trigger panic. A Vietnam veteran may automatically drop to the ground in panicked fear when hearing a helicopter overhead. He once heard the whirring sound of helicopter blades as he saw an enemy combatant lunge at him and thrust a bayonet into his shoulder.

Uncued panic is panic that comes out of the blue. However, if you monitor yourself when you experience the onset of panic, chances are you'll find sensory cues, such as a general weakness or a slight change of mood. These sensory changes could be caused by many things such as a flip-flop in your blood sugar or increases in stress hormones from recent conflicts. You might interpret a rapid heartbeat to mean "I'm going to die." Then fearing that your panic can hasten your demise, you could panic over your panic by thinking that you are doing yourself in, but that you can't stop.

Some who experience panic sensations go about their business without panicking about the panic. On the other hand, the dramatic change in the intensity of sensations associated with your life support processes invites catastrophic interpretations. This includes panicking over the panic.

Unexpected panic reactions can be especially troublesome. You simply can't predict when they will occur. Nevertheless, understanding the panic process can demystify it and make it less fearsome. You are also less likely to panic about the panic. If you know about the physical reactions that go with panic and know that they are normal for this type of state, there is no real need to worry.

Having the facts about the psychological and physical symptoms of panic reduces fears about panic (Rees, Richards, and Smith 1999). Knowledge about how the sensations of panic work can help diffuse a panic in motion, but it can also serve as a relapse prevention measure (DiFilippo and Overholser 1999).

Cognitive Ways to Address Panic

Panic is normally experienced as a dramatic change in a combination of normal sensations. Yet, there is no real physical danger in the sensations of panic. If you know that the sensations are not dangerous and will soon pass, you are less likely to panic over experiencing panic. But there can be no doubt that the combination of dramatic physical sensations compel attention. Here is some information about panic that can help put it into perspective, and decrease its frequency and impact.

In a panicked state, you are likely to feel dizzy. In the wake of this sensation, fear of fainting is common. Although dizziness can ordinarily correlate with fainting, during a panic reaction, it is highly unlikely that you will faint. There is a physical basis for this observation. With a rapid heartbeat, more blood rushes to your brain, which counterindicates fainting. Fainting occurs with a slow heartbeat and with less blood traveling to the brain.

The quickened heartbeat experienced in panic is dramatic compared to a resting heart rate. A dramatic change in perspective about your heart rate is likely to be more alarming than your actual heart rate would indicate, however. By taking your pulse and measuring your heart rate, you will probably discover that it is about what you'd expect if you were moderately exercising. Experientially obtaining data on your heart rate during panic can lead to a change in your thinking about the significance of this change.

Here are some suggestions for what to do if you feel panicked:

Relabel the panic sensations as a "temporary nervous system reaction." This relabeling can put panic sensations into perspective.

As you might deal with depressive thinking, you can outsmart panic thinking. Panic thinking includes such ideas as "I'm going to look like a fool in public." "I'll never be right again." "I can't cope with this experience." "I'm going to go crazy or die." You can outsmart such panic thinking with logic. Here is a sample approach:

- Next time you panic, count the number of people who focus their attention on you. The likelihood is that people around you will not notice you panicking. The sensations you find so dramatic are not dramatically visible to a casual observer.

- Ask yourself whether you have a crystal ball that tells you for certain that you will never feel right again. (If you really believed this prognostication, would you bet your home, automobile, or all your future earnings on the proposition that "I'll never feel right again"?)

- If you could cope, what would you do that is different? Even if you can't cope effectively enough in a specific situation, how is that a problem in other situations?

- Millions of people who experience panic think they are going crazy or will die. They don't go crazy. They don't die. (When you map out panicking about panic sensations in advance of their occurrence, this understanding can position you to assert greater control over the panic process.) Reassure yourself that, while very unpleasant, you will not die or go crazy from experiencing a panic reaction.

■   You can use the ABC method to create a blueprint for change that you can follow to help yourself blunt a panic reaction. See the sample at the end of this chapter.

Behavioral Methods for Addressing Panic

Behavioral strategies for addressing panic can be highly effective. Let's start with four basic techniques:

Get adequate exercise.   This often results in greater cardiac efficiency, increased lung capacity, the build up of endorphins (the natural feel-good brain chemical), physical confidence, improved body image, a boost in serotonin levels, and so forth. Exercise may take several weeks to start to show effects. However, exercise is not a guarantee to overcoming panic reactions. For example, athletes, such as National Football League running back Earl Campbell, can have panic reactions while in excellent physical condition. Exercise, however, raises the probability of reducing panic related to depression and depression that is related to panic.

Watch your breathing.   Some people with panic breathe about twice as rapidly as normal. Often breathing using the muscles of the chest, they forget to use their diaphragm in breathing. When this happens, psychological and physiological signs of apprehension can appear. To address this process, intentionally use your diaphragm when breathing. See if this helps override hyperventilation. For example, pretend that your stomach is a balloon. When you breathe in, your stomach expands. When you breathe out, it contracts. Experience the sensations of breathing in and out in a rhythmic way. When you breathe in, think the word "relax." As you breathe out, think the phrase "I'm going to be fine."

Exhale into a small paper bag.   The body's carbon dioxide level is thought to sometimes trigger a sensor in the brain that sends out signals that start a panic cycle. A technique for interrupting a panic reaction involves fooling the carbon dioxide detection sensor. Exhaling into a small paper bag for two or three minutes sometimes helps. Some people cup their hands over their faces and breathe into their cupped hands.

Time it.   Although the sensations of panic can be dramatic and terrifying, they are relatively short-lived. Panic sensations normally fade within one to ten minutes. But even a short-lived panic reaction can seem like eternity. To test this hypothesis, the next time you panic, look at your watch when the sensations start. Then check your watch again as the sensations subside. If you know that panic is time limited, this knowledge can counteract fearful thinking that the panic will never end. And forcefully remind yourself of the transitory nature of panic both during and between panic reactions.

Psychologist David Barlow (2004) asserts that different forms of distress may take different combinations of interventions to correct. He reports that you can help yourself overcome panic reactions through simulating some of the sensations of panic. Using these behavioral exposure methods, you reproduce the sensations of panic for purposes of calming yourself about each one. By taking planned steps to expose yourself to the different sensations of panic, you can teach yourself to avoid panicking over panic sensations.

Exposure exercises are practice sessions that involve evoking separate panic sensations and getting used to them without panicking. For example, dizziness and difficulty breathing are simple to duplicate. By parceling out these sensations, you can show yourself that the sensations are tolerable.

Although exposure techniques are ordinarily done in the presence of a skilled therapist, you can do the following exercises to determine if exposure methods hold promise.

- Demonstrate to yourself that you can survive the sort of dizziness that you experience during a panic reaction. Spin yourself around several times in a revolving chair to show yourself that however dizzy you get, the worst you'll feel is dizzy. You are not out of control!

- Simulate a hyperventilating experience. This can show you that shortness of breath in panic lasts only so long before you start breathing normally. For example, pinch your nose shut and breath through a straw for about a minute. This simulates the sensation of gasping for air. By desensitizing yourself to this sensation, you'll have one less symptom to fear.

You can include separating rational from irrational beliefs with exposure exercises. For example, if you believe that you'll lose control if you try to simulate panic in any phase of an exposure exercise, and that would be awful, examine the prediction. Question why it would be so bad to panic. Remind yourself that you've survived previous panics. Reassure yourself that the purpose of simulating conditions of panic is to desensitize yourself to the sensations that you associate with the panic.

A therapist can make these assurances to you, which can help reduce any anticipatory panic that you are likely to experience. However, self-initiated exposure exercises can have a more positive effect when you couple them with your own reassurances to yourself that you can survive the experience. Through this reassurance and your understanding of the intent of the exercise, you reduce the risk of panic and panicking over panic. In short, you act as your own therapist.

CHALLENGING PANIC THINKING

List some examples of your panic thoughts that you believe are irrational. Then challenge this panic thinking with techniques you've learned in this book and record some rational thoughts that you believe give perspective to your situation.

Personal examples of panic thinking:

Challenges for panic over panic thinking:

Rational thoughts that lead to a broader perspective:

TRAUMA AND DEPRESSION

Just as depression is an equal opportunity condition (people at all levels of society are eligible), people who develop what is called post-traumatic stress disorder (PTSD) come from all walks of life. Following a traumatic event, PTSD involves distressing images, thoughts, perceptions, dreams, flashbacks of the event, irritability, difficulties concentrating, sleep disorders, or a strong physical response to event-related cues. Such reactions can start immediately or months after the tragic incident(s), and this type of experience can trigger a fear of reexperiencing the trauma of the flashback.

What constitutes a traumatic event? Traumatic events include a job loss, a sudden death of a loved one, a violent assault, a financial setback, a natural disaster (losing a home due to a fire or storm), witnessing a crime or accident, early life stress, being in a combat war zone, and childhood sexual, verbal, or physical abuse.

Robert Moore (pers. comm.), a Florida marriage and family therapist, tells us that depression is sometimes a lingering aftereffect of a traumatic event. He goes on to say that "trauma is just the clinical term now used for the memory of a loss that continues to trigger sad feelings more than a reasonable while afterward."

According to the National Comorbidity Survey, people experiencing a catastrophic or traumatic event are eight times more likely to experience depression (Kessler, Davis, and Kendler 1997). Cognitive and behavioral therapies are effective for people suffering from the psychological aftermath of trauma (Harvey, Bryant, and Tarrier 2003).

Managing the Cognitions About Trauma

Following a traumatic event, a range of responses are possible. Believing that you did all you could under the circumstances is generally a positive response. Even if you believe that you could have done more, you can still conclude that imperfection is part of being human, and Monday morning quarterbacking can't change what happened. That conclusion is also positive. However, if months after the event your mind keeps retracing the horror, and you believe that you have failed in some way, and you retreat into a world of hopelessness, then you need to address these thoughts.

When the past is gone, all the "should haves" or negative self-statements over what happened won't put Humpty Dumpty together again. Grief and loss continue on their own volition. But when trauma rebounds, some distressful memories, images, and beliefs erupt that can be addressed.

PTSD often includes an etching of the experience onto the amygdala, the part of the brain that controls the fight-or-flight response. Through exposure to trauma-related sensations and accompanying emotive cognitions, you can train other parts of the brain to switch on and override a primitive amygdala reaction. This often involves working through the process using the ABC method to boost your chances for reducing or eliminating the associated raw nerve reactions.

Despite the power of trauma recollections and reactions, you can change your perspective on aspects of this process, even though the original event(s) and memories remain the same. While the event happened in the past, the upset is in the present moment. That is because of present-moment associations with painful images and sensations and because of irrational beliefs about these conditions as well as about the original event(s). It is in this theater of the mind that you come to grips with the meaning of the event and the feelings of terror or horror that accompanied it.

If you experience depression from trauma, the following exercise can be a start in the journey of managing the emotive cognitions of trauma:

- List examples of trauma thinking ("I can't cope with this experience." "I can't stand it." "I am a weak person.")

- Examine what you mean when you tell yourself such things as "I can't cope with this experience."

- Start with clarifications. What does "can't cope" mean? How does it apply in this instance? What are the exceptions to this line of thought? For example, is it possible to learn to live with a disaster without feeling consumed by it? By contrasting catastrophic self-talk with constructive alternatives, you can take away distress while grimly accepting this past experience.

If you are among the millions suffering from PTSD who also suffer from depression, do the following exercise to see if you can start to move yourself in the direction of freedom from the unpleasant sensations, thoughts, and images that accompany this stressful state.

CHALLENGING TRAUMA THINKING

List some examples of your trauma thoughts that you believe are irrational. Then challenge this trauma thinking with techniques you've learned in this book and record some rational thoughts that you believe give perspective to your situation.

Personal examples of irrational trauma thinking:

Challenges for trauma thinking:

Rational thoughts that lead to a broader perspective:

ANGER AND DEPRESSION

Between 30 to 40 percent of those suffering from dysthymic or major depressions are likely to simultaneously experience elevated states of anger. A depressed mood elevates the risk for anger (Harkness et al. 2002). This anger often finds expression in verbal or physical abuse (Koh, Kim, and Park 2002). The percentage of those experiencing anger may be higher among people with bipolar depression (Benazzi 2003).

The Freudian theory that depression is anger turned inward has many exceptions and is no longer a primary explanation for depression (Cox, Stabb, and Hulgus 2000). When anger is coupled with depression, this pattern often blends helplessness and hopelessness with patterns of internalizing and externalizing blame.

Depression appears to carry an increased vulnerability for anger that can mimic the physical and psychological sensations of panic. In this form of anger, the physical sensations include shortness of breath, sweating, or a racing heart. Psychological factors include fear of loss of control. But unlike panic, which feels like collapsing within, this facsimile of panic involves lashing out. These anger reactions are sudden, intensive, and inappropriate to the situation (Fava and Rosenbaum 1999).

Perfectionism, Blame, and Anger

Emotions can be divided into pleasant and unpleasant groupings. These hardwired reactions can further be subdivided into primary emotions such anger, sadness, and fear. Anger, or displeasure, is a hardwired emotion that probably came about through evolution to enhance survival. In primitive times, anger was probably an emotional catalyst for an aggressive expression to ward off enemies. In contemporary society, anger more often is a reaction to perceived unfairness or to threats to your image or way of life. This expression can be functional, but more often it grows from irrational ideas, such as "I should have my way, and anyone who doesn't give me what I want should be roasted." This form of anger is irrational (i-anger), as there is no universal law that says that you should be entitled to total obedience. What if everyone thought the same way?

In a complex society, anger is common. Some anger over the frustration of reasonable expectations is understandable, such as a friend stealing your wallet. The expectation is that friendship and trust are connected, and anger reflects a breach of that connection. Some forms of socially oriented anger, however, involve extensions of blame. Practically everyone has thought at one time or heard someone else say, "He shouldn't have done that. He's an idiot!" Blame extensions, such as declaring someone an idiot, reflect irrational expectations and demands that these expectations be met. Irrational anger includes the need to punish.

It is the damning form of blame that separates displeasure from irrational anger. If you don't like what someone has done, you are likely to experience displeasure. I-anger goes beyond displeasure. For example, if you have expectations for others that they don't meet, and then grow angry when your wishes are thwarted, you may have inadvertently extended blame into intolerance, condemnation, and punishment. This i-anger appears in many guises: brooding, irritability, resentment, vengefulness, intolerance, derogation, whining, crankiness, grouchiness, spitefulness, and outbursts.

As is typical for many depressed people, anger can be self-directed, such as when you demand perfection from yourself, feel intolerant about your failings, and then condemn yourself for real or imagined faults. In this state of internalized blame, you may doubt and down yourself for what you believe are your weaknesses, faults, or inability to control important events. You might blame yourself for failing to live up to your expectations. You might believe that you should act with perfect consistency. You may believe that you are only as good as what you accomplish and that what you accomplish is not good. Falling short of meeting perfectionist expectations, you are inclined to blame and degrade yourself. This perfection-linked inward directed anger can be as much of a sign of depression as a cause.

When i-anger blends with depression, short fuses are common. When your stress tolerance is low, such things as waiting too long in line, witnessing someone violate the rules, seeing trash on the street, or hearing a leaky faucet can trigger anger thinking. When powerful negative mood sensations surge through the body, they too can trigger i-anger thoughts.

Contending with I-Anger

If you count yourself among those experiencing anger and depression, the good news is that i-anger is recognizable and addressable. Assuming that you are interested in quelling i-anger, there are many ways to help yourself accomplish this result. You can disrupt the process through distracting yourself, such as by taking a walk. You can wait for the anger to subside through the passage of time. You can also seek new information and more effectively identify and question i-anger assumptions.

Seeking new information and identifying and questioning i-anger assumptions is a way to override and then to prevent i-anger. Here is an approach for addressing this emotive cognition.

1. Map the links in the anger-blame chain by identifying the situation and associated beliefs.

2. Separate legitimate from fictional blame. Legitimate blame is where there is a clear fault for a visible action or accident in which you can assign accountability and consequences. Fictional blame involves violations to your personal codes, where others can have rational, alternative views. You believe in saving every penny you earn. Your mate believes that spending for luxuries is desirable. You blame and condemn your mate for holding to a different view.

3. Address legitimate matters of blame through corrective action.

4. Question fictionalized blame through challenging its validity. For example, if you think that anyone who disturbs you deserves to roast, do some perspective flipping. Think about whether you'd deserve to be roasted for the same reason. If so, why? If not, why not?

5. Hold yourself and others accountable for truly blameworthy acts. But focus on the act rather than on the person.

CHALLENGING I-ANGER THINKING

List some examples of your i-anger thoughts. Then challenge this i-anger thinking with techniques you've learned in this book and record some rational thoughts that you believe give perspective to your situation.

Personal examples of i-anger thinking:

Challenges for i-anger thinking:

Rational thoughts that lead to a broader perspective:

DEPRESSION AND GUILT

During periods of depression, a subgroup of people who suffer from depression are also sensitive to emotions that commonly link to our social world, such as humiliation, embarrassment, and guilt. Each of these social-emotional experiences relates to a perspective on the self that involves self-consciousness. For example, you may feel embarrassed if you are made the brunt of someone's joke. You might experience shame if you eat alone at a restaurant and think that others see you as a loser. You might feel guilt if you think you have wrongfully offended someone. You might feel humiliated if you spill a drink on someone at a party and think that you made a fool of yourself.

When you experience rational guilt, this says that you recognize that you intentionally acted badly and that you have ethical or moral values and a conscience. Recognizing fault and making amends is a culturally prescribed way to rectify harm. The idea is to do the best you can to take corrective action. In this sense, guilt in the form of regret is socially functional, especially when this state motivates corrective actions.

Irrational guilt (i-guilt) is a radically different state of mind. I-guilt is peppered with perfectionism that often includes irrational demands and extensions of blame thinking. For example, you believe that you should not have done what you did and are both culpable and worthless. This view automatically superimposes a sense of self-condemnation over regret. It is the element of regret and worthlessness that differentiates i-guilt from i-anger.

Irrational guilt can feel devastating to the person who is trapped in this emotional state. The related self-condemnation is consistent with internally directed i-anger and worthlessness thinking. From a self-development standpoint, extracting the surplus meaning from this emotive cognition can alleviate a particularly unpleasant form of distress.

Contending with I-Guilt

Depression and i-guilt commonly involve perfectionist demands and worthlessness thoughts that you are only one way—a bad person! You can use i-guilt feelings as a signal to examine and question this line of thinking. For example, through this examination process, determine how you're a worthless person for erring. Convince yourself that even if you acted poorly, self-condemnation rarely leads to self-improvement, nor does it rectify a wrong. Recognize that both correction and self-improvement are rarely fostered following i-guilt. Such a global self-rating is illogical. For example, you cannot both be a complex changing person and, at the same time, worthless.

The purpose of the following exercise is to promote responsibility and to disengage from the extensions of blame that are part of i-guilt thinking.

CHALLENGING I-GUILT THINKING

List some personal examples of i-guilt thinking. Contrast them with constructive alternative thinking. For example, if you think you are a worthless person who deserves punishment, can you think of reasons to accept yourself while condemning your behavior? Challenge any negative thinking that is global, such as thinking you can only be one way—worthless. This is a fiction of the mind. Record new thoughts that you believe can give you a broader perspective.

Personal examples of i-guilt thinking:

Challenges for i-guilt thinking:

Rational thoughts that lead to a broader perspective:

SHAME AND DEPRESSION

Shame is a complex social emotion that involves self-consciousness, humiliation, and stress. When you feel shame, your entire self may seem tarnished.

Shame is a typical part of living within a society and can be functional. Following a wrongful or foolish behavior, shame is common. When you can avoid wrongful or foolish acts, you reduce the risk of social censure, blame, and shame. Accepting that you are also only human and cannot control the universe can lead to feeling uncomfortable following a public foible, without experiencing a global sense of worthlessness that is typically associated with shame.

Leading a reasonably ethical life, you'll have less to feel shame over, and you may rarely experience this emotion. By treating others with respect, you are less likely to experience the sort of social censure risked by those who act contemptuously and disrespectfully toward others. However, into everyone's life, occasions arise where it is in their best interest to take a firm stand and to speak with an unwavering truth that can disadvantage others. Such situations commonly occur when there is an irreconcilable conflict of basic interests. Rarely will anyone experience shame under such circumstances. Here the difference between shame and assertion lies in intention and perspective.

Shame is inane when it derives from self-consciousness–evoking conditions that are primarily meaningful to the individual but not to most reasonable persons:

- You are ashamed of the shape of your nose. When you look into a mirror, you focus on your nose. Then, you think ill of your entire self.

- You think you have to keep your body fat below 11 percent of your total weight to look right to the public. Your body fat goes to 13 percent. You wear baggy clothes to hide your shape. Meanwhile, you binge eat to avoid thinking about yourself and then feel ashamed of yourself for binge eating.

- You feel shame because your neighbor has a newer automobile, your children's grades don't match your expectations, or you are too short, tall, skinny, or fat, or the person you are dating isn't drop-dead handsome.

Although shame can exist without language, our "shoulds" can spark a global sense of shame-related worthlessness. Thinking that you should be perfect, you might experience shame if you made what you thought was a dumb-sounding statement.

When shame thoughts are active, they compound the misery of depression. When you're depressed, inane shame can aggravate depression, and depression can increase your sensitivity to inane shame.

Inane shame reflects the sort of reasoning that can easily slide beneath your rational radar. When this happens, it is not accessible to self-correction.

In depression, inane shame can be circular. Here is an example of this circularity: "I have an unusual nose. That is why I feel depressed. I feel depressed because I have an unusual nose." In a depressed state of mind, the inane can sound rational. However, you can expose the folly in this circularity by flipping the issue about and asking such questions as "Does depression cause my nose to look as it does?"

Inane shame can be an offshoot of the blame game, where a person or group attempts to control another through blame and shame. For example, Mother tells Johnny that he should be ashamed of himself for getting a C in math, as that disgraces the family. She adds, "You can do better than that."

And because she thinks he can do better, she implies that he should. This combination of should and shame can fertilize self-doubts and self-downing.

Some people lead lives where they are prone to experience shame. This form of self-consciousness can arise from social training where early on you learn what is wrong with you, and have little positive feedback to fall back upon. Shame-sensitive people tend to recall negative messages, such as "You'll never amount to anything." "You are a useless burden." "You're a failure." "You can't do anything right." "You look like a slob."

The founder of multimodal therapy, Arnold Lazarus (pers. comm.), notes, "To my mind the shame game is predicated on views that are inculcated by parents and teachers. Nevertheless, it is far better, I think, to have someone who is capable of shame than to deal with psychopaths who have none."

Contending with Inane Shame

One way to deal with inane shame is to introduce chaos into inane shame thinking by challenging the self-conscious ideas associated with it. For example, if you are caught in an embarrassing moment and hear yourself say, "I'll never live this down," take a second look at this self-statement. The idea "I'll never live this down" is the type of statement you can challenge. You can shift from such a shame perspective by

- Balancing cultural shame phrases with another common cultural phrase such as "life goes on." Then, consider which statement has the greater validity.

- Evoking a musical contrast, such as putting some music to a phrase: "When dawn next comes, that shame is done." (Some of my clients have made progress by mentally singing shame-challenging phrases in an upbeat tune.)

- Questioning the assumption that you are only one way, totally worthless, because you exposed a weakness, acted foolishly, or acted wrongfully. Although you can condemn the actions that legitimately led to feeling uncomfortable with yourself, you can stay out of the contingent-worth trap by addressing the act rather than dressing yourself down.

- Engaging in efforts to give yourself self-acceptance while at the same time recognizing that inane shame habits of mind are practiced and automatic. Altering automatic habit processes normally requires time, tolerance, and constructive corrective actions.

Try Stepping Out of Character

Inane shame can be counteracted through stepping-out-of-character exercises. These exercises are designed to confront shame-evoking conditions under controlled conditions and to innoculate yourself against inane shame and shame excesses.

If you find that you excessively inhibit yourself by doing such things as not asking for directions when lost or not asking for change when you need to make a phone call, you may be a prime candidate for these stepping-out-of-character exercises. The purpose of the exercises is to work on reducing excessive or inane shame thinking in order to free yourself from shame excesses.

- Many restaurants offer "two eggs any style" on the menu. When ordering eggs, most people ask for two fried eggs, scrambled eggs, or poached eggs. If you expect to feel embarrassed asking a waiter or waitress for one fried and one scrambled egg, this is an example of excessive shame. Try doing it the next time you're out for breakfast. You'll be surprised to find it's really no big deal.

- If you are self-conscious about what you think others think of your appearance, wear a belt for a day that does not match the rest of your outfit, wear a T-shirt in reverse, or wear two different colored socks. By the end of the day, you probably will feel less self-consciousness about these mismatches. Some discomfort may be reasonable, at first.

- If you grow embarrassed at the thought of inconveniencing others, take off your watch, go to a local mall, and ask twenty people for the time of day. Before you go, make a prediction as to how many people will give you the time of day and not appear to be put out of their way. Match what happens against what you predicted. Most people will probably be happy to give you the time. In the unlikely event that twenty people refuse to give you the time of day, you can still ask and answer this question: "How does this make me less of a person if a group of twenty refused to give me the time of day?" If you are honest with yourself, you'll conclude that although you didn't get the time, you can still accept yourself. You may also wonder if you subconsciously selected people who appeared less likely to be helpful.

Stepping-out-of-character experiments can have a disrupting impact on both shame and depression. You've created an opportunity to activate negative thinking under conditions that you can control and where you can question these thoughts once they surface. You've introduced an element of chaos into the automatic nature of inane and excessive shame thinking. By observing what happens when you follow through with stepping-out-of-character exercises, you can experience a shift in perspective from shame thinking to acceptance thinking. This adjustment in thought counteracts the worthlessness component of depressive thinking.

CHALLENGING INANE SHAME THINKING

List some examples of your inane shame thoughts. Then challenge this thinking with techniques you've learned in this book, and record some rational thoughts that you believe give perspective to your situation.

Personal examples of global shame thinking:

Challenges for global shame thinking:

Rational thoughts that lead to a broader perspective:

ABC METHOD FOR DEFUSING EMOTIONAL REASONING

Many emotions that arise from irrational thinking have a catastrophic component. Catastrophic thinking, for example, can promote fear, such as when you can't control a situation and think that others will hate you for that lack of control. A catastrophic pattern of thought can emerge in a situation where you make a mistake and believe it's too much for you to take and that the mistake is you! Catastrophic thinking can erupt into a depression, such as when you lose a job and tell yourself that you will be financially ruined, will lose everything, and will have to go on welfare forever.

Catastrophically inspired stressful emotions can be interpreted in such a way as to validate the ideas associated with them. For example, when depressed, you might experience distressful emotional sensations, then think of yourself as helpless or worthless. The helplessness or worthless thinking can explain anxious, demoralized, or depressed feelings, but they can also add to this stress. This circularity is a form of emotional reasoning.

June awoke on the "wrong side of the bed." She explained her distressed sensations by associating back to a harsh comment an acquaintance made years earlier about her artwork. She believed that the comment evoked the negative sensations that she experienced. She told herself that this person's comment deprived her of a career in art, which was why she was depressed. June now had an explanation for her depressive sensations and depression. Her problem, however, derived from her circular emotional reasoning, not the event she told herself was the cause.

Joe felt angry at his wife when she cooked his pancakes too long. He thought that his mate's cooking caused his anger and that he would not have been angry were it not for her cooking. Almost instantly, he screamed at her and berated her for her cooking. His reasoning was circular. The anger-evoking problem was neither the pancakes nor Joe's mate. Something else happened in between that told the real story behind his anger. Joe demanded that his wife behave infallibly. He thought that she deserved punishment for her imperfection because it affected him. This demand thinking was automatic; it skipped under his conscious awareness but was associated with his angry feelings and outburst.

Psychologist Carroll Izard (1993) thinks that to assure our survival, we have many triggers for an emotional response, and that emotion and cognition are highly interactional. This survival process can go amuck when reasoning and emotions become intertwined into a distressful form of circular logic. In this circle, feelings validate the ideas that accompany them. For example, if you think you are helpless and feel anxious, the anxiety can validate helplessness thinking. Although the emotion is real, the accompanying thinking can be false.

By uncoupling distressful thinking from distressful sensations and emotions, you put yourself in the advantageous position of disengaging from emotional reasoning. The following ABC method addresses the circularity in worry.

Activating event (experience): "A friend does not arrive on time for a luncheon meeting at a restaurant. The friend is already five minutes late."
Rational beliefs about the event: "The friend may have been unexpectedly delayed."
Emotional and behavioral consequences for the rational beliefs: "Acceptance but some annoyance about the lateness. Remain waiting. Plan to call friend's cell phone if friend doesn't arrive in the next five minutes."
Irrational beliefs: "My friend has no respect for my time. My friend got into a terrible accident."
Emotional and behavioral consequences for the irrational beliefs: "Mixed feelings of anger and worry."
Disputes for irrational beliefs: "(1) How does my friend's lateness prove the friend has no respect for my time? Sample answer: In this form of emotional reasoning, a discomfort about the delay involves jumping to the conclusion that the delay is both intentional and shows inconsideration. How does the feeling prove the premise? Emotional reasoning can be contrasted with other information. The friend has a history of promptness. The facts contradict the 'lack of respect' view. How can one be both inconsiderate for 'lateness' and at the same time be normally prompt? (2) How can I know for sure that my friend got into an accident? Sample answer: In this form of emotional reasoning, the feeling of worry supports the accident theory. But how does a feeling prove a theory? The answer is, it does not! However, the relief that typically follows when worrisome thoughts are found false provides a reward for the worry. By addressing the circularity in the worry, the reward can be a reduction in tension from such thinking."
Effects of the disputes: "Continuing annoyance about the delay, but a mind that is free from self-talk that relates to resentment and worry. Less stress that can evoke depressive thoughts. Fewer depression-provoking thoughts."

When emotional reasoning is linked with your depressive sensations, use the following chart as a guide to map and put a stop to this thinking.

Activating event (experience):

Rational beliefs about the event:

Emotional and behavioral consequences for the rational beliefs:

Irrational beliefs:

Emotional and behavioral consequences for the irrational beliefs:

Disputes for irrational beliefs:

Effects of the disputes:

KEY IDEAS AND ACTION PLAN

What are the key ideas that you got from this chapter? What actions can you take?

Key Ideas

What are the key ideas that you found helpful?

1. _____

_____

2. _____

_____

3. _____

_____

Action Plan

What actions can you take to progress?

1. _____

_____

2. _____

_____

3. _____

_____

POSTSCRIPT

Although your beliefs and attitudes may fall under your conscious awareness, they can powerfully influence your emotions and behaviors. Some cognitive emotions, such as i-anxiety and i-anger, can evoke, reflect, and support a depressive mood and accompanying depressive sensations and thinking. By making these associated attitudes and beliefs conscious, you can subject them to observation and evaluation. By defusing erroneous beliefs associated with such states, you position yourself to gain a sense of emotional freedom from their impact and are in a stronger position to deal with the other aspects of depression and prevent its recurrence.

CHAPTER 16

Special Cognitive and Behavioral Techniques

When you feel smothered by depression, you can experience yourself as immobilized. It's not that you absolutely can't, say, sharpen a pencil. You might just think you can't. You might focus on your fatigue, for example, and distract yourself from the task at hand.

Rather than wait for a depressed mood and, say, fatigue, to lift, consider the value in accepting that you'll sometimes need to push yourself to do some of the smallest activities of daily living when you don't feel like doing them.

Is it possible for you to imagine yourself engaging in an important activity of daily living, even when you don't feel like it, and even when you operate at a lower efficiency? Can you imagine yourself doing what you are currently delaying, such as taking a shower, wearing newly ironed clothing, or bringing your vehicle in for an oil change? If you can imagine doing these things, you can do what you can imagine.

Engaging in such activities as sharpening a pencil is an important part of a process of bootstrapping yourself up from depression. But how do you do something when every fiber in your body yells out, "I can't"?

This chapter will look at some practical cognitive and behavioral methods for coping with depression. It starts with an evolutionary view and ends with a values view. In between, you'll find many imagery and behavioral methods for ridding yourself of depression and some techniques that you can use to improve your sleep.

As your activity level gradually increases, your depression should gradually lift.

EVOLUTION AND DEPRESSION

Psychology Today contributing editor and clinical psychologist Nando Pelusi (2003) notes that most people find that overcoming their depression can prove especially challenging when they blame themselves and down themselves for being depressed. He suggests a two-step evolutionary perspective to eliminate self-blame and self-downing as a secondary aspect of depression.

As a first step, Pelusi (pers. comm.) suggests that you evoke a "contemporary" explanation for blame thinking. For example, if you catch yourself involved in secondary depressive thinking—where you think you should not be depressed, blame yourself for how you feel, then down yourself—think again. Telling yourself something like "I'm worthless if I'm depressed" does not change the depression and can deepen this state.

Because such secondary depressive thinking often glides below the threshold of awareness, this line of thought can rage unchecked. This double trouble of experiencing depression and demanding that you don't feel as you do can lead to an added stress that worsens your depression.

The following chart describes questions and answers for addressing a secondary depressive thought:

Secondary Depressive Belief	Two Questions to Challenge Secondary Belief	Sample Answers to Challenging Questions
"I must not be depressed. Feeling how I must not feel shows I'm to blame and worthless."	When you feel depressed, where is the law that says you should not feel as you do?	A depressed mood is there for a reason. Regardless of the reasons, however, you still feel as you do. This acceptance view is an intermediary step in correcting secondary depressive thought.
	Why should a habit of mind disappear by decree?	A depressed mood practically never changes by decree. But you can encourage yourself to take steps to address your secondary depressive thinking—such as that you should not feel depressed. Self-encouragement, followed by action, can go far to eliminate distresses evoked by unrealistic decrees.

Pelusi's second step involves what he sees as an "ultimate" explanation for taking the onus of blame away from feeling depression. He notes that early humans may have inherited tendencies to depression that may have been functional in primitive periods where 99 percent of our ancestors lived among small bands of kin.

Depression may have had a survival value in the early days of our evolution. For example, feelings of depression among some people in northern climates could routinely occur a few months before the winter solstice. Preliminary feelings of depression could trigger a migration impulse to travel to a warmer climate. Then, when spring grew near, a biological depressive impulse could trigger a northerly migration. Under this scenario, depression wasn't a flaw but, in some cases, served an adaptive function.

With the growth of civilization and language, certain philosophies, such as a need for approval, could attach to this survival mechanism with unfortunate results. This "modern" adaptation is like evolution in reverse.

COGNITIVE IMAGERY TECHNIQUES

Through positive imagery, you can prepare yourself for positive changes. By visualizing the future in constructive terms and by visualizing the types of changes you'd like to make, you can gear up your mind for change. This can include imagining yourself engaged in activities that can help free you from the bonds of depression. The following time projection and mental rehearsal exercises illustrate two ways to use imagination to overcome depression.

Using Time Projection

When pessimism and gloom trump reason and optimism, you can act like a naysayer and negate whatever you accomplish in the present and deny there will be any positive future. Who wouldn't feel hopeless and depressed under such circumstances?

Hopelessness seeks its own evidence. So if you take a test and get a high grade, you say this was a fluke. It was the failing grade that you got on your seventh-grade English test that attests to your true abilities. Anything else you've accomplished came about because you faked people out. As to the future, nothing can be done to change the gloom that you foretell.

Now, if you were not in a depressed state of mind, you would probably think differently—perhaps somewhat optimistically. How might you shift from a pervasively gloomy point of view to one that is sprinkled with some optimism or, at least, a wait-and-see attitude?

There is no magical way to quickly shift from depressive thinking to a realistically optimistic outlook. Like a granite block that is inscribed with pessimistic thoughts, gloom has staying power. But with a symbolic hammer and chisel, you can clear away symbolic depressive thoughts as you inscribe realistic new ones onto the granite block.

Rutgers Professor Emeritus Arnold Lazarus (1971) suggests a *time projection* chiseling tool. If you are depressed by oppressing circumstances, ask yourself, "What will I be doing in one, five, or ten years?" and "What positive things could happen?" The future offers opportunities. Sprinkling the future with a variety of potential positive choices can help counteract a generalized sense of gloom.

TIME PROJECTION EXERCISE

In the following chart, sketch in probable positive things that can happen to you over the next year, five years, and ten years.

Possible One-Year Positive Occurrences	Possible Five-Year Positive Occurrences	Possible Ten-Year Positive Occurrences

When gloom seems impenetrable, and time projections do little to dampen prophesies of gloom, you can augment the time projection with *backward planning* (Knaus 1998). Suppose that you report that as you try to think of positive future occurrences, the occurrences seem blurred and you see yourself fading into darkness. If that happens, here is another step.

If you see only doom for yourself, you are likely to filter out ideas that are inconsistent with that gloomy perspective, thus perpetuating the gloom. It is a typical tendency for people to engage in such filtering. Nevertheless, you can skip past the negativity through a backward planning technique. This backward planning exercise is a "let's pretend" sequence that is like reviewing the steps you took in sequence back to the beginning.

Imagine that this is one year from now. You have overcome your depression. Think backward from that event. What happened just before your depression lifted? What did you do to help make that happen? What steps did you take before the last step? What decisions did you make in the beginning to start an antidepressant process in motion? For example, your actions just prior to defeating depression could involve challenging depressive thinking. Before that you structured your day and pressed yourself to follow through on what was reasonable and within your capacity to do. The first step you took was to decide that you might be able to defeat depression by taking antidepressive actions.

A backward planning process can help to counter pessimistic thoughts about the future. With a competing set of images in place, you have an argument to rebut the pessimistic view.

Doing Mental Rehearsals

Mental rehearsals can help in areas of personal development. For example, you are alone and feeling isolated. You associate this condition with your depression. You'd prefer to have more contact with others. But, you find that you get tongue-tied when meeting with acquaintances. You don't see yourself communicating well, and you believe that this is a partial reason for your sense of isolation. This represents a self-development opportunity.

Suppose you lack confidence in your ability to engage people in small talk, and you'd prefer to more comfortably engage in informal conversations. To prepare your mind for a change in this area, experiment by mentally rehearsing the change. In this mental rehearsal phase, you would do the following:

1. Imagine a situation when you are with a person you want to act friendly toward. Create the scene in your mind (a grocery store, restaurant, your living room) where a brief conversation can take place.

2. Imagine making small talk, asking "how is your family?" and "how are things going at work?" (People who ask questions that inspire others to speak about what they want to speak about are typically viewed as good conversationalists.)

3. Imagine the rational thoughts you'd prefer to think, such as "asking people questions that I think they'd enjoy answering is a reasonable form of small talk."

4. Imagine the feelings that would flow from such a rational perspective.

5. Next, imagine yourself engaged in small talk with a specific person.

6. Imagine communicating to different people you know in different locations such as a restaurant, beside the watercooler, or over a backyard fence. (Doing multiple practice sessions is a way of gearing the mind for actually chatting with others).

7. Imagine making passing conversation with friendly looking strangers at malls, grocery stores, and other places where people gather. Passing conversation can include asking for the time or making comments about something in the surrounding environment. (You are likely to find that some people will not respond, others will respond in kind, and others will try to engage you in conversation.)

If small talk stalls, what would be a rational way of viewing this drop off? Try viewing it this way: "If the conversation falls flat, so be it. Communications are a two-way street. You can't win them all." Can you think of anything more reasonable than that? If so, use it. Simultaneously, imagine the feelings that can flow from this rational perspective. Is it the sort of feeling that comes from acceptance? Is it the sort of feeling you associate with confidence? Try to conjure that feeling as you visualize yourself in a situation where a conversation "drops off." If you can accept that not all conversations go as planned, you'll probably feel more relaxed about engaging in small talk.

What if someone wants to talk about something personal? Rehearse that scenario in your mind as well. Eventually you will put what you rehearsed to the test.

BEHAVIORAL METHODS FOR CURBING DEPRESSION

When depressed, you may show little interest in the activities of daily living. You may trudge along slowly. You may experience more frequent feelings of anxiety, anger, or sadness. You may think more negative thoughts that relate to helplessness and hopelessness. In addressing depression from a behavioral angle, the idea is to decrease the frequency of depression-related behaviors while increasing the frequency of constructive behaviors.

Some visible behaviors are simpler to increase than others. If you find your movements sluggish, force yourself to pick up your pace. If under a slackened pace it takes you fifteen minutes to put the laundry into the washer, set a timer to do it in twelve minutes.

Here is a sampling of some behavioral methods to help defeat depression:

Create a contingency contract with yourself to increase an activity.   The contract defines the priority activity, how you will structure the activity (dates, times), what you will do to work on the priority, and the type of rewards you will give yourself following the completion of specific phases of the activity. Write up the contract. Date it. Sign it. Follow it. Set up a penalty that you agree to impose on yourself if you fail to carry out the contract. Your penalty could be as simple as making a donation to some cause or political candidate that you do not like. Find someone who is willing to monitor your contract. His or her job will be to make sure that if you fail to carry out the contract, you will impose the penalty on yourself.

Create another contingency contract for an activity to decrease.   Activities to decrease can involve sitting inactively in a corner, associating life with a painful experience, or avoiding contact with friendly people. By decreasing the frequency of such activities, you will increase positive activities. For example, by not sitting inactively in a corner, you may instead compose e-mail notes to friends. Instead of associating life with painful experiences, you can look for ways to contribute to relieving the despair of others, say, through volunteer work. Instead of avoiding contacts with others, you can make phone contacts, arrange for a luncheon, and so on.

Break the contracted activity into relatively smaller components.   Give yourself a reward following each phase. Although it is questionable whether you can really reward your own behavior, you can arrange a kind of self-reward with your monitor. You could, for instance, give away a sum of money to the monitor and then earn it back—in units or in one lump sum—by passing the contract or contract components that you design for yourself. Frequent rewards are likely to prove more motivational than one long-term reward. However, do include a desired bigger long-term reward following the completion of the project.

Use a penalty system to discourage negative behaviors.   If you complain to your friends about how rotten you feel, this can be a turn off to them. Some may avoid you. If you set up an agreed self-penalty with your monitor, this will help you to decrease this behavior. For example, if you enjoy drinking coffee, you can ask your monitor to help you make sure you deprive yourself of drinking coffee for a day following a complaint session. If your monitor does his or her job, this will help you to avoid complaining.

Create a list of positive things to look forward to experiencing.   Admittedly, this step can prove challenging. When the future looks dismal, any positive expectation may seem like a meal of gruel. Nevertheless, the future can contain a rerun of a once favored movie. It is possible that you can purchase the antique chair you wanted at an upcoming auction. You may meet a favorite relative for lunch when that person comes to town. So, instead of negating things that the future may hold, look for ways to anticipate something out of the ordinary that can have value.

Try counting how many positive statements you make about yourself.   Include the number of positive statements about your future prospects that you make to yourself. Try to increase these and to decrease negative statements about yourself and negative statements about your future. Set up one or more rewards with your monitor for increasing the rate (number per day) of positives and decreasing the rate of negatives.

Pace yourself.   There is no universal law that says that you must operate like a dynamo, especially when depressed. During times when depression seems lighter, you may be in a better position to concentrate. That may be the time when you look closer into solving problems associated with depressive thinking. When depression deepens, doing mechanical activities can help disrupt the depression. These activities can include washing a car, moving furniture, weeding a garden, buying a quart of milk, or cleaning a bathtub.

Engaging in behavioral activities can help promote a sense of command over your own actions. When you use your muscles, you are simultaneously acting to change negative thoughts that say "you can't do this; after all, you are depressed."

CHART YOUR GOALS

Use the following chart to identify behaviors that you think are useful to increase, behaviors that you think are useful to decrease, and how you will reward yourself for progress in each area. Since what may be rewarding to one person may be unrewarding to another, an individualized program of rewards is best. A sample idea is included for each area. You fill in the rest.

Behaviors to Increase	Rewards for Progress	Behaviors to Decrease	Rewards for Progress
Resolving disagreements with family members	Watching television for one hour following each resolution	Moping and complaining to family members	Watching birds at bird feeder for fifteen minutes for each mope-free day

Premack's Principle

Finding ways to reward yourself can seem daunting when you feel depressed. You may want to disappear into the darkness rather than do something to get a reward which may seem meaningless at the time you get it. When depressed, reinforcing yourself for doing something constructive does not necessarily mean that you will repeat the behavior for which you were rewarded. However, establishing a routine where you break daily activities into achievable parts—and following each part with something that you might ordinarily do when you are not depressed—can help tip the balance in your favor. The Premack principle can provide a structure for this purpose.

Psychologist David Premack's (1965) principle is that any action that a person engages in frequently can serve as a reward to increase infrequent but desired behaviors. Frequent behaviors are usually readily available, which is the appeal of this reinforcement system. When you are depressed, however, you can experience a dramatic behavioral shift where you drop some activities that are normally frequent, such as reading the newspaper or calling friends. Normally infrequent behaviors, such as withdrawal, encroach upon time and become time hogs because they capture attention but produce little in the way of positive outcomes. Depressive thinking, perfectionist ruminations, angry preoccupations— all substitute for the normal activities of daily living. Nevertheless, it is possible to normalize your life by reengaging in high frequency behaviors that you previously enjoyed.

Find something that you normally do or did that is or was pleasurable. Make doing this activity contingent upon doing something specific to deal with your depression. Suppose you decide to take one hour to write out your depressive thoughts so as to make them more visible. At the end of this time, do something that you normally find pleasing. It can be catching up on the news or drinking a cup of coffee.

If drinking coffee is a high frequency behavior, you can follow logging and disputing your depressive thoughts with a cup of coffee. This form of reinforcement increases the probability of exploring and disputing depressive thinking. Additionally, you could receive an additional reward in the form of relief from depressive thinking.

The Premack principle qualifies as a procrastination technology technique that can aid in defeating depressive thinking. When a high frequency behavior follows a normally low frequency behavior, it means that you have acted rather than put off a useful action. There is another benefit. Structuring your time to reward normally low frequency (or new) behavior with an established behavior is a way to act against a depressive process. So whether the Premack approach proves initially rewarding or not, you are still taking steps to establish a momentum that can compete with the lethargy of depression.

USING PREMACK'S PRINCIPLE

The following chart describes two examples for using the Premack principle. Use the remaining spaces to fill in your own plan.

Counter-Depression Activity	Positive Activity That You Ordinarily Do
Thought log recording.	Read local news.
Twenty minutes questioning depressive ideas.	Drink cup of coffee.

MAINTAIN ROUTINES

How you structure your life when depressed can make a difference. Structuring your time and activities to follow through on normal activities of daily living is like a ladder up from depression.

If you lose ground on your routines when you are depressed, reestablishing them can counteract the pull of depression. The Premack principle can be used to target specific areas where you want to increase the frequency of a certain behavior that can compete with a depression-related inactivity. Normalizing your routine is broader in scope.

- Getting back to normal schedules can seem daunting when you feel depressed. Yet gradually rebuilding normal routines into your life and sticking with those basic routines can create a sense of structure, familiarity, and stability that eventually can help mute depression. This scheduling process can include assigning times for basic routines such as exercise, showering, eating, shopping, returning phone calls, and sleeping.

Making Checklists

Organization is a mechanical process. You can use procrastination technology to mechanically structure normal routines. This technology includes using checklists.

- To start, put your priority daily activities on a list. Then order them according to the sequence that you plan to do them in. The list can include showering, attending to toiletries, dressing, eating breakfast, and so on.

- You can structure your time to make normal high-probability behaviors follow those that you want to encourage in yourself. Checking off the activities that you complete signals an accomplishment and a sense of control.

- You can assign a fixed time for each activity of daily living, such as exercise starting at 8:30 A.M. As you complete the items on the list, check them off. (You can make printouts of this routine, so you have a new list each day.)

Checking off accomplishments is a measure of progress, and such measures can be viewed as rewarding. And even if whatever you do doesn't feel rewarding, marking these accomplishments provides visual evidence that you can act to normalize your life. This behavioral message translates into a cognitive one. You can assert control over certain activities, even when depressed.

Using a Weekly Planner

A weekly planner is another way to structure time and activities. To use the following chart, you would list your daily routines (activities) in the order that it makes the most sense for them to get done. You can use the boxes under each day of the week to check off activities as you do them.

Routine and Time	Mon.	Tue.	Wed.	Thur.	Fri.	Sat.	Sun.

The above planner makes sense for redundant activities that you can do daily. But not all days are the same. You may have some activities to do on Tuesday that you don't have on Monday. If that is the case, create different planners for different days. There are many ways to create daily planners. Computerized daily planners provide flexibility for changing the scheduling of some daily routines. Your local bookstore or drugstore will have daily planners that allow for structuring activities by day and time.

A simple check mark can be all that you need to signal progression. Adding color can give a new visual dimension to the process. By using a highlighter, you can cross off activities that you accomplish. You can use different colors to signal different levels of accomplishment.

As items get crossed out, this observation can feel rewarding. But even when depression trumps any feeling of reward, remember that you are still acting in a way that can bring long-term relief from depression. Paddling upstream does not have to feel rewarding. You just have to get to where you want to go. When you commit yourself to establish and maintain daily routines, plan for lapses. Practically everyone lapses from time to time on even the best conceived self-help plan. If you lapse, start again.

Scheduling systems are far from universally effective. However, for a subgroup of people with depression, they can be of significant benefit.

Project by Project

Although some people prefer to operate following a defined schedule, others prefer to work by projects where they stick with something until the project is advanced or done. Then they shift to something else. If you do better working by project, you can break the preliminary stages down into phases. If your project is to recognize and defeat depressive thinking, you can combine this with the Premack principle. For example, follow one hour of reviewing key areas of this book with a normal activity of daily living, such as showering.

Depression is a wild card in any routine scheduling program. Nevertheless, you can use the schedule as a tool to compete against depression where it is understood from the start that substituting scheduled events for depression-related lethargy and related behaviors is a jagged process rather than a straightforward event.

Depression retards normal activities. So it is wise to see the schedule as an experiment. As you engage in this experiment, you are likely to come across stumbling blocks, delays, and other interferences that can be identified and worked at along the way. The time it takes you to recognize and address such depressive interferences is the time it takes.

Strategic Delays and Procrastination

Unlike procrastination, where you impulsively put off a relevant activity, delays can be strategic. When depressed, some activities on your list might best be put off.

Suppose you feel stressed by your current job and want to get another. You are able to plod through the day on the job, but you really don't like what you do. When depressed, your mood will be downtrodden. Although some people with depression can present as though they were upbeat, depression can dampen your chances for interviewing effectively.

If you decide to put off a job search because of a lack of energy and enthusiasm, waiting until you get over feeling depressed can be a strategic choice. That is not procrastination. Procrastination would be putting off dealing with the depression or putting off the job search once depression passes.

GET MODERATE EXERCISE

Exercise is among the top of the list of antidepressant activities. Still, exercise is often at the bottom of the list of what most people with depression normally do.

Understandably, exercise can be challenging to start and to maintain, even when you are not depressed. Building exercise into your routine often involves a struggle that comes at a time of high pessimism and low energy. But you can have an added incentive when depressed. You are not only acting to get into better shape—good for general health reasons—but also to alleviate a distressful depressive state.

To get the benefits from exercise, you have to decide to do it. Assuming that you make this choice, next, you'll need to put one foot before the other to get the process started. Expect to stumble in this area at first, but do try to persist. You are likely to overcome the side effects of antidepressant medications through exercise.

Sometimes exercising with a group or buddy can serve as an incentive to continue. If that's not feasible, consider exercise as an individual pursuit. Some people are likely to do better as a solitary long-distance runner than as a member of a team.

> Start slowly. Build your exercise routine to a level that is realistic to do and to maintain.

Looking beyond depression can be a remarkably effective way to start, then to sustain, an exercise program. For example, imagine it is sixteen weeks from now. If you could get relief from depression within sixteen weeks, would you exercise for that purpose only?

Are there any short-term benefits that can serve as an immediate incentive to start an exercise program? You can normally experience an improved mood for a time following either aerobic or anaerobic exercise (Yeung 1996). For example, immediately following twenty-five minutes of treadmill walking, women with major depressions experienced less automatic depressive thinking and a better mood. Following this exercise routine, people with the greater degree of depression tended to experience the greatest magnitude of positive change (Lash 2000).

What Is Moderate Exercise?

Moderate exercise can reduce fatigue, increase energy, boost your immune system, and reduce symptoms of depression. But what constitutes moderate exercise? This partially depends on your health, physical condition, gender, and age. Although there is no single standard, the answer to this question comes in four parts: type, intensity, time, and frequency.

- Moderate exercise activities include jogging in place, walking on treadmills, climbing stairs, swimming, walking, bicycling, rowing, or light weight lifting. You can work on your own, with a group, or at a health facility with exercise equipment and professional instruction. Both aerobic exercises (walking, swimming, or biking) and anaerobic (weight training and stretching) exercises are equally effective for improving your mood. Low intensity exercises (where you don't grunt, groan, and strain) tend to be better tolerated.

- You are moderately exercising when you raise and maintain your heart rate 20 to 30 beats above your normal level. If your normal heart rate is 80 beats per minute, 100 to 110 beats per minute can be your target range.

- The amount of time for exercising involves sustaining an approximate 105-beat rate for between twenty to thirty minutes.

- A reasonable frequency is to exercise every other day. But there is some evidence that exercise is cumulative. You can break exercise sessions into five-minute segments and spread the effort throughout the day.

If you have any question about your physical condition concerning exercise, a health check and stress test can be the place to begin. If you choose an exercise approach to address depression, and you're not sure what will work best for you, experiment.

BEHAVIORAL TECHNIQUES FOR SLEEP PROBLEMS

When your depression feels severe, you'll feel fatigue, yet you may have trouble sleeping. About 90 percent of those with a major depression have fitful sleep patterns. Insomnia, awakening in the middle of the night (middle insomnia), interrupted sleep, paradoxical dreaming, and early morning awakening are common signs of depression. Disruption in sleep patterns is normally a psychobiological issue with a strong biological component, as described in the following list.

- The rapid eye movement (REM) phase of sleep is associated with dreaming. When the latency for this stage of sleep is short, relative to nondepressed sleepers, it is associated with depression (Giles et al. 2003).

- Negative, fitful dreams are called *paradoxical*: sleep loses some of its normal benefits. As depression starts to lift, there is a change in dream patterns from more negative dreams during the first half of sleep to fewer negative dreams during the second half of sleep (Cartwright et al. 1998).

- Some who also suffer from anxiety might have difficulty falling asleep.

Restorative sleep correlates with reductions in a depressed mood, depressive thinking, and other common symptoms of depression. Some sleep medications can prove productive. However, if you've tried medication to restore sleep without significant success, here are some cognitive and behavioral methods that you can try for restoring healthy sleep patterns.

- Follow a regular sleep schedule. Go to bed just when you are likely to feel sleepy. Give your body cues associated with sleep, such as listening to a favorite soothing song about fifteen minutes before you are scheduled to retire.

- If you routinely fall asleep on the couch while watching TV, then awaken a few hours later and stay awake for the next several hours, you need to change the routine. Do something active where you will stay awake until a regular bedtime.

- Spend about a half hour in direct daylight each day. In the morning, go out in the sun for about fifteen minutes. This can help set your sleep-time clock.

- Do moderate exercises (aerobics, for example) during the afternoon every day. Since it takes a few hours for the body to go back to normal, avoid exercising two to four hours before you go to bed. After exercising, your cardiac output and your ability to attend, concentrate, and vigilance increases. However, there is some research to say that mild to moderate exercise in the evening might aid sleep. Use your experience as a guide.

- Avoid ingesting coffee, cola, tea, or chocolate (or other caffeine-containing substances) seven hours before your regular bedtime.

- If you smoke, refrain from doing so several hours before going to bed. (Because of demonstrated health risks, it is a good idea to stop permanently.)

- Avoid alcohol for three hours before going to bed. A glass of wine in the evening may cause you to feel relaxed, which may make it easier for you to fall asleep. However, as the body breaks down alcohol, your sleep is likely to be disturbed.

- Associate your bed with sleeping. Avoid reading or watching television in bed or doing work in bed.

- Sleep is associated with a drop in body temperature. Sleep in a well-ventilated room with the room temperature around 65 to 68 degrees.

- Take a warm bath about two hours before sleeping. This can be relaxing as well. The two-hour time gives your body ample time to cool down before sleeping.

- Massage your feet for ten minutes immediately before going to bed.

- Use relaxation as a sleep aid. Relaxing muscles creating relaxed images can help dull some of the sharp edges of sleeplessness. (For descriptions of relaxation methods, see chapter 14.)

- Reduce controllable external noises that can serve as distractions to sleep. Try using white noise to muffle outside sounds that can't be eliminated. A white noise may be a low-volume sound from a nonoperating television channel.

- If you relax your body during periods of interrupted sleep, you will do better than if you worry about how well you are doing trying to fall asleep. Your body will gain some benefit.

- Some pundits advise sleeping with your head facing north. The theory is the pineal gland responds to magnetic forces with increases in melatonin production. (I'm unconvinced that this makes any difference, but turning your head north can't hurt.)

- If you are inclined to watch a clock to see when you awaken, use one without an illuminated dial or light. You are less likely to preoccupy yourself with how much sleep time you might be losing.

- If you have difficulty sleeping because you reflect on the trials and tribulations of the day, this is a signal that you can profit from resolving daily conflicts as they arise.

- There is a significant scientific literature on the relationship between sleep problems and negative content of thought. One direction of this thought is worry over lack of sleep and anxiety about performing less well following interrupted sleep. Worry is distracting and anxiety creates arousal. Challenging negative thinking related to sleep can help alleviate those tensions.

- Wakefulness can come about from telling yourself something like "I've got to fall asleep, I've got to fall asleep." Should this "command to sleep" process occur, question the demand that you have to fall asleep. Explore the possibility that the worst thing that is likely to happen is that you'll feel tired the next day, and how is that so bad?

- Teach yourself to defuse negative thinking that can contribute to disrupted sleep patterns. For example, learning to decrease cognitive distortion through rational examination can, over time, reduce the frequency and intensity of thoughts that promote depressive arousal and disrupted sleep patterns.

- If you have difficulty falling asleep because you anticipate a negative occurrence tomorrow, flip things around and concentrate on best outcomes.

- When you are unable to sleep, a tested behavioral approach is to get out of bed. The idea is to avoid associating the bed with wakefulness. Return when you are ready to sleep.

- Count backwards from one thousand by threes.

- Play barely audible soft background music that you associate with restfulness and sleep.

- Plan to rise between 6:00 A.M. and 7:00 A.M. There is some evidence that sleeping late increases the risk for depression (Olders 2003).

Melatonin and Sleep

What about using melatonin to get a good night's sleep? Melatonin is associated with sleep. It is a hormone secreted by the small pine-cone shaped, pea-sized pineal gland located near the center of the brain. Light and darkness presumably cue the gland to produce melatonin. The rise and fall of melatonin production presumably regulates the twenty-four-hour circadian rhythms that relate to sleep. The highest melatonin levels peak at about 2:00 A.M.

Melatonin in small amounts may improve sleep patterns. However, health store varieties may not be pure. There is no meaningful evidence affirming the effectiveness of melatonin pills sold in health food stores or through mail-order marketing organizations.

Pecans, bananas, turkey, rice, tomatoes, oats, sweet corn, milk, and barley are rich sources of tryptophane, which is thought to boost melatonin levels. Meditation may also boost melatonin levels.

BEHAVIORAL TECHNIQUES FOR SAD

Seasonal affective disorder commonly occurs in northern climates at around the time the days grow short. In addition to defusing the depressive thinking that ordinarily accompanies this form of depression, light therapy can help reduce SAD effects.

There are specialized lighting systems for treating SAD. Research shows that florescent light bulbs with an intensity of 10,000 lux (about ten to twenty times as bright as ordinary inside light) is a therapeutic level. Dim light filtered through a slightly red-tinted visor worn directly over the eyes has also been found effective.

Light therapy procedures produce about a 75 percent remission rate. Changes may be notable between three days and two weeks of daily exposure to extra light.

In some cases, people obtain the same effects of light therapy by going out for a walk on a sunny morning. Exercise correlates with depression reduction. Walking, the light of day, or walking plus the light of day can make a difference.

The use of light has promise as a general way to curb depression (Tuunainen, Kripke, and Endo 2004). The technique also has promise for reducing depression among pregnant women who are prone to depression (Epperson et al. 2004).

A VALUES APPROACH FOR DEFEATING DEPRESSION

Chapter 2 looked at how certain people, such as Abraham Lincoln, found beacons to lead them through dark periods of their lives. Beacons can be viewed as values, or what an individual conceives as a highly important means of giving guidance to actions.

What is this thing called "value"? Values are core beliefs that represent what is important to you. They can be what you believe is right or wrong; what is ethical and moral. Values sometimes appear in the form of abstract ideas such as integrity, responsibility, freedom, and friendship. However you label or define your values, they are matters of importance to you.

Your values can occur in combination to give direction to your life. One value direction is to contribute your gifts, engage in appealing activities, and remove barriers that stand in the way of such valued activities. Following this combined value direction, you are likely to address depression if it gets in the way of the expression of your values.

Virginia psychologist Leon Pomeroy (2005) observed that we view the world through the external values of society. This includes our views of rules, regulations, and authority. Our internal valuations refer to individuality, uniqueness, and self-concept. Internal values are lenses to the outer world. The interaction between external and internal value systems partially determines the quality of our relationships with others, what we find important in our work, and the directions we follow as we move through time and space.

Values serve as organizing principles around which we can structure a significant part of life. Whether you feel depressed or not, if you value responsibility, you are likely to organize your activities around responsible steps to address depression. When the pull of responsibility dominates the pull of a depressive retreat, you are more likely to act responsibly even when the going feels sluggish and slow. Thus, exercising responsibility is an establishment of control that opposes helplessness thinking.

Your family and social experience help shape your beliefs and values. When you are depressed, many positive beliefs and values can become subservient to depressive beliefs. Nevertheless, even when depressed, you can reactivate values that you believe are functional. You can pick new values to pit against depressive thinking, moods, and behavior. For example, you can promote responsibility over withdrawal. Thus, you act to counter the pull of depression because "it is the responsible thing to do." The following exercise shows how the value of responsibility applies to social situations (external) and self-development (internal) factors.

EXERCISING YOUR VALUES

First, list what you believe are important social rules and regulations that you believe are important responsibilities to follow, and then list what you anticipate from expressing these values. These values can involve paying bills on time or volunteering to help disadvantaged children learn literacy skills. Next, list the values that represent what you think is important from a self-development perspective, and then list what you anticipate from expressing these values.

External values to follow:	Anticipated results for following the value:
Internal values to follow:	**Anticipated results for following the value:**

Next, as a thought exercise, consider if there is a relationship between what you value that is external and the values that you hold that are internal. You may come to see that the value of responsibility intersects with both external and internal directed actions.

By setting upon a path paved with desirable values, you can leapfrog over many false beliefs and apprehensions. That's because your values define what's important to you. Many decisions will then fall into values categories, which can simplify the choices that you make and reduce much uncertainty and indecisiveness that so often accompany depression.

KEY IDEAS AND ACTION PLAN

What are the key ideas that you got from this chapter? What actions can you take?

Key Ideas

What are the key ideas that you found helpful?

1. _____

_____

2. _____

_____

3. _____

_____

Action Plan

What actions can you take to progress?

1. _____

_____

2. _____

_____

3. _____

_____

POSTSCRIPT

Although there is no universal law that says that you must work at becoming undepressed, making a choice to address depression is normally an enlightened one. By choosing to engage in antidepressive behaviors that compete with depressive behaviors, you can come to change thinking and emotions that interact with a depressed mood and related physical conditions.

While you are not depressed, rewards can prove encouraging. In depression, you may profit by staggering your actions in a way that includes "normal" activities following new counter-depression activities, the use of multiple short-term rewards for incremental progress, and larger rewards for milestone accomplishments.

CHAPTER 17

A Multimodal Way to Defeat Depression

Rutgers University Psychology Professor Emeritus Arnold A. Lazarus (1992) developed a BASIC-ID anagram that applies to addressing depression:

B = Behavioral

A = Affective

S = Sensations

I = Imagery

C = Cognitive

I = Interpersonal

D = Drugs

Lazarus views comprehensive change as involving the correction of self-defeating behaviors, dysfunctional affects, unpleasant sensations, troublesome images, cognitive distortions, interpersonal difficulties, and possible biochemical imbalances. You can use Lazarus's BASIC-ID modality approach to identify the components of your depression and for prescribing change. Depression frequently involves an interaction between two or more of the BASIC-ID modalities.

EXPANDING THE ANALYSIS

Lazarus's goal is to create conditions whereby people with mild to moderate depressions achieve a relatively rapid remission of their depression symptoms and can prevent relapse. Here is a sample BASIC-ID applied to depression:

- Depressive *behaviors* include activities such as avoidance and escapist routines, withdrawal, procrastination, decreased work performance, fidgeting, complaining, and outbursts. Lazarus sees a connection between increased positive behavioral activity and a drop in melancholic mood. Thus, action exercises for defeating depression are prescriptive remedies. Even a monotonous activity, such as filling out an insurance form, can temporarily distract you from depressive thinking and a negative mood.

- *Affects* are the emotions you experience, such as joy, happiness, frustration, and love. Depressive affects commonly include sadness, anxiety, anger, shame, and guilt. Lazarus suggests relaxation, meditation, and calming statements to help reduce the tensions associated with negative affects. Assertiveness skill development can serve as an inoculation against future depressions. Recognizing and questioning depressive thinking can cause an improvement in mood.

- *Sensations* include tension, fatigue, pain, or feeling relaxed, cold, hot, dull, and so forth. Scheduling pleasant events for positive sensory stimulation can help when you feel dull or lack sensory stimulation. As a remedy, for example, schedule times to view something visually appealing; listen to calming music, an upbeat song, or to waters tumbling over rocks; smell a scented candle; get a massage, take a warm bath, or do muscular relaxation to stimulate tactile sensations; taste a drop of honey.

- *Imagery* includes fantasies, dreams, and self-image. Some depressive images are metaphorical, such as imagining yourself frozen in a block of ice. You can create positive images that clash with depression imagery. Imagine yourself in a block of ice in the warm summer sun. Can you feel the ice melting away? Here are other examples for positive imagery: imagine when you met a challenge and felt good. Imagine when you lived beyond a disappointment. Imagine yourself bathing in a pool of tranquility. Lazarus also suggests time projection imagery. You visualize yourself taking positive steps as you approach your future.

- Our *cognitive* processes involve knowing, memory, reasoning, reflection, imagination, believing, and more. We live our lives primarily through our habits, along with our beliefs, perceptions, and thoughts. In a depressive mind-set, beliefs take the form of schemas, or organized thought patterns. "I am useless" can be part of a depressive schema, or core belief. This schema can have mental tentacles, such as "I'll never change." These gross exaggerations distort conception and perception. Uprooting them includes Socratic ways of arguing, the PURRRRS system, and the ABCDE method for disputing irrational beliefs.

- The *interpersonal* modality includes managing relationships at work, home, or elsewhere. Depending on social circumstances, this can involve avoidance of complaining; selecting words and phrases that convey positive messages; initiating small talk with others, such as asking "how are things going?"; resolving conflicts before they fester; developing a pleasant style of speaking; and avoiding criticizing others.

- The *drug* modality refers to both drugs and the biological dimensions of depression. This modality involves an evaluation for antidepressant medication, actions to eliminate the abuse of addictive substances, a physical examination to rule out physical causes for depression, actions to improve appetite and sleep, and physical exercise.

The modalities overlap and interact. Anger in depression, for example, can involve negative images, misconceptions, dysphoric sensations, interpersonal conflict, and alcohol abuse. Sometimes you have to approach depression from several angles to diminish or end a persistent dysphoric mood.

APPLYING THE SYSTEM

Lazarus's BASIC-ID acronym is a good memory device. However, you don't have to follow the modalities in succession. The BASIC-ID order is flexible. For example, you can order the modalities according to their impact. If cognitive and drug modalities predictably head the list of problem features in your depression, then you would normally address them first. If you have no depressive imagery, then there is no need to reduce negative imagery. However, you could create positive images where you view yourself meeting the challenges of implementing the other modalities. The following story illustrates how this system can help defeat depression.

■ *Joan's Story*

Joan was twenty-five, single, and unemployed. She suffered from a moderately severe depression for about one year. When she first came to therapy, at the insistence of her parents, she said she had neither the hope nor the energy to come on her own.

She had previously tried antidepressant medication and had had unpleasant side effects. "After a while," she said, "I felt like a chemistry experiment with drugs prescribed to counteract the effects of other drugs."

Joan said she had no confidence in cognitive approaches. Her parents had brought her some information, read it to her, and she concluded it could work for others but that she was too far gone. Her therapist asked if she had heard about a multimodal approach. She said, "What's that?" Since she didn't know about the system, she was hardly in a position to discount it, so the door was open for her to consider Lazarus's broad-spectrum approach to positive change.

Prior to the onset of her depression, Joan had socialized with a group of friends from her high school days and others from work. She said that her job could be stressful at times, but she generally enjoyed her career. At a time just prior to her depression, she had reestablished a relationship with her high school sweetheart. She said that the relationship had gone well, though she pointed out, "I used to worry if my relationship with Don would last." (Joan described herself as a worrier.)

Shortly before her company downsized, Joan started to feel depressed. Then she was among many who lost their jobs. Thereafter, her depression worsened. Once out of work, she put off writing her resumé. She avoided looking in the newspapers or talking to her friends about jobs. She gradually stopped answering telephone calls and e-mail messages. Her off-and-on exercise program abruptly ended. She increasingly spent time shopping online to distract herself but stopped when her money ran out. She complained of eating too much junk food, oversleeping, and lacking energy. She felt she was no longer fun to be around. She described spending several hours each day in her bedroom, especially in the morning when she had trouble getting herself out of bed. Also conspicuous were the omissions in her life. She had previously enjoyed hobbies, such as gardening and golf. Viewing herself at one time as organized, she had rarely addressed priority activities. She described a sense of mental tenseness that she thought caused muscular tension. She described herself as living in a dark pit.

Joan had broken up with Don shortly after her job ended because "I didn't want to burden him with my troubles." She also felt shame that she drained her parents' finances after they assumed responsibility for her expenses. She described a negative self-concept, great pessimism that she'd ever feel normal again, and a pervasive helplessness. She said she cried a lot, sometimes for no reason. She reported feeling "dull," which translated into feeling a lack of sensory stimulation.

Joan's BASIC-ID modality came from several sources: a depression inventory (see chapter 2), her own self-reflections, and her therapist's observations from her initial screening interview. Her main themes were dealing with basic priorities, staying out of the bedroom during waking hours, reestablishing hobbies, dealing with crying, overcoming shame, managing stress and tension, decreasing her sense of dullness, exiting the dark pit, questioning negative thinking, reestablishing previously valued relationships, and taking actions to reduce the biological symptoms of depression. From this list, she classified her information under the BASIC-ID modalities. She next sketched a plan for addressing each modality issue. Here are Joan's examples for each modality and her prescriptive action plans:

Modality	Example	Action Plan
Behavior	"Priority activities go by the wayside."	"Make 'to do' list. Do daily priority. Update resumé."
	"Spend long periods of time in bedroom by myself."	"Use bedroom for sleeping only during the time normally set aside for that purpose."
	"Omissions in areas that once brought pleasure, such as golfing, gardening, reading, warm baths, comedies."	"Do one thing a day to improve garden. Take warm bath every other day. Add new activity each month."
	"Neglect personal care and appearance."	"Make extra effort each day to keep up with personal care and appearance."
	"Crying."	"Accept as a symptom."
Affect	"Shame"	"Shame is a self-conscious negative evaluation of global self-worth based on a vacuous idea that a complex self can be only one way. A pluralistic view of self mutes shame: Punch holes in a shame belief that the self is one way and worthless."
Sensations	"Tension, stiff muscles."	"Massage, stretching exercises, swimming, and biking. Jacobson's muscular relaxation technique (see chapter 16)."

	"Fatigue and loss of energy."	"Avoid napping during the day. Repetitive low-energy garden weeding (lift spirits)."
	"Sense of dullness."	"Burn favorite scented candles. Open curtains to let in light. Paint on canvas. Listen to relaxing music. Fill an eyedropper with a mix of honey and fresh lemon, put drop on tongue. Use foot massager three times a day."
Imagery	"View self as spiraling deeper into a dark pit."	"Imagine an upward spiral staircase with each stair marked by activities of daily living (daily shower, brush hair, change clothing, put dishes in dishwasher, etc.) Put this saying on refrigerator: *Climbing the spiral stairs each day prepares for the challenges that lie ahead.*"
Cognition	"Pessimism."	"Look at pessimism as a symptom, not a fact."
	"Sense of worthlessness. Helplessness."	"Inventory positive attributes. Match each helplessness example against a positive action, such as arising and making breakfast."
Interpersonal	"Self-isolating."	"Reestablish e-mail contact with friends: Send out one new e-mail per day. Attend niece's upcoming birthday party. Plan at least one activity each day where others are present: walking through mall, asking for directions. Record event and what resulted."
Drugs	"Lethargy; lack of exercise."	"Moderate exercise program: bicycling to post office box each day. Every other day resume home aerobic program for twenty minutes."
	"Sleep."	"Slight decrease in oversleeping (from ten hours per night to eight hours per night). Use two alarms to awaken. See if pattern changes as depression lifts."
	"Diet."	"Plan and eat three balanced and nutritious meals a day."

Joan constructed her BASIC-ID plan during three therapy sessions. Thereafter, she chiefly worked on her own. Joan kept in contact with her therapist by phone, calling weekly for fifteen weeks, every other week for four weeks, and then once a month for the next three months, and thereafter as she saw fit.

Her exercise program required encouragement. A breakthrough came at week seven when she agreed to bike with her mother to an aerobics class. She did this consistently thereafter.

When she first began to address her depression, Joan reported feeling mostly depressed and discouraged. At times she felt doing better was going to be an effort in futility. But at about week eight into her program, this hopelessness and worthlessness thinking started to fade.

Joan faced a special challenge in week ten. At that time, she developed a morbid fear of relapsing. Now that she no longer felt so depressed, Joan viewed with dread a reawakening of depressive sensations. When she experienced a wave of depression, she focused on the sensation with fear. Thoughts of hopelessness followed. Because she had made progress, however, she had something to fall back from. That was the good news.

Fear of relapse is common among those coming out of a depression. This can be a favorable fear. It is also addressable. Normally, when people start to worry whether the ground they gained will last, they lose ground because of the worry. Still, they are nicely positioned to bounce back because they now have tools to use that were neither present nor used before.

In dealing with her tension magnification, Joan learned to accept the depressive sensations (admittedly challenging to do) and to question and debunk her doomsday prophesy about relapsing. Thereafter, when she experienced a wave of tension and negative thinking, she first labeled the negative thinking "depressive thinking." Then she went for a walk. The labeling exercise was especially helpful. She saw depressive thoughts as symptoms, not facts.

Joan made a significant breakthrough at week eighteen. She learned about a new job opportunity. Understandably, she was at first apprehensive about explaining to an interviewer why she had been out of work for over a year. However, her worry went beyond normal apprehension. She entered the realm of anxiety as she contemplated failing the interview. In this realm of anticipation, she had heart palpitations, tension headaches, and gastrointestinal symptoms.

Once she settled on a plan for answering questions about her recent unemployment, her strain diminished. Her plan was to say that a down economy made it difficult for her to find work, emphasize why she thought this opportunity was a good fit for herself and the company, and describe how her work skills could benefit this employer. To Joan's surprise, the interviewer did most of the talking and said nothing about the employment gap. She got the job.

Reflecting on her anxiety, Joan learned that she received a reward for worry. Although this was not the type of reward that many would want, it was still a reward. When the worst she predicted didn't happen, she felt relief. This relief was Joan's reward for worry.

Because of this possible worry-reward connection, Joan made a conscious effort to develop a wait-and-see approach. In situations where she couldn't prove that her fortune-telling was factual, she considered a range of possibilities. These predictions included the worst thing that could happen, the best thing that could happen, and possibilities in between. The wait-and-see approach reduced her worry thinking.

At week twenty, Joan contacted Don. She wanted to see if she could reestablish a relationship with him. In advance of the meeting, she worked to maintain an optimistic perspective. But she primarily worked to minimize worrying about the meeting.

When she met Don, she found he was happily involved with another woman. She felt saddened. But she also felt happy that she had tried. Not all things work out as we wish they would.

A STRUCTURE FOR POSITIVE CHANGE

Using the BASIC-ID involves gathering and organizing information that fits the modalities. You can take information from your thought logs (chapter 4), the depression inventory (chapter 2), and key idea sections throughout this book as well as from general self-knowledge, and organize the relevant information according to a multimodal framework.

BASIC-ID EXERCISE

In the following modality framework, fill in examples for the categories that apply to you.

Once you've identified the modalities, what do you do? The next step is to extend the assessment phase of the exercise into action prescriptions. The following framework can be used to pencil in your multimodal design for positive change.

Modality	Example	Action Plan
Behavior		
Affect		
Sensations		
Imagery		
Cognition		

Interpersonal		
Drugs		

As a final step, number each modality according to its importance (impact). Then, address each modality according to its priority by following the prescription. To avoid putting off the priority, set a time to start. Refuse to procrastinate.

RELAPSE PREVENTION

Lazarus recommends the following multimodal method to prevent relapse: "Relapse prevention of depression from the multimodal perspective calls for vigilance in checking one's BASIC-ID every few weeks. Thus, depression can creep up on one, but a BASIC-ID checklist may discover, say, negative images, more than unusual untoward sensations (e.g., tension), and pessimistic cognitions. It may be advisable to return (to a counselor) for a therapeutic tune-up, or assuage these negative events by systematically going through the BASIC-ID process and taking specific steps to remedy problems" (Lazarus pers. comm.).

KEY IDEAS AND ACTION PLAN

What are the key ideas that you got from this chapter? What actions can you take?

Key Ideas

What are the key ideas that you found helpful?

1. _____

_____

2. _____

_____

3. _____

_____

Action Plan

What actions can you take to progress?

1. _____

_____

2. _____

_____

3. _____

_____

POSTSCRIPT

By taking steps to face depression through the applicable modalities, you've started down the yellow brick road to where you can become your own wizard. By following a multimodal approach, you can help yourself pin down and address key elements in your depression. This approach to defeating depression can be more thorough than other methods.

CHAPTER 18

Five Changes to Defeat Depression

Aristotle saw power as the ability to make things happen. Moving from a depressive perspective to one that is free from the stresses of depressive thinking involves a series of changes that represent an assertion of this power. A five-phase awareness, action, accommodation, acceptance, and actualization process sets the direction for making things happen.

Purposeful change is a process that involves visualizing and engaging in problem-solving activities. When you define a change process and assert control, you give yourself the power to guide your destiny.

The five phases of change provide a different structure to gain freedom from depression. This purposeful process includes leaving the arctic chill of depression behind you as you move forward to experience a growing command over yourself. When you view yourself in command of yourself, you can better take charge of the events that take place around you.

AWARENESS

Awareness is an ongoing process that covers a broad area of your psychic life. It can involve your conscious perceptions and perspective that you are cognizant about at any moment. Part of the process can be an awakening experience where you bring to consciousness beliefs, values, and preferences that can subconsciously influence your choices, emotions, and behaviors. Awareness can also be a goal, such as boosting self-understanding.

From a self-development perspective, an enlightened awareness includes factual self-knowledge, being tuned into your thinking, and trusting your emotions and actions because you know they are grounded. Enlightened awareness, like a good spaghetti sauce, takes many ingredients and time to simmer and blend. It involves some labor, but ideas can spontaneously come to mind and insights can emerge, as you add ingredients to the sauce.

An enlightened awareness is the mirror opposite of depressive awareness. With a depressive awareness, you can experience yourself marinating in a sauce of mental misery. As the sauce thickens, you darkly congeal negative ideas about how others feel about you, your capabilities, and your future.

Constructive incubation can activate enlightened awareness where you get yourself out of the sauce of misery. This incubation is like planting a seed in your mind, and fertilizing it. In coping with depression, this enlightened activation process can occur at practical, empirical, and core levels.

At a *practical level* you look for common sense solutions for depression, or advice, such as what your grandmother might give: get rest, eat right, and exercise. You gather information about depression. You compile a thought log and list your depressive thoughts. Boosting your practical knowledge about depression opens down-to-earth options that you can use to overcome depression.

At the *empirical level* of awareness, you put on the hat of a scientist. Your scientist observes and analyzes information in order to advance your understanding of the depression you experience. Through this analytic process, you position yourself to recognize and to address the irrationalities of depressive thinking. You examine how depressive hypotheses differ from fact. You examine an alternative reality where you see that your life includes experiences where depressive pessimism does not apply. This enlightened perspective is a typical by-product of an empirical way of knowing and experiencing. It is a perspective that can soften the connection between depressive thinking and a depressed mood.

At a *core level* of awareness, you've made connections between depression and factors such as self-doubt and self-downing, perfectionism, and low frustration tolerance. You may even have done a point-of-origin assessment and connected the dots between your early life experiences and current depressive vulnerability. For example, if when you were a child, your parents made promises to you that they rarely kept, this could set the stage for a reaction to disappointment where you depress yourself following a disappointment. Such connections can set the stage for reflecting, rather than reacting, when you face a major disappointment. Core issues, however, are individual, not universal. Highly similar childhood experiences can be perceived differently by different people.

Practical, empirical, and core awareness often flow together like sugar, cream, and coffee. Each part of the combination can exist separately, but as a practical matter, each process can complement the other.

AWARENESS EXERCISE

Awareness of depressive thinking sets the stage for actively culling out depressive distortions from your thoughts. You can use the following checklist to illustrate your growing awareness:

Enlightened Awareness	Yes	No
"I'm aware of my depressive thoughts."		
"I'm aware of how these thoughts affect how I feel and what I do."		

"I'm aware that I can accept depressive thoughts and still contest them."		
"I'm aware that my worth does not depend on ridding myself of depressive thoughts."		
"I'm aware of the adaptable things that I do even when I feel depressed."		

The checklist illustrates key points of awareness regarding your inner world of depression. You can use it to illustrate the progress you have made in kindling your awareness with reasonable thoughts and principles that have the power to soak the embers of depression.

ACTION

Action is doing something, such as lifting a book, closing a window, or thinking out a problem. When conscious, we can't escape taking actions. Intentionally thinking out a problem is a thinking form of action. Knitting is a coordination between the mind and fingertips. The question is, what actions do you choose to take when you feel depressed, and why?

How to Take Action

While awareness involves understanding, action involves mental and behavioral activities directed to attain outcomes. A by-product of actions directed to decrease depressive thinking can be testing new rational understandings, which can lead to positive new actions.

In the area of defeating depressive thinking, many of the actions you take will be rational corrective actions that oppose depressive cognitive processes. The five exercises that follow address depression by looking for loopholes, testing hypotheses, and using the index card technique, the role experiment technique, and the simple activity technique. These action exercises can help blunt depressive thinking and promote positive alternative thoughts and actions.

FINDING LOOPHOLES IN DEPRESSIVE LOGIC

People with multiple depressive thoughts can separate them, label them, and address them through finding and eliminating loopholes in their depressive logic.

First break the sequence of depressive thoughts into separate components, then independently investigate the processes. For example, if helplessness thoughts trigger irrational anger (i-anger), start with helplessness and investigate this pattern. Then, move on to i-anger.

Say your first depressive idea relates to helplessness. Once you have this idea separated out, examine it.

- In what way are you helpless? List your evidence.

- Question the validity of the evidence by seeking credible alternative explanations, such as that helplessness in one area doesn't predict helplessness in all areas of your life.

- Examine the possibility of choice. What are your options in different areas of your life? (Whenever you have options, you can't be helpless.)

Changing Depressive Thoughts to Hypotheses

When depressed, positive experiences can morph into negatives. In a depressed mind-set, you might brush aside experiences that contradict your depressive ideology. Seeing doom and gloom everywhere you look, you are likely to deepen a depressive mood, and the depressive stresses can provoke more bleak thinking. It is here where your work to develop your practical awareness skills and empirical ways of knowing translate into functional ways of doing. For example, by redefining depressive thoughts as hypotheses, you take the certainty out of them and prepare them for a test.

The modern way to test a hypothesis is to try to disconfirm it. For example, if you believe you will stay depressed forever, restate the problem in the following way: "I hypothesize that I will stay depressed forever." You've now taken a certainty and turned it into a guess. Next, see if you can find an exception to this forever belief. You might feel better on a day when you effectively challenged your depressive thinking, and that would be an exception. If you find exceptions to the hypothesis, then you know that an extremist view of staying depressed forever has exceptions.

Based upon how you define them, some situations are hopeless. If you once danced for a living, and you need to be thirty years younger to play the role of a teenager in a play about teenaged dancers, that option is out. It's a fact that you are thirty years too old for the role. Suppose you think that you are too old to play the role of a teenaged dancer and therefore there is no hope to ever earn a living from your dance training. That is a hypothesis that is likely to turn out to be a bad guess. As a performing artist, you have other alternatives, such as becoming a dance teacher. By seeking reasonable alternatives, you've shifted from "no way out" thinking to a productive form of alternative thinking.

CONVERTING DEPRESSIVE THOUGHTS

The following chart is a framework for converting depressive thoughts into hypotheses. Sometimes the act of defining a depressive thought as a hypothesis can change the meaning and significance of the thought. This exercise starts with an example. You fill in the rest.

Depressive Thought	Conversion of Thought into a Hypothesis
"I can't do anything right."	"I hypothesize that whatever I undertake will turn out badly."

As most human qualities and potential include errors and variances, the vulnerability in fixed depressive ideas lies in their inflexibility. Depressive thoughts are fixed ideas. Framed as hypotheses, the definition changes from a certainty to a testable proposition of truth.

THE INDEX CARD TECHNIQUE

A practical reminder system can help contrast depressive thoughts with their opposite coping statements. On an index card, list three prime depressive thoughts on one side and three coping statements on the flipside. This card serves as an awareness reminder.

Depressive Thoughts
1. "I'm helpless to escape misery."
2. "I can see no future."
3. "I'm a loser."

Coping Statements
1. "Helplessness is a myth."
2. "My future is what I want to make it."
3. "I can see myself in more than one way."

You can also use a personal digital assistant to input and retrieve depressive thoughts and coping statement alternatives. Whatever approach you take, reminding yourself that you have alternatives to depressive thoughts takes the certainty from them.

Self-Management Role Technique

George Kelly (1955), the founder of the psychology of personal constructs, predicts that people who act to change their behavior are likely to change their thinking in line with the behavior. The idea is that positive changes in thinking can be encouraged by experimenting with different roles. These roles involve practicing new behaviors. One role is to operate like a scientist who makes discoveries through experimentation.

We play many roles in life. At first, we are a child playing the role of a son or daughter, student, or friend. Later, we assume roles of parent, specialist, club member, writer, investigator, negotiator, chauffeur, gardener, and so on. Some roles develop as a result of cultural exposure, such as gender roles within a family. Others are self-defined, such as the protector, gadfly, or martyr. If your self-assigned role ceases to make sense, you can define and teach yourself to take on other roles that benefit you and others.

One of Kelly's techniques is to write a new role script that addresses a specific area of your life that you think is in your best interest to develop. The script can include new thinking that goes along with acting out new role prescriptions.

Sometimes by adopting a role with a title, it is easier to perform the job. The title defines the responsibilities inherent in the role. Here is a job description for a person who plays the role of *the questioner*.

- The questioner monitors and records depressive thinking.

- The questioner raises questions about depressive thoughts, perhaps following Socrates' prescription of first defining the terms, then obtaining examples and exceptions.

- The questioner raises questions as to whether alternative evidence-based or rational thoughts exist and what they might be.

- The questioner matches the depressive thoughts against their evidence-based counterparts. For example, there is a statistical probability of 80 percent that you'll gain significant relief or overcome depression. How does this evidence-based view compare to a depressive thought such as "I can never get over feeling depressed?"

Following Kelly's approach, you play out the script as though you were an actor playing the part. You test the script for a few weeks. You make modifications using the feedback you receive. Based upon the results, you can quit the new role, modify it, or embrace it as part of the way you operate in life.

The Simple Activity Technique

Simple activities are those that you can do even when highly frustrated or depressed. They don't require much concentration, just a bit of persistence.

If activity is a remedy for depression, then what simple activities can you execute? Any healthy activity that interrupts the flow of depressive thought makes sense to try. The following activities are examples:

- Use a toothbrush to brush a rug or scrub a kitchen floor.

- Do dishes the old-fashioned way; wash them by hand.

- Remove your stored groceries and reorganize them.

- Dye a pair of socks.

- Remove and clean your lightbulbs.

- Walk in place for fifteen minutes and count your steps.

The simple activity technique is a palliative technique. This means that it serves as a distraction and can sometimes have a calming effect. Although this is not an elegant way of addressing depression, the simple activity technique can create a break from an active flow of depressive thinking. It can sometimes promote an increase in energy, which will allow you to address more challenging activities.

ACCOMMODATION

Accommodation is the *conceptual integration* phase of change, where you adjust to new information or to different ways of looking at old information. This is part of learning. You eat a chocolate bar for the first time and quickly adjust to the idea that it tastes good. The accommodation process involves constructing, destroying, and reconstructing knowledge. It involves developing understanding by connecting the dots between your initiatives and their results.

Accommodation overlaps with awareness and action, but it has its own unique feature of integrating the results of experience. This can be an automatic process that is something like digesting food. It also can be intentional and active.

The accommodation process can be done with intent, as when you play with paradoxes and with juxtaposing ideas. These contrasts—especially those involving inconsistencies and incongruities in your thinking—can be powerful stimuli for doubting the certainty typically found in depressive thought.

> The poet Walt Whitman once said, "So you say I contradict myself, so I contradict myself."

An accommodation approach can be especially useful in altering a mental filtering process where you exclude information that won't fit your preconceptions. For example, accommodation can include intentionally contrasting depressive thinking with alternative rational thinking and then adjusting your thinking to accommodate to the more realistic view. This accommodation phase can be especially useful in uncloaking the fallacies in depressive thinking.

Accommodation Paradoxes

Paradoxes suggest that we can have coexisting but opposite abilities. For example, being both relaxed and anxious at the same time is a paradox. Both processes are controlled by different nervous systems that typically do not operate in unison. They coexist but don't emerge at the same time.

There are many incongruities within us. We can be passive and active. We can think rationally and irrationally. We can reflect and react.

Some intellectual paradoxes are self-contradictory and based upon word games. The Greek philosopher Zeno of Elea (circa 450 BC) pit an intellectual assumption against an observation. Zeno's famous paradox is that an arrow shot toward a target continually travels half the distance and so never strikes it. Because space is infinitely divisible, we can repeat the "half the distance" requirements forever. But the arrow does hit. How is this to be explained? The time it takes for an arrow in motion to hit a target is finite, not infinite. It takes a set time to go half the distance to the target and a set time to go the rest of the way.

Zeno's paradox of the arrow in motion is a word game that has nothing to do with physical reality. In a sense, depressive thinking is a word game that sounds logic tight but is inconsistent with many aspects of what we call reality.

Telling yourself that you are useless is a word game that centers on the overgeneralizing verb "to be." Because the "I'm worthless" idea is without an anchor, it can float unimpeded through your thoughts. A more specific definition may be "I think I am useless when I can't lift a hundred-pound sack of potatoes onto a shoulder-high shelf." That definition is concrete and can be tested.

You can examine any paradox where there is an inconsistency between depressive and rational thinking. For example, how can you be both useless and useful? Is it not the acts you describe and not your self that better defines useful or useless?

Paradoxes can have curative effects. The Arabian physician Avicenna (980–1037 AD) used paradoxical psychology with a depressed man who had a delusion that he was a cow ready for slaughter. He told the man that he was too lean for a feast. The man ate to gain weight. With proper nutrition, the man's depressive delusion broke. Of course, this technique raises questions. Why would someone who thought he was a cow eat to fatten up for a slaughter? However, a delusional state of mind is a distorted and irrational state of mind that is like a waking dream. In a delusional world, the irrational can seem rational, and paradoxes can seem real until something happens to change that view.

Accommodation Process

In the following exercise, you'll explore incongruities in depressive thinking by matching opposing depressive and clear-thinking ideas. This clarifying process can release more of the powers of your rational mind.

Listed below are four incongruities that are common among people with depressive thinking habits. Your challenge is to justify the depressive side of the paradox, respond to an incongruity-promoting question, and then decide what idea makes the most sense, and why.

INCONGRUITY EXERCISE

1. "I'm helpless to change" vs. "I'm to blame for all my troubles."

   Justification for helpless position: _____

   How can you be helpless and still totally blameworthy?

   Response to blameworthy question: _____

   Which position makes the most sense, and why? _____

2. "I have no worth" vs. "People are complex with literally thousands of different traits, qualities, and characteristics."

   Justification for "no worth" position: _____

   How can you be worthless and still have thousands of traits and characteristics of different strengths and visibilities?

   Response to strengths question: _____

   Which position makes the most sense, and why? _____

3. "Unless I'm perfect, I'm nothing" vs. the concept of human fallibility that says that learning is part of life so no one can be a finished product.

   Justification for perfectionism position: _____

   How can a fallible human ever reach perfection?

   Response to fallibility question: _____

   Which position makes the most sense, and why? _____

4. "I can't do anything right" vs. the idea that there is no way that overgeneralizing about millio[ns] of performances can be right.

   Justification for incompetence position: _____

   How can a single depressive idea define your life?

   Response to definition question: _____

   Which position makes the most sense, and why? _____

By exploring the incongruities between these statements, you can give yourself a different way to understand the significance of life's inconsistencies and give yourself the chance to adjust your thinking accordingly.

This accommodation exercise can add to your storehouse of techniques. There is no law to say that you must scuttle the irrational side of a paradox and adopt a rational point of view, but, statistically, it seems to work better that way.

ACCEPTANCE

For the purposes of this book, acceptance means that you need never put yourself down, but you can judge and change your thinking and your actions if you are displeased with the process and the outcome. If you try to make a change, and your plan proves premature or fruitless, you can try again or try another. The spirit of acceptance is that you accept yourself regardless of whether or not you think depressively or whether your plans succeed or fail. This is a value choice.

Psychologist Albert Ellis (1994) suggests that self-downing and self-acceptance represent value choices. There is no universal law that says you must choose one over the other. The determination can be in which philosophy provides the better options according to what you value. You can act with acceptance and tolerance without giving up any of your rights and responsibilities.

Another useful aspect of acceptance is that of ridding yourself of the double trouble of putting yourself down for putting yourself down. This acceptance view links to building tolerance. People who build such tolerance generally find that they have more flexibility. Thus, acceptance is the *preparation* phase of change.

Self-Acceptance

Here are two acceptance exercises that support the position that you can always accept yourself and find some of what you do unacceptable. The first exercise compares acceptance with tolerance. The second compares a static view of life with a fluid one.

Both exercises include an accommodation factor. The accommodation factor blends depressive ideas and more evidence-based ideas to help you develop a sense of acceptance regardless of the prescription you follow.

COMPARING DEPRESSIVE BELIEFS WITH AN ACCEPTANCE PHILOSOPHY

Self-acceptance is a cognitive process that relates to the way you view yourself. Acceptance influences behavior and vice versa. The following chart contrasts the nonaccepting results of depressive thinking with an acceptance philosophy. This comparison illustrates the choice between the inflexibility of depressive beliefs and the fluidity of self-acceptance beliefs.

Depressive Idea	Acceptance Belief
Depressive thinking binds us to a turnstile of despair by accepting this negativity as a fixed reality.	Acceptance involves viewing limitations, conditions, and attributes from a realistic perspective.
Depressive thinking blinds us with a sense of bleakness.	Acceptance unleashes the idea that bad times pass and new, good times begin.
Depressive thinking forecloses on life as a miserable experience.	Acceptance partially involves acknowledging that life continues even when you are depressed and that you can participate in that continuing process.
Depressive thinking magnifies the significance of a disturbing event or possibility and makes that the essence of life.	Acceptance makes the most untoward experiences of life more tolerable without diminishing their significance.
Depressive thinking makes it hard to let go of the misery and adds distress to an already sad or unfortunate condition.	Acceptance of unpleasant, unfortunate, and catastrophic experiences leaves us with a sense of sadness for what was, what is, or what can never be.

Contrasting depressive with acceptance beliefs provides a way to see through the shallowness of some forms of depressive thought. It shows an alternative way of defining experience that is softer in tone and stronger in logic.

The Depression Photo Exercise

In depression, your views of the world and yourself may be fixed. This is like a snapshot where your image is captured at a point in time, but you move beyond the time the shot was taken.

As you accommodate to the ebb and flow of the events around you, you may come to see that you cannot be like a photograph of depression, forever fixed in one pose. Rather, your essence is more like a river that flows along channels that may be different from before. While changing, there is still a consistency about that river that characterizes you.

Knowing that you can change less attractive parts of yourself, such as depressive thinking, helps support the spirit of acceptance. If you find yourself posed in a depression photo, the following exercise can help you extract yourself from this static picture by moving beyond depressive photo ideas, such as "life is hopeless." The idea is to see through reason and experience that life reflects a process (life in motion).

DEPRESSION PHOTO EXERCISE

In the first part of this exercise, describe a static fixed view of the depression photo. Next, contrast this with a life-in-motion view. Then, after considering the differences between depressive thinking and self-acceptance views, think about which view would hold up before a jury in a court of law and why. This exercise starts with two examples. You fill in the rest.

The Depression Photo	Life in Motion	Which view would hold up in court and why?
"I am helpless."	"Conditions in life are ever-changing and calling forth different capabilities as the view changes."	"The life-in-motion view would probably hold up in court. It comes closer to reflecting reality. 'I am helpless' represents a fixed view in time that does not correspond to reality."
"I am worthless."	"Although people can define themselves according to their theory of worth, it is impossible that their worth can be viewed in only one way. While it is fair to describe yourself in some single ways, such as human, pejorative labels are inconsistent with reality."	"The life-in-motion view comes closer to reflecting reality. 'I am worthless' represents a fixed view in time that does not correspond to reality."

Can you come up with an argument that could convince a jury of reasonable people to accept a depression photo theory that you are helpless and worthless? If you believe you are able to make a convincing case, the fact you could argue that point paints a picture of a competent debater.

With a high level of self-acceptance, you are likely to trust your thoughts, feelings, and actions and to see them as constructive extensions of yourself. This is a buffer against depression. But it is also a jumping off point for experiencing more of what you want in life.

ACTUALIZATION

At the level of actualization, you have integrated awareness, action, accommodation, and acceptance phases of change, and you typically experience yourself as grounded in what you think, feel, and do. This is a *cognitive, emotional, and behavioral integration* phase change.

Psychologist Abraham Maslow (1987) views self-actualization as the expression of personal attributes in pursuit of achieving goals and ambitions. This view applies to defeating depressive thinking. If you want to get past the darkness of depression, you have to act to go through portals to a world where you feel free of depression. Thus, ridding yourself of depressive thinking involves doing something else first, such as stretching your resources to actualize specific parts of yourself.

Defeating depressive thinking includes stretching your clear-thinking resources to develop these competencies in pursuit of the goal of gaining relief from depression. At this phase of the process, you have already stretched to develop your self-monitoring skills in recognizing depressive thinking, and you will continue to refine your skills in confronting depressive thinking.

This actualization process involves making self-development efforts that, while varied, include improving your communications, seeking positive opportunities, facing meaningful challenges, initiating ways to build more quality experiences into your life, and preferring choices that yield long-term advantages. Throughout your life, the comforts of procrastination may periodically occur but would best be overtaken.

STRETCHING YOUR RESOURCES

The following stretch technique provides a way to actualize your resources to overcome and then to prevent a future depression. Simultaneously, the exercise provides sample ways to extend your resources to meet the ordinary challenges of life.

Define three personal resources that you can stretch to help you to address and prevent depression, as well as advance your vital self-interests. These resources can include your reasoning skills.

1. Identify three personal resources that, when extended, proved a positive expression of your capabilities. This can include problem solving, communications, and tolerance.

2. Stretch these resources by applying them to depressive thinking as well as to positive alternative activities. This approach involves putting your mind and muscles in motion to go through the paces of forming a positive change.

3. Note what you learned from the experience. This learning can point to adjustments to make and where you can stretch next.

The following chart provides a framework for this activity.

	Activity 1	Activity 2	Activity 3
Personal resources			
Stretch actions			
Learning			

Perfectionism and Actualization

Do not confuse perfectionism with stretching your resources. By actualizing efforts, you work to achieve quality. This stretching process involves persistence and acceptance of inevitable setbacks. Perfectionism can involve stretching but more often involves distressing ideas and needless laments.

Stretching to do as well as you can, given the time and resources available to you, is a different path from that of striving for perfection. While perfectionism and actualization can both involve high standards, perfectionism involves a pressured need to meet expectations that are often so lofty as to be out of reach. In actualizing your capabilities, you approach a challenge as a learning experience.

Although it is true that perfectionist striving can lead to driven successes, more often fear of failure, procrastination, and other forms of avoidance accompany this pursuit.

Variability in mood, conditions, knowledge, timing, and experience are immaterial in a perfectionist world. Only one idea counts, which is that you should perform with perfect consistency. The only thing that matters is achieving the impossible. That attitude is the opposite of an actualizing view.

> *I walk endlessly through long corridors toward nowhere. I see a light which I had not seen before. It beckons to me. I take the step. Now I look back amazed that I could have walked the darkened way before.*
>
> **—W.K.**

PROGRESS REPORT

The following outline can help you to determine where you have progressed and where you still have work to do. To complete the progress report, place a check mark on or between yes or no. The yes represents areas to reinforce; the no represents areas to continue to work to improve. If your check mark is closer to the no, that represents an area to continue to develop.

Progress Question	Yes	No
"I have accepted that depression is a condition of mind, body, and spirit that can happen to anyone. It does not reflect my human worth."	Y —————————————— N	
"I have identified the major negative beliefs and cognitive distortions that help sustain my depression."	Y —————————————— N	
"I have engaged in problem-solving activities, such as actively disputing depression-sustaining beliefs."	Y —————————————— N	
"I have resolved the helplessness–self-blame paradox by proving to myself that I am not helpless and that self-blame wastes my time."	Y —————————————— N	
"I have shown myself that since I am not helpless, I can act to shape the future within my natural limits."	Y —————————————— N	

As a practical matter, the five phases of change blend and overlap, so the ordering of these phases may depend upon your unique situation. You might observe, for example, that you have contradictions in your thinking that you'd like to straighten out. So, you will start with an accommodation exercise. However, voluntary personal change typically starts at the level of awareness.

The journey up from depression has many twists and turns, advances, and lapses and periods of encouragement and discouragement. Nevertheless, self-development is an ongoing awareness and action process that builds upon positives and reduces negatives. It's just that simple. Nevertheless, something that is simple can prove challenging to accomplish and will involve stress. But this is the healthy kind of stress called "progressive stress."

Is the accomplishment of ridding yourself of depressive thinking worth the stressful effort? Consider the alternative. Working to maintain a depressive outlook takes distressful efforts. Either way, there is effort involved. You decide the direction of the effort.

KEY IDEAS AND ACTION PLAN

What are the key ideas that you got from this chapter? What actions can you take?

Key Ideas

What are the key ideas that you found helpful?

1. _____

_____

2. _____

_____

3. _____

_____

Action Plan

What actions can you take to progress?

1. _____

_____

2. _____

_____

3. _____

_____

POSTSCRIPT

Change is a process, not an event. From a self-development standpoint, this process of engagement is a prime way to meet promising challenges, as well as to defeat needless fears and depressive preoccupations. The enactment of this process opens opportunities to experience a growing command over yourself. When you view yourself in command of yourself, you can better command the events that take place around you.

As a practical matter, change takes time and is often accomplished progressively in small steps, with many lapses and relapses along the way. By committing yourself to take time to progress slowly and to accept lapses and relapses, you are less likely to get slowed by urgency and desperation. Paradoxically, a positive change process can quicken. One passage from the ancient Chinese book of changes might help this perspective: "At the darkest of times, change is near."

References

Adamson, K. 2002. *Kate's Journey: Triumph Over Adversity*. New York: Insight Publishing.

Ainslie, G., and J. R. Monterosso. 2003. Building blocks of self-control: Increased tolerance for delay with bundled rewards. *Journal of the Experimental Analysis of Behavior* 79 (1): 37–48.

Alloy, L. B., L. Y. Abramson, M. E. Hogan, W. G. Whitehouse, D. T. Rose, M. S. Robinson, R. S. Kim, and J. B. Lapkin. 2000. The Temple-Wisconsin cognitive vulnerability to depression project: Lifetime history of Axis I psychopathology in individuals at high and low cognitive risk for depression. *Journal of Abnormal Psychology* 109: 403–418.

Alloy, L. B., and C. M. Clements. 1992. Illusion of control: Invulnerability to negative affect and depressive symptoms after laboratory and natural stressors. *Journal of Abnormal Psychology* 101: 234–245.

Allport, G. W., and H. S. Odbert. 1936. Trait names: A psycho-lexical study. *Psychological Monographs* 47 (211).

American Psychiatric Association. 2000. *Diagnostic and Statistical Manual of Mental Disorders*. 4th ed. Text rev. Washington, DC: American Psychiatric Association.

American Sunday School Union. 1848. *The Folly of Procrastination*. Philadelphia: American Sunday School Union.

Apodaca, T. R., and W. R. Miller. 2003. A meta-analysis of the effectiveness of bibliotherapy for alcohol problems. *Journal of Clinical Psychology* 59: 289–304.

Ari, S., D. A. F. Haaga, C. Brody, L. Kirk, and D. G. Friedman. 1998. Priming irrational beliefs in recovered-depressed people. *Journal of Abnormal Psychology* 107: 440–449.

Balfour, D. J. K. 1991. The influence of stress on psychopharmacological responses to nicotine. *British Journal of Addiction* 86: 489–493.

Barlow, D. H. 2004. Improving outcomes in patients with generalized anxiety disorder and panic disorder: Role of psychological treatments. *CNS Spectrums* 9 (11 Suppl. 13): 1–8.

Barr, J. T. 1857. *Too Late: The Fatal Effects of Procrastination*. New York: Carlton and Porter.

Beck, A. T. 1963. Thinking and depression: Theory and therapy. *Archives of General Psychiatry* 10: 561–571.

———. 1976. *Cognitive Therapy and the Emotional Disorders*. New York: The New American Library.

Beck, A. T., and B. F. Shaw. 1977. Cognitive approaches to depression. In Vol. 1 of *Handbook of Rational Emotive Therapy*, edited by A. Ellis and R. Grieger, 119–134. New York: Springer.

Beers, C. 1908. *A Mind That Found Itself*. New York: Longmans and Green.

Beevers, C. G., and I. W. Miller. 2005. Unlinking negative cognition and symptoms of depression: Evidence of a specific treatment effect for cognitive therapy. *Journal of Consulting and Clinical Psychology* 73: 68–77.

Benazzi, F. 2003. Anger in bipolar depression. *Journal of Clinical Psychiatry* 64: 480–481.

Berne, E. 1964. *Games People Play: The Psychology of Human Relations*. New York: Grove Press.

Braverman, E. 2004. *Balanced Brain Advantage: The Edge Effect*. New York: Sterling.

Bruder, G. E., J. W. Stewart, P. J. McGrath, G. J. Ma Guoguang, B. E. Wexler, and F. M. Quitkin. 2002. Atypical depression: Enhanced right hemispheric dominance for perceiving emotional chimeric faces. *Journal of Abnormal Psychology* 111 (3): 446–454.

Burns, D. D. 1999. *Feeling Good*. New York: Avon Books.

Burns, D. D., and S. Nolen-Hoeksema. 1991. Coping styles, homework compliance, and the effectiveness of cognitive-behavioral therapy. *Journal of Consulting and Clinical Psychology* 59: 305–311.

Burton, R. 2001. *The Anatomy of Melancholy*. New York: Review Books Classic.

Cartwright, R., M. A. Young, P. Mercer, and M. Bears. 1998. Role of REM sleep and dream variables in the prediction of remission from depression. *Psychiatry Research* 21: 249–255.

Cooley, C. H. 1902. *Human Nature and the Social Order*. New York: Scribner.

Cox, B. J., and M. W. Enns. 2003. Relative stability of perfection in depression. *Canadian Journal of Behavioral Science* 35 (2): 124–132.

Cox, D. L., S. D. Stabb, and J. F. Hulgus. 2000. Anger and depression in girls and boys: A study of gender differences. *Psychology of Women Quarterly* 24: 110–112.

Cuijpers, P. 1998. A psychoeducational approach to the treatment of depression: A meta-analysis of Lewinsohn's "coping with depression" course. *Behavior Therapy* 29: 521–533.

Dalai Lama. 2002. *A Simple Path*. London: Thorsons.

Deldin, P. J., and P. Chiu. 2005. Cognitive restructuring and EEG in major depression. *Biological Psychology* 70: 141–151.

DiFilippo, J. M., and J. C. Overholser. 1999. Cognitive-behavioral treatment of panic disorder: Confronting situational precipitants. *Journal of Contemporary Psychotherapy* 29: 99–113.

Dollard, J. 1942. *Victory over Fear*. New York: Renyal and Hitchcock.

Edelstein, M., D. R. Steele, and D. Ramsey. 1997. *Three Minute Therapy: Change Your Thinking, Change Your Life*. Centennial, CO: Glenbridge.

Ellis, A. 1962. *Reason and Emotion in Psychotherapy*. Secaucus, NJ: Lyle Stuart.

———. 1987. A sadly neglected cognitive element in depression. *Cognitive Therapy and Research* 11: 121–145.

———. 1988. *How to Stubbornly Refuse to Make Yourself Miserable*. New York: Kensington.

———. 1994. *Reason and Emotion in Psychotherapy*. Rev. ed. New York: Kensington.

———. 2003a. *Ask Albert Ellis*. Atascadero, CA: Impact.

———. 2003b. Similarities and differences between rational emotive behavior therapy and cognitive therapy. *Journal of Cognitive Psychotherapy: An International Quarterly* 17 (3): 225–240.

Epperson, C. N., M. Terman, J. S. Terman, B. H. Hanusa, D. A. Oren, K. S. Peindl, and K. L. Wisner. 2004. Randomized clinical trial of bright light therapy for antepartum depression: Preliminary findings. *Journal of Clinical Psychiatry* 65: 421–425.

Fava, M., and J. F. Rosenbaum. 1999. Anger attacks in patients with depression. *Journal of Clinical Psychiatry* 60 (Suppl. 15): 21–24.

Flavell, J. H. 1979. Metacognition and cognitive monitoring. *American Psychologist* 34: 906–911.

Frankl, V. 1963. *Man's Search for Meaning*. New York: Washington Square Press.

Freud, S. 2005. *On Murder, Mourning, and Melancholia*. London: Penguin.

Gilbert, D. G., and C. D. Spielberger. 1987. Effects of smoking on heart rate, anxiety, and feelings of success during social interaction. *Journal of Behavioral Medicine* 10: 629–638.

Giles, D. E., N. H. Hoffman, D. J. Kupfer, and M. L. Perlis. 2003. Short REM latency predicts the first episode of depression in unaffected relatives of unipolar depressed probands. Unpublished manuscript, Sleep Center, University of Rochester.

Glassman, A. H. 1997. Cigarette smoking and its comorbidity. *National Institute on Drug Abuse. Treatment of Drug-Dependent Individuals with Comorbid Mental Disorders*. Monograph No. 172. Rockville, MD: U.S. Department of Health and Human Services, Public Health Service, National Institutes of Health, National Institute on Drug Abuse. NIH publication no. M172, 52–60.

Goldapple, K., Z. Segal, C. Garson, M. Lau, P. Bieling, S. Kennedy, and H. Mayberg. 2004. Modulation of cortical-limbic pathways in major depression: Treatment-specific effects of cognitive behavior therapy. *Archives of General Psychiatry* 61: 34–41.

Gould, R. A., and G. Clum. 1993. A meta-analysis of self-help treatment approaches. *Clinical Psychology Review* 13 (2): 169–186.

Gregory, R. J., C. S. Schwer, T. W. Lee, and J. C. Wise. 2004. Cognitive bibliotherapy for depression: A meta-analysis. *Professional Psychology: Research and Practice* 35: 275–280.

Harkness, K. L., R. M. Bagby, R. T. Joffe, and A. Levitt. 2002. Major depression, chronic minor depression, and the five-factor model of personality. *European Journal of Personality* 16: 271–281.

Harvey, A. G., R. A. Bryant, and N. Tarrier. 2003. Cognitive behavior therapy for post-traumatic stress disorder. *Clinical Psychology Review* 23: 501–522.

Heider, F. 1958. *The Psychology of Interpersonal Relations*. New York: Wiley.

Heller, W., and J. B. Nitschke. 1997. Regional brain activity in emotion: A framework for understanding cognition in depression. *Cognition and Emotion* 11: 637–661.

Hewitt, P. L., G. L. Flett, E. Ediger, G. R. Norton, and C. A. Flynn. 1998. Perfectionism in chronic and state symptoms of depression. *Canadian Journal of Behavioral Science* 30 (4): 234–242.

Hollon, S. D., M. E. Thase, and J. C. Markowitz. 2002. Treatment and prevention of depression. *Psychological Science in the Public Interest* 3 (2): 39–77.

Horney, K. 1950. *Neurosis and Human Growth*. New York: Norton.

Izard, C. E. 1993. Four systems for emotion activation. Cognitive and noncognitive processes. *Psychological Review* 100: 68–90.

Jacobson, E. 1929. *Progressive Relaxation*. Chicago: University of Chicago Press.

John, U., C. Meyer, H. J. Rumpf, and U. Hapke. 2004. Depressive disorders are related to nicotine dependence in the population but do not necessarily hamper smoking cessation. *Journal of Clinical Psychiatry* 65: 169–176.

Johnson, S. 1962. *The Yale Edition of the Works of Samuel Johnson: Selected Essays from the "Rambler," "Adventurer," and "Idler."* Edited by W. J. Bate. New Haven: Yale University Press.

Johnson, W. 1946. *People in Quandaries*. New York: Harper and Brothers.

Judd, L. L., R. C. Kessler, M. P. Paulus, H. U. Wittchen, and J. L. Kunovac. 1998. Comorbidity as a fundamental feature of generalized anxiety disorder. Results from the National Comorbidity Study. *Acta Psychiatrica Scandinavica* 98 (Suppl. 393): 6–11.

Keightley, M. L., G. Winocur, S. J. Graham, H. S. Mayberg, S. J. Hevenor, and C. L. Grady. 2003. An fMRI study investigating cognitive modulation of brain regions associated with emotional processing of visual stimuli. *Neuropsychologia* 41: 585–589.

Kelly, G. 1955. *The Psychology of Personal Constructs*. Vol. 2. New York: Norton.

Kessler, R. C., C. G. Davis, and K. S. Kendler. 1997. Childhood adversity and adult psychiatric disorder in the U.S. National Comorbidity Survey. *Psychological Medicine* 27: 1101–1119.

Kessler, R. C., K. A. McGonagle, S. Zhao, C. B. Nelson, M. Hughes, and S. Eshleman. 1994. Lifetime and twelve-month prevalence of DSM-III-R psychiatric disorders in the United States. Results from the National Comorbidity Survey. *Archives of General Psychiatry* 51: 8–19.

Klein, D. N., J. E. Schwartz, S. Rose, and J. B. Leader. 2000. Five-year course and outcome of dysthymic disorder: A prospective, naturalistic follow-up study. *American Journal of Psychiatry* 157: 931–939.

Klopfer, B. 1957. Psychological variables in human cancer. *Journal of Prospective Techniques* 31: 331–340.

Knaus, W. J. 1982. *How to Get Out of a Rut*. New York: John Wiley & Sons.

———. 1998. *Do It Now: How to Break the Procrastination Habit*. New York: John Wiley & Sons.

———. 2000. *Take Charge Now: Powerful Techniques for Breaking the Blame Habit*. New York: John Wiley & Sons.

———. 2002. *The Procrastination Workbook*. Oakland, CA: New Harbinger Publications.

Koh, K. B., C. H. Kim, and J. K. Park. 2002. Predominance of anger in depressive disorders compared with anxiety disorders and somatoform disorders. *Journal of Clinical Psychiatry* 63 (6): 486–492.

Kupfer, D. J., E. Frank, V. J. Grochocinski, P. A. Cluss, P. R. Houck, and D. A. Stapf. 2002. Demographic and clinical characteristics of individuals in a bipolar disorder case registry. *Journal of Clinical Psychiatry* 63: 120–125.

Lash, J. M. 2000. The effects of acute exercise on cognitions related to depression. *Dissertation Abstracts International: Section B: The Sciences and Engineering* 60 (12-B): 6371.

Lazarus, A. A. 1971. *Behavior Therapy and Beyond*. New York: McGraw-Hill.

———. 1992. The multimodal approach to the treatment of depression. *American Journal of Psychotherapy* 62: 50–57.

Mahalik, J. R., and D. M. Kivlighan. 1988. Self-help treatment for depression: Who succeeds? *Journal of Counseling Psychology* 35: 237–242.

Maiuro, R. D., T. S. Cahn, P. P. Vitaliano, B. C. Wagner, and J. B. Zegree. 1998. Anger, hostility, and depression in domestically violent versus generally assaultive men and nonviolent control subjects. *Journal of Consulting and Clinical Psychology* 56 (1): 17–23.

Margaret. 1852. *Thoughtless Little Fanny or The Unhappy Results of Procrastination*. London: Milner.

Marrs, R. W. 1995. A meta-analysis of bibliotherapy studies. *American Journal of Community Psychology* 23: 843–870.

Maslow, A. 1987. *Motivation and Personality*. 3rd ed. New York: HarperCollins.

Meyer, A. 1948. *The Commonsense Psychiatry of Dr. Adolf Meyer: Fifty-two Selected Papers*. Edited by Alfred A. Lief. New York: McGraw-Hill.

Murray, C. J. L., and A. D. Lopez, eds. 1996. *The Global Burden of Disease: A Comprehensive Assessment of Mortality and Disability from Diseases, Injuries, and Risk Factors in 1990 and Projected to 2020*. Cambridge: Harvard University Press.

National Institute of Mental Health. 1999. Depression research at the National Institute of Mental Health. National Institutes of Health. U.S. Department of Health and Human Services. http://www.nimh.nih.gov/publicat/depresfact.cfm.

Nezu, A. M. 1985. Differences in psychological distress between effective and ineffective problem solvers. *Journal of Counseling Psychology* 32: 135–138.

Okasha, A., and T. Okasha. 2000. Notes on mental disorder in Pharaonic Egypt. *History of Psychiatry* 11 (44, Pt. 4): 413–424.

Olders, H. 2003. Average sunrise time predicts depression prevalence. *Archives of General Psychiatry* 60: 817–826.

Parker, G., and K. Parker. 2003. Influence of symptom attribution on reporting depression and recourse to treatment. *Australian and New Zealand Journal of Psychiatry* 37: 469–478.

Patten, S. B. 2003. Recall bias and major depression lifetime prevalence. *Social Psychiatry and Psychiatric Epidemiology* 38: 290–296.

Paul, R. 1990. *Critical Thinking: What Every Person Needs to Survive in a Rapidly Changing World*. Rohnert Park, CA: Center for Critical Thinking and Moral Critique.

Pelusi, N. 2003. Evolutionary psychology and REBT. In *REBT Theoretical Developments*, edited by W. Dryden. New York: Brunner-Routledge.

Penava, S. J., M. W. Otto, K. M. Maki, and M. H. Pollack. 1998. Rate of improvement during cognitive behavioral group treatment for panic disorder. *Behaviour Research and Therapy* 36 (7–8): 665–673.

Peterson, C., M. E. P. Seligman, and G. E. Vaillant. 1988. Pessimistic explanatory style is a risk for physical illness: A thirty-five-year longitudinal study. *Journal of Personality and Social Psychology* 55: 23–27.

Plath, S. 1972. *The Bell Jar.* New York: Bantam Books.

Pomerleau, C. S., A. N. Zucker, and A. J. Stewart. 2003. Patterns of depressive symptomatology in women smokers, ex-smokers, and never-smokers. *Addictive Behaviors* 28: 575–582.

Pomeroy, L. 2005. *The New Study of Axiological Psychology.* Amsterdam-New York: Rodopi.

Potter, S. 1952. *One-upmanship.* New York: Holt.

Premack, D. 1965. Reinforcement theory. In *Nebraska Symposium on Motivation,* edited by D. Levine. Lincoln, NE: University of Nebraska Press.

Rees, C. S., J. C. Richards, and L. M. Smith. 1999. The efficacy of information-giving in cognitive-behavioral treatment for panic disorder. *Behaviour Change* 16: 175–181.

Reinach, J. 1977. *Goose Goofs Off.* New York: Holt, Reinhart, and Winston.

Renouvier, C. 1842. *Manuel de philosophie moderne.* Paris, Paulin, S.l., Un Volume.

Riso, L. P., and C. F. Newman. 2003. Cognitive therapy for chronic depression. *Journal of Clinical Psychology* 59 (8): 817–831.

Riso, L. P., P. L. du Toit, J. A. Blandino, S. Penna, S. Dacey, J. S. Duin, et al. 2003. Cognitive aspects of chronic depression. *Journal of Abnormal Psychology* 112 (1): 72-80.

Robins, L. N., and D. A. Regier, eds. 1997. *Psychiatric Disorders in America: The Epidemiologic Catchment Area Study.* New York: The Free Press.

Ruhmland, M. M. J. 2001. Efficacy of psychological treatments for panic and agoraphobia. Abstract. *Verhaltenstherapie* 11 (1): 41–53.

Sartorius, N., T. B. Üstün, Y. Lecrubier, and H. Wittchen. 1996. Depression comorbid with anxiety: Results from the WHO study on psychological disorders in primary health care. *British Journal of Psychiatry* 168 (Suppl. 30): 29–34.

Schacter, S., and J. E. Singer. 1962. Cognitive, social, and physiological determinants of emotional states. *Psychological Review* 66: 379–399.

Simon, G. E., M. VonKorff, M. Piccinelli, C. Fullerton, and J. Ormel. 1999. An international study of the relation between somatic symptoms and depression. *New England Journal of Medicine* 341: 1329–1335.

Smith, G. R. 2001. Somatization disorder and undifferentiated somatoform disorder. In *Treatments of Psychiatric Disorders,* 3rd ed. Edited by G. O. Gabbard. Washington, DC: American Psychiatric Publishing.

Solomon, A., B. A. Arnow, I. H. Gotlib, and B. Wind. 2003. Individualized measurement of irrational beliefs in remitted depressives. *Journal of Clinical Psychology* 59: 439–455.

Stage, K. B., A. H. Glassman, and L. S. Covey. 1996. Depression after smoking cessation: Case reports. *Journal of Clinical Psychiatry* 57: 467–469.

Stein, M. B., J. R. McQuaid, C. Laffaye, and M. E. McCahill. 1999. Social phobia in the primary care medical setting. *Journal of Family Practice* 48: 514–519.

Sullivan, P. F., M. C. Nealee, and K. S. Kendler. 2000. Genetic epidemiology of major depression: Review and meta-analysis. *American Journal of Psychiatry* 157: 1552–1562.

Tang, T. Z., R. J. DeRubeis, R. Beberman, and T. Pham. 2005. Cognitive changes, critical sessions, and sudden gains in cognitive-behavioral therapy for depression. *Journal of Consulting and Clinical Psychology* 73: 168–172.

Teasdale, J. D., R. G. Moore, H. Hayhurst, S. Pope, M. Williams, and Z. Segal. 2002. Metacognitive awareness and prevention of relapse in depression: Empirical evidence. *Journal of Consulting and Clinical Psychology* 70: 275–287.

Tolman, E. C. 1922. A new formula for behaviorism. *Psychological Review* 29: 44–53.

Tsao, J. C., M. R. Lewin, and M. G. Craske. 1998. The effects of cognitive behavioral therapy for panic disorder on comorbid conditions. *Journal of Anxiety Disorders* 12: 357–371.

Turner, R. W., M. F. Ward, and D. J. Turner. 1979. Behavioral treatment for depression: An evaluation of therapeutic components. *Journal of Clinical Psychology* 35: 166–175.

Tuunainen, A., D. Kripke, and T. Endo. 2004. Light therapy for non-seasonal depression. *Cochrane Database System Review* 2: CD004050.

van Gool, C. H., G. I. Kempen, B. W. Penninx, D. J. Deeg, A. T. Beekman, and J. T. van Eijk. 2003. Relationship between changes in depressive symptoms and unhealthy lifestyles in late middle aged and older persons: Results from the Longitudinal Aging Study, Amsterdam. *Age and Ageing* 32: 81–87.

Vandergrift, L. 2005. Relationships among motivation orientations, metacognitive awareness and proficiency in L2 listening. *Applied Linguistics* 26: 70–89.

Wampold, B. E., T. Minami, T. W. Baskin, and S. C. Tierney. 2002. A meta-(re)analysis of the effects of cognitive therapy versus "other therapies" for depression. *Journal of Affective Disorders* 69: 159–165.

Waraich, P., E. M. Goldner, J. M. Somers, and L. Hsu. 2004. Prevalence and incidence studies of mood disorders: A systematic review of the literature. *Canadian Journal of Psychiatry* 49: 124–138.

Weissman, M. M., P. J. Leaf, C. E. Holzer, J. K. Myers, and G. L. Tischler. 1984. The epidemiology of depression. An update on sex differences in rates. *Journal of Affective Disorders* 7: 179–188.

Yeung, R. R. 1996. The acute effects of exercise on mood states. *Journal of Psychosomatic Research* 40: 123–141.

Ziegler, D. J., and J. L. Hawley. 2001. Relation of irrational thinking and the pessimistic explanatory style. *Psychological Reports* 88: 483–488.

William J. Knaus, Ed.D., is a licensed psychologist with more than forty years of clinical experience in working with people suffering from depression. He has appeared on numerous regional and national television shows including the **Today Show,** and over 100 radio shows. His ideas have appeared in national magazines such as *U.S. News and World Report* and *Good Housekeeping,* and major newspapers such as the *Washington Post* and the *Chicago Tribune.* He is one of the original directors of training at the Albert Ellis Institute. He is the author of twelve books including *Overcoming Procrastination* and *Do it Now.*

Foreword writer **Albert Ellis, Ph.D.,** is a pioneering theorist of cognitive behavioral therapy and the founder of rational emotive behavior therapy (REBT). He is the author of many best-selling books including *A Guide to Rational Living* and *Reason and Emotion in Psychotherapy.*

self-help workbooks from new**harbinger**publications

real tools for real change since 1973

THE ANXIETY AND PHOBIA WORKBOOK FOURTH EDITION

complete strategies for overcoming all types of anxiety disorders

$19.95 • Item Code 4135

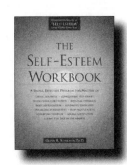

THE SELF-ESTEEM WORKBOOK

the book most-recommended for building healthy self-esteem

$18.95 • Item Code 2523

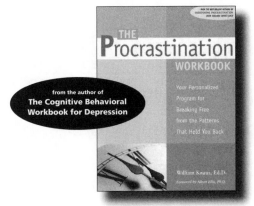

THE PROCRASTINATION WORKBOOK
Your Personalized Program for Breaking Free from the Habits That Hold You Back

the one book you need to stop putting off 'til tomorrow the empowering, positive changes you can make today

$17.95 • Item Code 2957

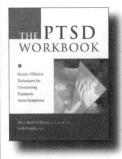

THE PTSD WORKBOOK
Simple, Effective Techniques for Overcoming Traumatic Stress Symptoms

help for victims of trauma

$17.95 • Item Code 2825

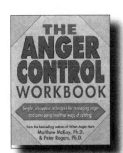

THE ANGER CONTROL WORKBOOK

a powerful, step-by-step program for anger management

$17.95 • Item Code 2205

available from new**harbinger**publications
and fine booksellers everywhere

To order, call toll free **1-800-748-6273**
or visit our online bookstore at **www.newharbinger.com**

(V, MC, AMEX • prices subject to change without notice)